Dialogues in Urban Planning

Towards Sustainable Regions

Edited by
Tony Gilmour and Edward J. Blakely
with Rafael E. Pizarro

SYDNEY UNIVERSITY PRESS

Published 2008 by SYDNEY UNIVERSITY PRESS

Sydney University Press
Fisher Library F03, University of Sydney, NSW 2006 AUSTRALIA
Email: info@sup.usyd.edu.au

National Library of Australia Cataloguing-in-Publication entry
Title: Dialogues in urban planning : towards sustainable
                    regions / editors, Tony Gilmour, Edward J. Blakely,
                    Rafael E.Pizarro.
ISBN: 9781920899127 (pbk.)
Notes: Includes index.
                    Bibliography.
Subjects: City planning.
                    Regional planning.
                    Sustainable development.
                    Sustainable urban development.
Other Authors/Contributors:
                    Gilmour, Tony.
                    Blakely, Edward James, 1938-
                    Pizarro, Rafael E.
Dewey Number: 307.1216

Front cover photograph by Tony Gilmour

Design by University Publishing Services, the University of Sydney

CONTENTS

FOREWORD BY PROFESSOR ALAN PETERS

When the word 'sustainability' first started entering the standard planning lexicon, it was widely seen as an essentially environmental or ecological concept. Sustainability had to do with the ability of macro-environments to reproduce themselves over the longer term. However, over the years there has been increasing recognition that environmental sustainability requires major changes in human behaviour, including human economic behaviour. In planning, there has been a slow realisation by the profession that much of what urban planners do, has a profound effect on regional sustainability. Among other things, planners regulate settlement patterns. They accommodate and guide growth, and help manage the externalities that derive from that growth. They help plan the housing and infrastructure, including the transportation infrastructure, needed to accommodate that growth. In addition, they regulate the building of housing and infrastructure. All these activities have a huge impact on the sustainability of regions.

The changes needed to promote sustainability are difficult since they so often seem at odds with the demands of economic growth and with the affluent lifestyles that growth allows. Moreover, even if it is possible to move to cleaner and greener models of economic growth, that move will produce winners and losers, and the losers may very well be those already poor. At the local and regional levels, it is clear that low-density settlement patterns, common throughout the western world, have encouraged a reliance on car travel. Planners need to encourage new developments to be denser and closer to workplaces and built using sustainable technologies, but they also need to find mechanisms to retrofit older suburbs so that these places function in more sustainable ways. These changes will prove very expensive.

All over the world, urban planning curricula are being updated and changed to take more notice of the need to promote the sustainability of places. Certainly this is true of the University of Sydney, as this book amply demonstrates with chapters reflecting research projects, academic writing and doctoral dissertations by the academic staff, adjunct faculty, and doctoral students at the Urban and Regional Planning program of the Faculty of Architecture, Design and Planning.

CONTRIBUTORS

Santosh Bista is a postdoctoral research fellow in the Faculty of Architecture, Design and Planning at the University of Sydney. He is an urban and regional planner and policy analyst with expertise in urban and regional economic planning and modelling. He has researched, taught and published extensively in this area.

Deborah Black is an Associate Professor at the University of Sydney's Faculty of Health Sciences. Deborah has over 30 years experience as an applied statistician in the areas of survey design, fieldwork management, interpretation of social data and planning based on survey outcomes.

John Black served on the Commonwealth Government Ecologically Sustainable Development Transport Working Group and has held a Japan Society for the Promotion of Science Fellowship to research sustainable urban transport policies. In 2005–7 he directed an international collaborative research project on employment and transport in Australian and Asian cities.

Edward J. Blakely is Professor of Urban and Regional Planning and Policy at the University of Sydney and Director of the Planning Research Centre. He is an internationally known planner with extensive professional practice experience. He is currently on leave serving as Executive Director of Recovery for the City of New Orleans.

John Dee is an environmental planning academic teaching and researching in the area of environmental science, planning and politics at the University of Sydney. His main interests are in planning theory, its relevance to practice and specifically the development of normative decision models capable of delivering more ecologically and socially acceptable outcomes.

Ken Doust is an experienced planning and engineering manager. He has a passion for the role of infrastructure planning and urban infrastructure in a climate change future. Ken's research topics include performance metrics and modelling of sustainable land use and transport systems.

Tony Gilmour is Research Policy Manager at the University of Sydney's Planning Research Centre. His current doctoral research focuses on the capacity of non-profit housing organisations to increase the supply of affordable housing, comparing approaches in Australia, England and America. Tony is author of *Sustaining heritage: giving the past a future* published by Sydney University Press (2007).

Nicole Gurran is an Associate Professor in the Urban and Regional Planning Program at the University of Sydney. She is the author of *Australian urban land use planning: introducing statutory planning practice in NSW* published by Sydney University Press (2007). Her research focuses on local planning, housing, and managing urban development in highly sensitive environmental contexts.

Richard Hu is an urban planning doctoral student at the University of Sydney. His doctoral research compares the transformations of the central cities of Sydney and San Francisco in the context of globalisation. Richard's other research interests include global cities, central city revitalisation and the creative class.

Godfrey Lubulwa works as Manager, Maritime and Rail Statistics at the Bureau of Infrastructure, Transport and Regional Economics. He is an economist with expertise in quantitative economic modelling. Godfrey has also worked as a Regional Research Economist in the same institution for many years.

Alan Peters is Professor of Urban and Regional Planning at the University of Sydney. His research and teaching interests are economic development policy, the application of GIS to urban planning and the simulation of land use change using three-dimensional visualisation environments. Alan has worked in a number of countries both as a planner and as an academic.

Peter Phibbs is the coordinator of academic programmes at the University of Western Sydney's Urban Research Centre. His main research interest is affordable housing but he is also exploring the use of short courses, films and the Internet to educate planning professionals about key policy issues such as climate change.

Rafael E. Pizarro is a lecturer at the University of Sydney teaching postgraduate courses in sustainable urban environments, urban design and development controls, and advanced urban design-planning studios. His research interests include sustainable urban development, climate change, planning in the developing world, and the image of the city in entertainment media.

Ashutosh Sarker is an ecological economist, employed as a postdoctoral research fellow at the University of Queensland. His areas of interest include common property, ecosystem services and institutional economics, specialising in Australia and Japan.

Krishna K. Shrestha is a human geographer, employed as a lecturer in Environmental Planning and Management at the University of Sydney. His interests are in the political ecology of community-based environmental planning, socio-environmental justice and sustainability, particularly in Australia and South Asia.

The chapters in this book have been refereed using a double peer review process. Each contribution was refereed by two of the editors of the book for acceptance, acceptance subject to modification or rejection. Final chapters were checked by the lead editor as having met their referee report requirements before being cleared for publication.

LIST OF FIGURES

Introduction

TOWARDS SUSTAINABLE REGIONS

Edward J. Blakely and Tony Gilmour

This book highlights how the notion of sustainability has permeated all the research and teaching activities of the Planning Research Centre and the Urban and Regional Planning program at the University of Sydney. In line with the trend in major international planning faculties in the United States, Australia and Europe, Sydney University is integrating sustainability as a core approach across specialisations.

It is, therefore, entirely fitting that the theme for this year's *Dialogues in Urban Planning* should be sustainability. The concept is taken in the most global and holistic fashion by the authors. Each of the chapters reflects how sustainability is understood by the author and the context of that term with reference to the subject matter addressed. Clearly, few ideas represent as great a challenge intellectually and practically as the notion of sustainability. In this book, the authors use the urban planning and policy paradigm to address the issues of sustainability. In some cases, authors attempt to define the term from an urban planning perspective and in others, the concepts of sustainability are incorporated in a plan or an exploration of a mechanism or means to plan.

The book is logically divided into two well integrated sections. In Part One, we look at theoretical roots and contexts for planning, starting with an interpretation by Krishna K. Shrestha and John Dee of the notion of sustainable planning as a 'wicked problem'. Surely sustainable planning is among the most wicked problems planners face since the trade-offs are so difficult to deal with and no one wants to make the necessary sacrifices, personally or collectively, to deal with such wicked problems as carbon emissions. While wealthy nations bemoan the developing world for practices that produce more carbon, no one in the developed world is suggesting we alter our lifestyles of air-conditioning and consumerism so the developed world can reach our level of income and opportunity. To illustrate the depth of a wicked problem, the authors provide not just theory but an actual case of difficult trade-offs.

The heart of wicked problems is sustainability of economic growth that consumes more natural resources and produces more carbon dioxide. The chapter by Ken Doust and John Black illustrates how these issues intersect with an examination of the forces and factors that communities must face as they produce more houses. The question is, what is the link between houses and jobs and how can a community induce the housing developer to become a job producer so that commutes to work reduce the car's domination of the suburbs. Clearly, placing jobs nearer to workers does not always ensure a one-to-one trade-off, as the authors acknowledge, but it does give workers the option to seek work closer to their homes and employers have the land and inducements to place jobs and housing closer together.

One answer to the development of sustainable planning is new forms of planning designed to consider the consequences of planning alternatives. In no area is this more sensitive than in the planning for and management of natural resources such as the Lockyer Catchment in Queensland. Krishna K. Shrestha with co-author Ashutosh Sarker offer an approach designed to prevent the destruction of the commons by using what they term 'ecosystem common-pool resource planning'. They use an illustrative case study to show how this very commonsense approach can be used to preserve and protect as well as to enhance the environment.

Sustainability in the largest sense requires an understanding of the industrial ecology that shapes regions and the world. It is industrial production that is altering the fragile global climate balance. Edward J. Blakely, Santosh Bista and Godfrey Lubulwa place the development of Sydney's economy through a set of rigorous analytical frames to provide a template for understanding how globalisation alters the opportunity structures at the community level. Regional plans must consider the differential impacts of moves to more sustainable practices on communities that previously produced regional wealth in the form of dirty producer industries, which are now viewed as social and economic 'evil'. So as we move to more environmentally friendly forms of production and consumption, we must be mindful of the new winners and losers in planning for sustainable outcomes.

Part Two translates theory into practice. Tony Gilmour offers the initial chapter in this section in which he looks at the production of social housing by the non-profit sector, a policy tool favoured by governments to produce sustainable community outcomes. His work deals more with the arrangements of the sector as a global learning community that is transferring knowledge on housing production and sustainable building and urban planning practices across the globe. This chapter is followed by an examination of the local planning regulatory environment in Australia by Nicole Gurran and Peter Phibbs. Their work sheds light on urban planning codes and practices as mechanisms through which more sustainable outcomes can and must emerge.

Health and particularly the advances in modern public health are the reasons we have a better standard of living and longer life spans. These advances have led to the reduction of communicable diseases to a very low level in the developed world. As people live longer, they have new health threats related to the environments in which they live, the way they eat and how settlement patterns are organised. Deborah Black and John Black look at Sydney through the template of a healthy place to live and find it wanting with respect to noise and related pollutants. They use the Sydney Airport noise issue as a way to get into this larger debate on how environmental health is increasingly the major dimension of health policy rather than just the development of life-saving medicines.

Black and Black's work relates to an advanced city in the developed world. In the succeeding chapter, Rafael E. Pizarro deals with sustainability issues in one of the least advantaged countries in the world. He points out how the developing world aspires to all of the unhealthy sprawled lifestyle of the developed world. But good urban design and planning which involves local people in Third World communities, as in the case he presents in Colombia, can lead to sustainable outcomes.

One of the most perplexing aspects of advanced nation development is the increasing dependence on car transport caused by the poor planning of suburban settlements. Santosh Bista shows how this beast might be tamed though the development of bus rapid transit as an alternative to expensive and inflexible new train or tram infrastructure. Bus rapid transit is something that advanced nations can learn from the developing world where it has been practised, by necessity, for many years. Using a case study of Blacktown in south-western Sydney, this chapter shows how bus rapid transit can be planned to overlay existing urban settlement patterns in order to promote environmental sustainability.

Some cities, like San Francisco – a world leader in urban planning – have been working on various aspects of urban sustainability for several decades. Richard Hu offers an insightful analysis of the evolution of San Francisco as a sustainable city model based on a study of significant metropolitan plans. He shows that San Francisco's coalition of government, environmental groups and businesses forged an uneasy alliance yet one that has yielded a remarkably liveable city.

In the final chapter, Edward J. Blakely offers the most challenging and sobering prospect on sustainable cities through his involvement in the re-planning of New Orleans post Hurricane Katrina. He shows the interweaving of social, economic and environmental aspirations into a single plan as the best course for a devastated city. Writing as Executive Director of Recovery for the City of New Orleans, Edward J. Blakely points out that this integrated approach to sustainability is an excellent strategy for all cities, no matter what their current status. Planning for a sustainable future avoids the Katrina-type tragedies and provides a template for recovery if a major man-made or natural disaster should arise.

Two important lessons can be derived from this book about how to build sustainable environments in both the developed and the developing world. First, as the chapters of the book show, the notion of sustainability can no longer just apply to that special subfield of planning called 'environmental planning'. It has to permeate *all* subfields of planning including housing, economic development, transport, regional coordination and urban design as they are all concerned with the economic, social and environmental wellbeing of society. Second, the neat conceptual boundaries between 'urban', 'suburban' and 'rural' planning, as determined by traditional geographical domains, have all but vanished. The notion of 'ecological footprint', the measuring stick of humanity's impact on planet Earth, tells us that what happens in the 'metropolis' deeply affects the 'rural' and the 'regional'. For example, the eco-footprint of Sydney, said to be over 20 million hectares, covers an area of land far greater than the 'real' physical boundary of the city estimated at just over 1 million hectares. The chapters in this book reflect this new understanding of 21st century planning.

Part One

THEORETICAL CONTEXT

Chapter 1

PLANNING FOR SUSTAINABLE DEVELOPMENT: 'WICKED PROBLEMS' AT SYDNEY'S MALABAR HEADLAND

Krishna K. Shrestha and John Dee

Planning decisions about sustainable development are often confronted with multiple and at times incommensurable interest sets that do not lend themselves to straightforward solutions through the application of scientific methods of rational planning theories. Rittel and Weber coined the term 'wicked problems' to describe this phenomenon. This chapter explores a set of wicked problems in the Malabar Headland in Sydney, Australia. By employing a mix of qualitative and quantitative methods, it was found that wicked problems were produced, reproduced and perpetuated in the Malabar Headland due mainly to two principal reasons: a) operational – relating to the complex and conflicting value-sets among stakeholders and multiple uses; and b) structural – relating to the institutional and interest group politics inherent within the layered federal system of government in Australia. As a result, the planning systems were unable to deliver decisions consistent with overarching environmental and social policy imperatives. The end result was a monumental planning stalemate. The chapter concludes by reflecting on the empirical findings of the Malabar case in relation to relevant theories of planning to gain an understanding of how planning systems can deliver outcomes that meet both environmental and social imperatives for sustainable development.

Introduction

Carson's 'Silent Spring', the Club of Rome's 'The Limits to Growth', Schumacher's 'Small is Beautiful' and Brundtland's 'Our Common Future' have all in different ways focused on conserving and protecting environmental values in the face of unprecedented growth. It was the Brundtland Report (WCED, 1987) that popularised the concept of sustainable development in both academic and policy vocabulary, and in

3

the political mainstream. The underlying argument was the notion of 'balance' between conservation and development objectives (Sachs, 1992) which has been endorsed by subsequent United Nations Conferences. Agenda 21 emerged from the Rio conference in 1992 and consists of a plan of actions to be implemented by each member country of the United Nations to achieve sustainable development objectives. It sets out required actions to be undertaken at supra-national (global), national, regional and local levels of the polity in each member country for 'balanced' economic growth and conservation to achieve sustainable development. Reconciling environmental objectives with those of development, however, have proven difficult due to underlying and opposed value-sets that inevitably lead to irreconcilable clashes of interests. The concept of sustainable development per se and the notion of 'needs' and 'development' and 'what is to be sustained' has been criticised as an oxymoron (Redcliff, 1995) because sustainable economic development and making the wealthy better off has neglected the real issue concerning conservation of natural resources (Sachs, 1992). Giddings et al. (2002: p. 188) make the same point in their comment that sustainable development is 'almost anything that anyone wants, so that beneath its covers lies a multitude of sins'. However, Conca et al. (1995: p. 207) perhaps came closest to defining the practicality of sustainable development in their comment that it is about 'reconciling divergent views to design environmentally friendly development … palatable to different interests'.

Planning is critical to achieving sustainable environments because it is where decisions are made about land use and development that requires practitioners to reconcile potentially irreconcilable environmental and development objectives (see Dubois, 2003). Environmental issues are now at the centre of a global political debate where the implications of climate change and global warming, for example, call for comprehensive thinking over intermediate and longer term timeframes. The corollary is that the current ways planning decisions are made, especially with respect to major development projects, must be radically changed because of their long-term potential environmental impacts. Planning agencies throughout the world are constantly called upon by governments of varying political persuasions to develop strategic plans for guiding decisions on development projects where there are multiple, competing and seemingly incommensurable interest sets that do not lend themselves to rational decision processes where there are clear choices about alternatives, mitigation and trade-offs. Solutions towards reconciling environmental and development issues and problems are also hampered by the fact that planning decisions must be made within a range of social, political and ecological complexities and uncertainties.

In coming to terms with these seemingly insurmountable problems, it is useful to recall Rittel and Webber's (1973) seminal paper, 'Dilemmas in a general theory of planning'. The authors conceived the term 'wicked problems' to describe planning decisions that do not lend themselves to the rational scientific methods which were prominent in the planning theories of the early post-World War II period, circa 1950–60s. Jacobs (1995), for example, argued that contemporary environmental philosophy presented a challenge to planning theory because it required a longer timeframe comprehensive type planning. But contemporary planning practice has progressively moved towards incremental approaches which by definition use shorter timeframes. The corollary is that planning decisions have not been particularly effective in accounting for overarching longer term policy intentions. This problem draws attention to planning theory and specifically those theories that try to explain practice.

This chapter is structured by first conceptualising the meaning of 'wicked problems' (see Rittel and Webber, 1973), followed by an analysis of the value clashes between environmental and development interests in the Malabar Headland case in Eastern Sydney. Finally, we reflect briefly on the empirical findings to throw forward insights about how planning systems can be made more responsive in terms of delivering outcomes consistent with overarching environmental policy imperatives.

What are 'wicked problems'?

Rittel and Webber's seminal paper emerged from the perceived limitations of the rational planning model, namely:

> The seeming consensus, that might once have allowed distributional problems to be dealt with, is being eroded by the growing awareness of the nation's pluralism and of the differentiation of values that accompanies differentiation of publics. The professionalized cognitive and occupational styles

that were refined in the first half of this century, based in Newtonian mechanistic physics, are not readily adapted to contemporary conceptions of interacting open systems and to contemporary concerns with equity. A growing sensitivity to the waves of repercussions that ripple through such systemic networks and to the value consequences of those repercussions has generated the recent re-examination of received values and the recent search for national goals (Rittel and Webber, 1973: p. 156).

The authors argue that the problems scientists are generally concerned with are 'tame' or 'benign' because the mission they seek is basically clear in terms of whether or not the problem can be solved. 'Wicked problems', on the other hand, do not have such clarity because they are essentially public policy issues that have complex future implications such as freeway locations, dam sites, parks and power plants. The authors use the term 'wicked' to mean 'tricky' or difficult to resolve. In contrast, 'tame problems' are those with a logical progression in relation to formulating the problem, information gathering, analysis, synthesis and solution. Hence, 'wicked problems' could be described as those that have no true or false answers because of the many interest sets involved in their ideological predilections and preferences (Rittel and Webber, 1973: p. 163).

Verma (1997) responded to Rittel and Webber (op cit.) by arguing that because planning decisions are essentially made by argument, they should be made argumentatively, more vigorously and in a structured way and that 'wicked problems' were basically unsolvable through the application of scientific method. The authors therefore believed that all that can realistically be done is to optimise (see Simon, 1976). 'Tame problems' on the other hand were generally considered to be solvable through the application of scientific method because they had relatively straightforward technical solutions. In the case of 'wicked problems', Rittel (see Verma, 1997) believed that if strategies such as 'doomsdaying' (i.e., putting forward worst-case scenarios and then acting on them) are employed we may be able to defuse some of these 'wicked problems'.

It is a truism to say that planning theory has experienced a somewhat tortured history in its attempt to establish a firm basis for practice. The master/blueprint planning approach (also called the comprehensive rational model) in the first two decades after World War II became the standard urban planning model. According to this model, professional experts, usually employed by government, are charged with identifying a comprehensive range of problems (requiring comprehensive knowledge) and devising broad solutions based on rational thinking. Little attention was given to the specific socio-political context in which such solutions were to be implemented. The plans were divided into broad statements of principles and details in the form of land use and development controls. The purpose of this division was to establish a more dynamic basis for a time-space sequence where, in the first instance, the broad-scale plan was perceived to focus on a highly generalised picture of spatial distributions, and then later concentrate on filling in the necessary detail as required (Hall, 1982). This comprehensive planning model was subjected to severe criticism because of an underlying assumption that viewed society as static, exhibiting little scope for change in its basic economic, social and political conditions.

In response to the comprehensive planning model, several competing theories emerged which attempted to correct its perceived weaknesses. McLoughlin (1969) and Chadwick's (1971) systems theory and Faludi's (1973a, 1973b, 1986) procedural theory were to gain considerable prominence in planning thought and practice in the late 1960s and early 1970s. Systems theory sought to establish a more rigorous scientific basis for planning practice by attempting to overcome the absence of dynamic elements in the essentially static master/blueprint planning approaches. This was done by introducing objectives to guide the plan-making process as well as to provide iterative feedback loops to better account for the dynamic nature of the variables it sought to model.

The scientific basis and methods of systems theory attracted severe criticism from the neo-Marxist urban studies perspective which focused on the power of the capitalist system and as a corollary the view that individual citizens are generally unable to participate in any meaningful way to influence its outcomes. Because Neo-Marxism adopts a position that sees the state as an active interest in the capital accumulation process, it argues that relevant research should focus on analyses of the impact of capital investment in the urban environment (see Castells, 1977; Harvey, 1981; Scott and Roweis, 1977). While recognising that this theoretical approach has significantly contributed to an understanding of the macro aspects of capital accumulation and its effects on urban environments, it has been criticised for its inability to provide a critical analysis of the role of institutions internal to the state.

The North American pragmatist theoretical tradition (see Dewey 1938; Schön 1983, 1992; Schön and Rein 1994) developed the reflective practice model which focuses on understanding how a practitioner may confront and analyse a complex set of 'wicked' planning problems through the employment of reflective frames and discourse construction so as to understand the planning problem and work through systematic approaches towards its resolution. While this approach can help practitioners clarify and refine proposals, its fundamental weakness is its reliance on the intelligence, skill, reasonableness and indeed good intentions of the practitioner(s) involved. In this sense, it can only offer a sound planning proposal on its own terms.

Communicative and participatory theories of planning emerged in the late 1980s and 1990s drawing on Habermas' theory of communicative action (Habermas, 1987), which attempts to explain the interconnection between the systemic side of human life and the value-driven side of human introspection – the latter being defined as the 'lifeworld'. Prominent writers such as Healey (Healey et al., 1988; Healey, 2006) and Forester (1989; 1999) have attempted to interpret and apply communicative action theory to planning decision-making where the latter focuses on the essentially value-laden political role of planning and on how planning decisions must take into account the language of practical conversation and communication. Interestingly, Innes (2004) argues that while collaborative planning is useful when acceptable solutions are not emerging from traditional decision-making processes, it should not be considered a panacea for all planning problems. In this sense, Innes believes that many critics of consensus building have not been fully informed about the nature of this practice.

Flyvbjerg (1998), in his critique of the Habermasian communicative models, argues that Habermas cut himself off from understanding real communication when, in developing his theory of communicative rationality and discourse ethics, he distinguished between 'successful' and 'distorted' utterances in human conversation. Flyvbjerg argued that success in rhetoric that is not based on rational argument is often associated with distortion – a phenomenon demonstrated repeatedly in the Aalborg project. He found that rationality is produced by action (i.e., the social forces that are revealed in the actual planning issues or confrontations during the implementation phase) and it is the rationality of a given activity by participants via that activity. The above theoretical approaches have all in different ways contributed to the theory and practice of planning. There is a clear division, however, between the rational planning theories and the reflective practice, consensus theories – the former relying on linear scientific methods and the latter on collaborative, participatory approaches. The responsible planning authorities in the Malabar case were confronted with finding solutions to a complex set of wicked problems which provides insights into the strengths and limitations of these theories.

Malabar Headland: a challenge for sustainable planning

The study in Malabar Headland in Eastern Sydney describes a complex range of 'wicked problems' which presented formidable constraints to the responsible planning authorities in terms of implementing policies and actions for environmentally sustainable planning outcomes. These principal problems concerned the history of the land and continuation of a range of uses that were incompatible with conservation objectives and disputes between the Commonwealth and state governments over remediation costs to remove environmental hazards.

Research method and data collection

We employed both qualitative and quantitative methods for data collection and analysis. An in-depth study was conducted between November 2006 and July 2007 (9 months) to explore the problems in the planning and management of Malabar Headland. It investigated how and why the federal government has failed to make decisions to solve critical environmental problems in the headland. It drew on primary data collected through oral history (=3), SSIs (semi-structured interview =15), group discussions (=4), purposive visits to the site (=7) and numerous informal discussions. To maintain the anonymity of respondents, the four alphabet codes are assigned to each oral history (HIST.1 to HIST.3), SSI respondent (SSIT.1 to SSIT.15), group discussion (DISC.1 to DISC.4) and field visit (VIST.1 to VIST.7).

9

Respondents were selected based on the 'snow-balling methodology'. Respondents selected were from Randwick City Council, a local environmental group Friends of Malabar Headland (FOMH), NSW Rifle Association, Malabar Riding School, bushcare groups and other community members who were interviewed for oral history and SSIs, and participated in discussions. Questions were asked about the past, present and future of Malabar Headland, focusing particularly on respondents' views of the problems and prospects of Malabar Headland. Field visits were carried out to ascertain the state of the land, heritage assets and vegetation (soil erosion, fire, leaches, noxious weeds, etc.), to take photos as evidence, to talk to people/visitors, and to find out the nature, extent and linkage between different land uses within the headland. Findings were checked with some key respondents of SSIs to ensure their accuracy and validity.

The data collection started with the field visits and informal discussions (which continued until the end), followed by oral histories, SSIs and group discussions. There was a deliberate overlap between some respondents. Three key respondents who provided oral histories were invited for SSIs, and three SSI respondents participated in group discussions. This was to link and crosscheck the data collected through different instruments by the help of respondents.

Secondary data on Malabar Headland were collected from three key newspapers in Sydney: *The Sydney Morning Herald*, *The Daily Telegraph* and *The Southern Courier* between 1991 and 2007. Relevant political statements, speeches, press releases and interviews were collected from the website of three local political representatives – Peter Garrett, Bob Carr and Michael Daly. Various publications on Malabar Headland including two plans – one prepared by Randwick City Council in 1990 and another by the FOMH in 2002 – were reviewed and analysed. A survey of 223 community members conducted by FOMH in 2001 was analysed with permission.

Environmental and heritage significance

Malabar Headland is a peninsula in eastern Sydney within the jurisdiction of Randwick City Council. It is about 12 km from Sydney Central Business District (Figure 1), beautifully located on the edge of the Pacific Ocean with Malabar Beach lying to the south and Maroubra Beach to the north. The Malabar Headland is owned by the Australian federal government and managed through the Commonwealth Government Department of Finance and Administration (DoFA) whose primary responsibility is to sell government properties assumed to be underperforming so as to enhance strong economic management (DoFA, 2006). A major part of the land is currently under lease to the NSW Rifle Association and Malabar Riding School for professional and recreational shooting and horse riding respectively.

Figure 1: Map showing Malabar Headland in eastern Sydney

Source: FOMH (2001)

The headland is within the municipality of Randwick and is subject to the planning provisions and controls of the Randwick Local Environmental Plan (LEP). It comprises three sections of land with a total area of 177 hectares. The eastern section is zoned National Park and contains 54 hectares of land with picturesque rocks, sandstone cliffs and coastal bushland. The central section (the largest land parcel) is zoned Private Open Space containing 108 hectares of open land locally known as the ANZAC Rifle Range (Figure 2). Currently, the main use of this land is recreation and professional shooting. The north-western section of the land is zoned 2B Residential and contains 15 hectares consisting of open space and bushland. It abuts existing residential areas to the north and west. Both the western and eastern parts of the site are covered by native vegetation. There are also several Aboriginal engravings and middens as well as significant World War II historic sites such as the gun emplacements and railway cutting (Randwick City Council, 1990). The north-west and central sections have significant waterfront views and as a result high value future development potential.

Figure 2: Malabar Headland zoning, 1988

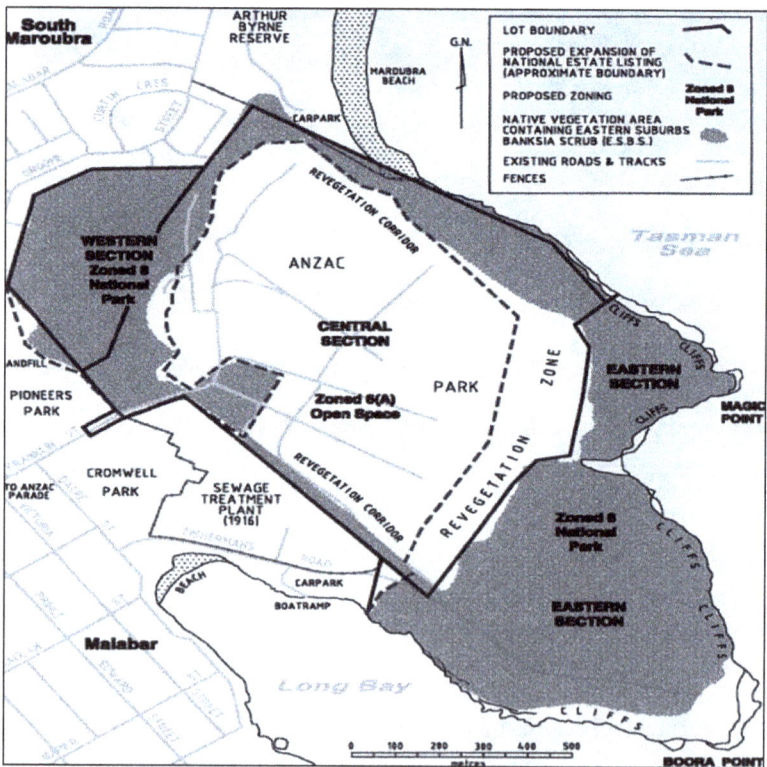

Source: SREP No.14 (NSW Department of Environment and Planning, 1998)

Malabar Headland is of national significance with important ecological, cultural and historical values. A Plan of Management developed by FOMH (2002) identified the headland as one of the most diverse and high quality coastal vegetation areas in the Sydney region supporting over 283 endemic native plant species and more than 200 bird species. It is also the home to the Eastern Suburbs Banksia Scrub (ESBS) – an endangered plant community listed under the *Commonwealth Environmental Protection and Biodiversity Conservation Act 1999* and the *NSW Threatened Species Conservation Act 1997.* The Commonwealth legislation lists ESBS as an endangered ecological community which must be protected; the state legislation contains a similar provision with specific details listings of the relevant vegetation species and ecological communities. The Australian Heritage Commission (1997) includes the site on the Register of National Estate for its cultural and natural heritage significance. Similarly, the NSW State Heritage Register includes the headland as a site of significant cultural and natural heritage significance. However, despite the above environmental and heritage listings, the Malabar Headland has been neglected over many years because no agreement has been reached between the Commonwealth and state governments for effective long-term management of the site.

History of Malabar Headland

Historical data collected from oral history respondents and from various other sources show that before 1929 the land was owned by the NSW government and as early as 1888 was used by fishermen, indigenous people, and recreational shooters. In World War I (1914–1918), the land was used for military purposes and in 1929 transferred to the Commonwealth government for defence purposes. During World War II (1939–1945), the headland supported various military installations, notably the Boora Point Battery (Randwick City Council, 1990). It is worth noting that between 1929 and 1986 the land was used for recreational and professional shooting in conjunction with the military operations.

From 1967 onwards, the planning and management of the land went through a critical phase. In 1967 the ANZAC (Australian and New Zealand Army Corps) Rifle Range at Liverpool closed and the NSW Rifle Association clubs were transferred from Holsworthy to Long Bay

Range (re-named ANZAC Rifle Range in 1970). The war veterans were very pleased to be 'closer to the city and particularly being in a place where some of the veterans were stationed during the War' (HIST.3). In 1986, the official use of the land by the military ceased. It is critically important to mention here that during the 1980s the Malabar Headland, particularly the central section, was used as a landfill where industrial wastes were dumped (Figure 2). One respondent commented that 'many trucks used to come here with [a] full load of garbage, [and] they dumped wastes without any problem' (SSIT.3).

As indicated above, in August 1987 the Australian Heritage Commission included the eastern and western sections of the headland on the Register of National Estate to acknowledge their heritage and conservation values. And significantly, the NSW government, with agreement for the Commonwealth government, gazetted Sydney Regional Environment Plan No. 14 – Eastern Beaches (SREP No. 14) in 1988 which proposed different uses. The Rifle Range had mixed recreation/tourism development and medium density housing (NSW Department of Environment and Planning, 1998).

The 14-hectare site in the north-western section was zoned Residential, one-third of the eastern section National Park and the central section Private Open Space (see Figure 2 above). Subsequent to the above zoning, the Commonwealth government announced that the central section (the Rifle Range) and the north-western bushland section would be sold to the highest bidders: 'effectively to generate cash for the struggling Hawke government' (HIST.2), and 'This was considered as an insult by the government to force the war veterans to vacate the land' (HIST.1). These respondents considered that 'both [the] NSW government and federal government overlooked their own policy requiring the conservation of natural, cultural and Aboriginal heritage of national significance' (HIST.2). This was the start of a bitter conflict.

In 1990, the NSW Rifle Association challenged the federal government's intention to sell the land, arguing that they were not given sufficient notice and a suitable relocation site (DISC.1 and DISC.4). The Association was granted an Injunction Order by the NSW Supreme Court to prevent the Commonwealth accepting or rejecting any tenders. In its deliberation the court states: 'The Commonwealth was within its rights to cause the Rifle Association to leave the site, but three years notice was necessary' (FOMH, 2002). In 1990, Randwick City Council took proactive action and employed consultants to prepare a plan of management for the headland which the federal government subsequently ignored because 'the council was against the intention of the federal government to sell the Headland to developers' (HIST.1). And 1998 saw Randwick City Council challenge the NSW government by proposing to amend its Local Environmental Plan:

> The aim of this plan is to bring the development of the private open space zoned land in the centre of Malabar Headland in line with that if [of] the other open space zoned land in the city, by omitting the provision allowing tourist accommodation (Randwick City Council, 1998).

It is widely believed that all the above initiatives triggered the sale announcement by the Commonwealth government. These events then prompted the Premier of NSW, Bob Carr, to call for the preservation of the headland as National Park and public open space. However, he later failed to back the Randwick City Council proposal. The legal battles between the Commonwealth government and the shooters and the conflicts between different levels of governments were to stall any long-term planning and management of the headland for much of the 1990s.

The Department of Finance and Administration (DoFA) announced in 2001 that the Commonwealth government would provide a $9 million grant from the Federation Fund to build a new shooting facility at Holsworthy for the relocation of ANZAC Rifle Range operation (SSIT.4). While this announcement was initially welcomed by the Association, it became wary of accepting the offer due partly to 'the delay by the federal government to act quickly ... [and] the rejection by its members ... to leave a historically (World War I and II veterans) important site for shooting' (HIST.2). Moreover, the Association felt there would be 'the need to travel a long distance for their activities at Holsworthy from Sydney central region' (HIST.3).

In 2001, the Friends of Malabar Headland – a group of people concerned with the conservation of the natural and cultural heritage of Malabar Headland – conducted a community survey of 223 residents around Malabar Headland to elicit their views, values and interests on how to best manage the site. A vast majority of respondents saw walking in the headland, whale and bird watching, dog walking and bush regeneration as immensely enjoyable and important activities, despite the official restriction on access to the headland. They were also overwhelmingly opposed to commercial development on the headland.

Figure 3: Respondents' views on use of Malabar Headland

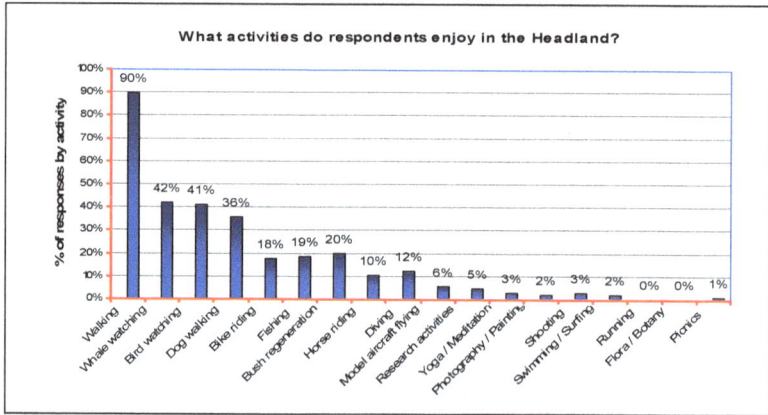

What activities do respondents enjoy in the Headland?

Figure 4: Respondents' views on access to Malabar Headland

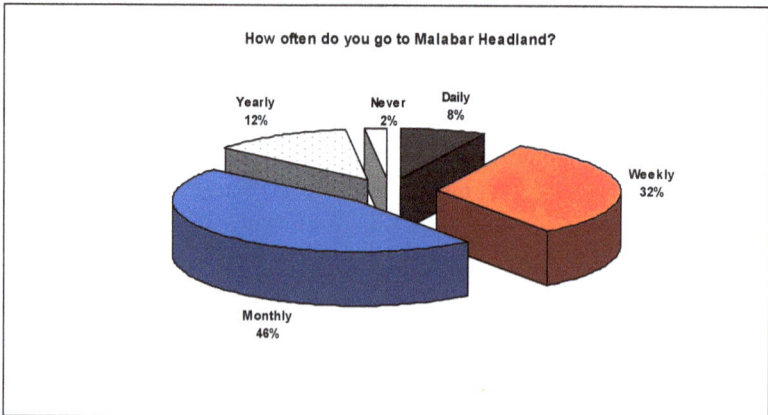

How often do you go to Malabar Headland?

Yearly 12%
Never 2%
Daily 8%
Weekly 32%
Monthly 46%

Source: FOMH (2001) for both figures

Figure 5: Respondents' views on commercial development

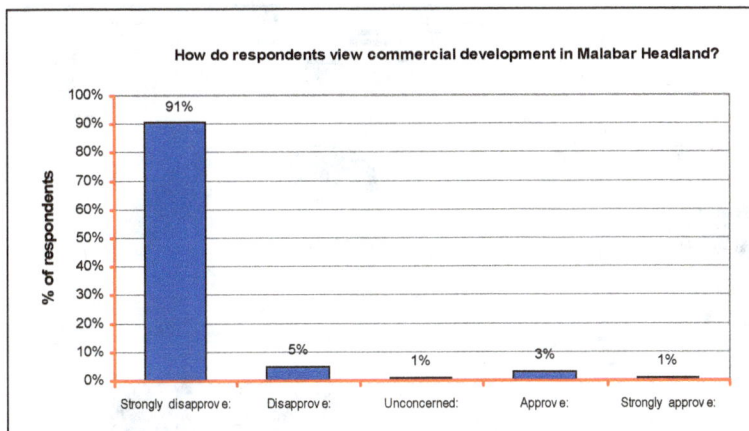

How do respondents view commercial development in Malabar Headland?

(Bar chart showing % of respondents)
- Strongly disapprove: 91%
- Disapprove: 5%
- Unconcerned: 1%
- Approve: 3%
- Strongly approve: 1%

Source: FOMH (2001)

As a result of this community survey, the FOMH prepared a Plan of Management in 2002, the principal management priorities being:

- The rezoning of the western section from Residential 2(B) to National Park/Nature Reserve 8.

- The transfer of management to the National Parks and Wildlife Service because of diverse and uncommon vegetation, high visual significance, potential contribution to local and regional open space systems and passive recreation.

- The rehabilitation and protection of the heathland vegetation communities and conservation of the coastal battery fortifications.

The above extracts from the Plan of Management are shown in Figure 6 below which compares two maps: SREP 14 Eastern Beaches REP with the FOMH proposal. The FOMH proposal rezones the central section (the ANZAC Rifle Range) from private open space to public open space with management responsibility administered by a Trust. This plan partially supports the 1998 Randwick City Council proposal to rezone the ANZAC Range from private open space to public open space which was 'not even acknowledged by the [federal] government' (SSIT.1).

Figure 6: Changes to zoning, 1988 and 2002

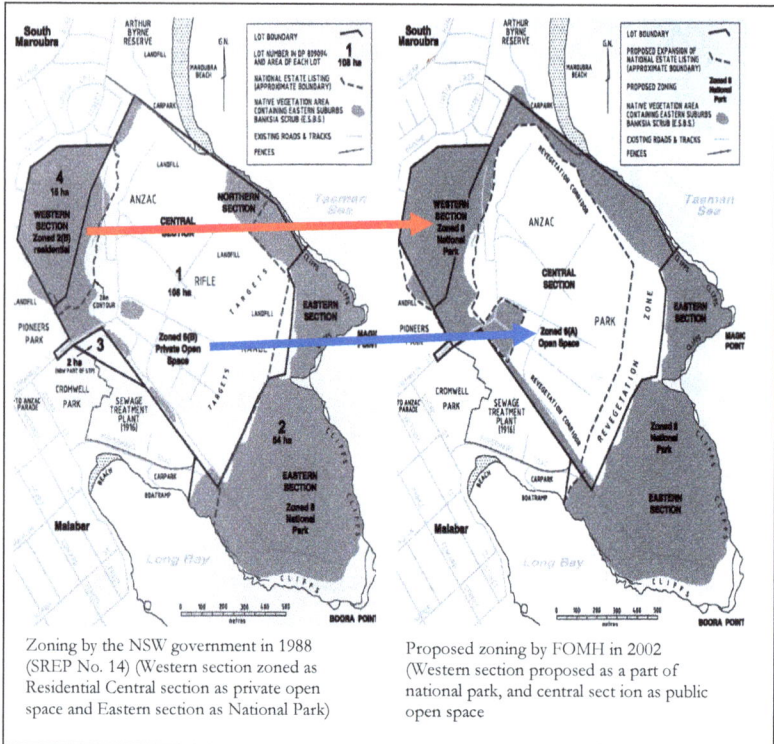

Zoning by the NSW government in 1988 (SREP No. 14) (Western section zoned as Residential Central section as private open space and Eastern section as National Park)

Proposed zoning by FOMH in 2002 (Western section proposed as a part of national park, and central sect ion as public open space)

Source: FOMH (2002)

In 2004 Bob Carr, the Premier of NSW, launched a petition calling on Prime Minister John Howard to hand the Malabar Headland over to the people of NSW. His petition brochure states:

> The federal government said it would hand Malabar Headland over to the people of NSW. That was six years ago. I have written eight letters to Canberra since 1998. Enough is enough. Now is the time to act. It's vital that the Malabar Headland is preserved as a National Park and this precious beach headland is preserved as public open space.

The above initiative was partly aimed at gaining certain approvals for the Randwick Local Environment Plan (LEP) amendment. The western section of the headland needs to become a collective endeavour shared by the state and local jurisdictions considering the Eastern Suburb Banksia Scrub still remains in a residential zone.

On May 3, 2007 Malabar Headland Community Forum (MHCF) was organised by Federal MP Peter Garrett comprising representatives of community groups, residents and Federal MP, the Honourable Peter Garrett. Garrett's website states that: 'Despite the long-running saga with the Federal Government [it is] still not … prepared to hand back the land to the people of NSW [and] the forum came to a clear consensus: it's time the headland was returned to the people of NSW'. The MHCF passed a motion which:

- Reaffirms the commitment of the local community to the preservation and conservation of the Commonwealth-owned land within Malabar Headland.

- Calls upon the Commonwealth government to complete Part 2 of the Facilities Management Plan currently underway.

- Calls upon the Commonwealth government to:
  - honour its commitment to the relocation of shooting activities currently conducted on the Malabar Headland;
  - confirm that $9 million allocated from the Federation Fund in 1998 is still available to be utilised as previously announced by Finance Minister John Fahey for the relocation of the shooters and the provision of open space on the Malabar Headland;
  - recommence discussions with the NSW Government without delay to bring about the relocation of shooting activities currently conducted on the Malabar Headland; and,
  - ensure the return of Malabar Headland to the people of NSW for its use as National Park and public open space.
- Calls on Randwick City Council to re-investigate rezoning of the western portion – currently zoned 2B residential – to National Park. (Source: Garrett, 2006).

Malabar Headland's current situation

The headland is partially fenced around the boundary, particularly on the areas adjacent to the residential areas and Maroubra Beach. The fences are signposted with restricted access signs listing possible fines up to $46,000 for significant damage to the environment. However, field visits found that the signposts have been erased by graffiti and the fences have been broken in many places. This, as one respondent said, is 'a form of protest undertaken by walkers and residents' (SSIT.13). This indicates that for some people, it is probably a conscious action by way of protest, while others might have just ignored the signs.

The NSW government, Randwick City Council, politicians from Labor, Liberal and Green parties, community groups, environmental activists, the Shooters Association, the Riding School and significantly the developers have called for urgent action by the landowner: the Commonwealth government. One respondent said: 'rumours have been in the air [that] the government [has been] preparing a plan for the headland for some years, but no one expect[s] it coming sometime soon' (SSIT.4). Another respondent added: 'we heard that a facility management plan has been finished, but it is kept secret, we don't know its details' (SSIT.13). It is significant to mention that the eastern and western sections of the Malabar Headland were listed on the NSW State Heritage Register in 2005, further highlighting the conservation value of the site.

During on-site visits, discussions with interested parties and user groups, it was found that the north-east of the headland contained a number of constructed wetlands supposedly built for controlling and treating harmful leachate to prevent it from flowing into the children's swimming pool south of Maroubra Beach. One respondent claimed: 'water in the wetlands is poisonous, fish and birds have died' (SSIT.1). Another respondent added: '[the] environmental protection authority issued a warning for residents some years ago' (SSIT.7). In response to the leachate pollution, the NSW Environment Protection Authority declared a Draft Significant Risk of Harm in April 2001 which still remains in force. A common theme from the study was that the former Liberal federal government wasted a lot of money on management of leachate and surface water flows at the Mayan Step sites without much success. Yet, the responsibility to remediate the land lay with the landowner (the Commonwealth government), but they had failed to do.

Shooting and horse riding continue together with degradation and pollution from sites used as dumping grounds for hazardous materials such as car tyres and so on. Numerous gullies, especially in the north-eastern section, have been badly burnt by wild fires and vegetation damage resulting from extensive trail-bike jump pads. In addition, some infestation has occurred due to noxious weeds, despite regular voluntary work by enthusiastic bushcare groups. The cultural and historical sites have been subjected to urination, vandalism and vulgar graffiti. Hence uncertainty exists, as one respondent pointed out: 'no one knows what is going to happen in the Headland' (SSIT.15). And finally, the Australian Liberal National Coalition Government was defeated at the polls on December 24, 2007. Part of Kevin Rudd's election 07 policy document 'Caring for Our Coasts' clearly indicated that the Malabar Headland will be handed over to the New South Wales Government for protection as national park and public open space. The new Labor government has yet to announce its position in relation to the Malabar Headland and to date there is still no management plan in sight.

Conclusions

All three levels of government in Australia aim to implement a draft of environmentally sustainable development policies. The Malabar case demonstrates, however, that well intentioned as these policies may be, they do not always translate into the intended implementation outcomes. The case is also revealing in showing that the history of the land was critical to understanding how the underlying value conflicts coalesced into 'wicked' planning problems in relation to its future planning. The residential zoning in the north-west section, for example, reflected past Defence Department intentions for war veteran housing. This historical fact kept the future residential housing use on the federal government's agenda long after both state and local governments and the community had shown little support and in some cases outright opposition. The history of user rights of land in the central section together with the continued illicit dumping of contaminated materials added yet another dimension to the planning problems because of the high costs associated with remediation and relocation. These costs made the state government reluctant to accept the legal transfer of the land unless the Commonwealth Government allocated funds to cover site remediation and clean-up. Also, the Commonwealth Government's existing property regime, which included unenforceable access restrictions, poor surveillance and monitoring, allowed the above problems to continue almost unabated. Until these problems are resolved, the conflict and dissatisfaction about decisions in relation to the planning and management of the headland will persist. The various plans proposed by different stakeholders have been ignored and there is no viable plan in sight from the federal government's perspective.

In the Malabar case, we can discern the root cause of the above 'wicked problems' as structural. This refers to the position of the former Liberal Commonwealth Government that essentially saw part of the headland as an economic asset – a position reinforced by placing responsibility for the management of the land under the auspices of the Department of Finance and Administration whose *raison d'être* is managing and disposing of government assets. As a result, the conservation and heritage values of the land were not given sufficient priority, most likely because the required planning and environmental expertise did not reside in the Department of Finance and Administration.

It can be speculated further that had responsibility for the long-term management of this land been placed within the Department of the Environment, Water, Heritage and the Arts, the management approach may have been entirely different because of the different culture and expertise within this department. In this respect, the new incoming Labor government may present a positive change in the way that the Malabar Headland and the 'wicked problem' associated with it are approached in terms of developing a long-term environmental plan rather than an assets management plan (or facilities management plan). But the decision in this respect ultimately rests with the landowner, the Commonwealth Government, because it must pay the costs of cleaning up the contaminated areas and then decide to either transfer the land to the state of NSW or develop it in its own right as the landowner.

Reflecting on the Malabar case, it is evident that the communicative approaches alone offered no real solution to the 'wicked problems' in hand. In this sense, Flyvbjerg's (1998) finding that rationality is produced in action by participants via that activity has some validity. It may be useful, therefore, to reconsider some earlier planning theories such as procedural, strategic choice and the constructivist/ reflective practice approaches which are seldom highlighted in planning literature today. While we are aware of the sustained criticisms of these theories, it is our belief that they should be reappraised because of their central concern with planning practice. Ultimately, planning knowledge is eclectic in the sense that no single theoretical tradition will provide a satisfactory explanation for the complex planning phenomena involved in cases such as Malabar Headland.

The principal point is that the practitioner, in trying to resolve such problems, must ultimately be guided by the planning and environmental policies and legislation applying to the land in conjunction with the context specific societal values, needs and expectations, and the ecological conditions. These in turn must be situated within a changing global political, economic and ecological landscape. Finally, this points to the policy implementation problem endemic to planning practice where statutory decisions are often inconsistent with policy and strategic intentions. The abovementioned theoretical traditions attempted to grapple with these issues and are well worth revisiting for their contributions to understanding practice.

Notes

The authors are indebted to Associate Professor Rob Cramb from the School of Natural and Rural Systems Management at the University of Queensland, who was the supervisor of the first author, for his valuable insights, comments and suggestions. We are also grateful to Friends of Malabar Headland for giving access to their community survey results and other information. We thank our respondents including community members and government officials for the time and information given during interviews and open discussions. We are especially grateful to Ms Bettina Digby from Randwick City Council and Mr Brian Vazey and Mr Peter Ryan from FOMH for giving valuable time and information during this research. We also thank the Randwick City Council, particularly the Bushcare Office, for providing access to their documents. We are also grateful for useful comments provided by colleagues and audiences at the Institute of Australian Geographers Conference in Melbourne (2007).

References

Australian Heritage Commission (1997) *Register of the National Estate database report: Long Bay area.* Canberra: Commonwealth of Australia.

Castells, M. (1977) (trans.) *The urban question: a Marxist approach.* London: Edward Arnold.

Chadwick, G. F. (1971) *A systems view of planning: towards a theory of the urban and regional process.* Oxford: Pergamon Press.

Conca, K., Alberty, M. and Dabelko, G. (eds.) (1995) *Green planet blues: environmental politics from Stockholm to Rio.* Boulder: Westview.

Department of Finance and Administration (DoFA) (2006) *Website: www.finance.gov.au* (consulted 17th December 2006).

Dewey, J. (1938) *Logic: the theory of inquiry.* New York: Henry Holt.

Dubois, O. (2003) 'Trade-offs between conservation and development in forestry: setting the stage and some guiding principles,' in *Forests, source of life,* the XII World Forestry Congress, 21–28 September 2003, Quebec City.

Faludi, A. (1973a) *A reader in planning theory.* Oxford: Pergamon Press.

Faludi, A. (ed.) (1973b) *Planning theory.* Oxford: Pergamon Press.

Faludi, A. (1986) *Critical rationalism and planning methodology.* London: Pion.

Flyvbjerg, B. (1998) (trans.) *Rationality and power: democracy in practice.* Chicago: University of Chicago Press.

Forester, J. (1989) *Planning in the face of power.* Berkeley: University of California Press.

Forester, J. (1999) *The deliberative practitioner: encouraging participatory planning processes.* Cambridge: MIT Press.

Friends of Malabar Headland (FOMH) (2001) *Questionnaire survey results of the Malabar Headlands community groups.* Sydney: FOMH.

Friends of Malabar Headland (FOMH) (2002) *A proposal for Boora National Park on Malabar Headland: draft community plan of management.* Available at www.malabarheadland.org.au (consulted 17th December 2006).

Garrett, P. (2006) *Website: www.petergarrett.com.au* (consulted December 2006).

Giddings, B., Hopwood, B. and O'Brien, G. (2002) 'Environment, economy and society: fitting them together into sustainable development.' *Sustainable Development.* vol. 10: pp. 187–196.

Habermas, J. (1987) (trans.) *The theory of communicative action, volume 2: life world and system.* Boston: Beacon Press.

Hall, P. (1982) *Urban and Regional Planning*. London: George Allen and Unwin.

Harvey, D. (1981) 'The process under capitalism: a framework for analysis,' in M. Dear. and A. Scott (eds.), *Urbanisation and urban planning in capitalist society*. London: Methuen. pp.116–124.

Healey, P. (2006) *Collaborative planning: shaping places in fragmented societies*. Basingstoke: Palgrave McMillan.

Healey, P., McNarmara, P., Elson, M. and Doak, A. (1988) *Land use planning and the mediation of urban change: the British planning system in practice*. Cambridge: Cambridge University Press.

Innes, J. E. (2004) 'Consensus building: clarifications for the critics.' *Planning Theory*. 3(1): pp. 5–20.

Jacobs, H. M. (1995) 'Contemporary environmental philosophy and its challenge to planning theory,' in S. Hender (ed.) *Planning ethics: a reader in planning theory, practice and education*. New Brunswick: Centre for Urban Policy and Research, Rutgers University.

McLoughlin J. B. (1969) *Urban and regional planning: a systems approach*. London: Faber and Faber.

NSW Department of Environment and Planning (1998) *Sydney Regional Environmental Plan No.14 – Eastern Beaches*. Available at www.legislation.nsw.gov.au.

Randwick City Council (1990) *Malabar Headland: draft plan of management, volume 1 and 2*. Prepared by Manidis Roberts Consultants, Sydney.

Randwick City Council (1998) *Randwick Local Environment Plan (Amendment No 35)* Sydney: Randwick City Council.

Redcliff, M. (1995) *Sustainable development: exploring the contradictions*. London and New York: Routledge.

Rittel, H. and Webber M. M. (1973) 'Dilemmas in a general theory of planning.' *Policy Sciences*. 4. pp. 155–69.

Sachs, W. (1992) 'Introduction,' in W. Sachs (ed.), *The development dictionary: a guide to knowledge as power*. London: Zed Books, pp. 1–5.

Schön, D. A. (1983) *The reflective practitioner: how professionals think in action*. New York: Basic Books.

Schön, D. A. (1992) 'The theory of inquiry: Dewey's legacy to education.' *Curriculum Inquiry*. 22(2): pp. 119–139.

Schön, D. A. and Rein, M. (1994) *Frame reflection: toward the resolution of intractable policy controversies*. New York: Basic Books.

Scott, A. J. and Roweis, S. T. (1977) 'Urban planning in theory and practice: a reappraisal.' *Environment and Planning A*, vol. 9: pp. 1097–1119.

Simon, H. A. (1976) *Administrative behaviour: a study of decision making processes in administrative organisations.* New York: The Free Press.

Southern Courier (2005–7) 7th June 2005, 6th February and 28th May 2007.

Verma, N. (1997) 'Arguing about wicked problems: putting Horst Rittel's works in perspective.' *Planning Theory.* vol. 18, Winter Edition. pp.95–113.

WCED (1987) *Our common future: report of the World Commission on environment and development.* London: Zed Books.

Chapter 2

METRICS OF ENVIRONMENTAL SUSTAINABILITY, SOCIAL EQUITY AND ECONOMIC EFFICIENCY FOR EMPLOYMENT LOCATION AND COMMUTING

John Black and Ken Doust

A definition of a sustainable urban transport and land use system that is supported by decision makers is one that provides access to goods and services in an efficient way for all inhabitants of an urban area, protects the environment, cultural heritage and ecosystems for the present generation, and does not endanger the opportunities for future generations to reach at least the same welfare level as those living now (May et al., 2001: p. 12). Objectives for sustainability include economic efficiency, protection of the environment, and equity and social inclusion.

The scope of this chapter is employment location and commuting for the journey-to-work travel from origins in the outer western suburbs of Sydney to all other destinations, and journey to home from major employment centres such as Parramatta. The equity aspect of urban development, as measured by accessibility to land uses, has been a long-standing research theme of one of the authors (Black, 1975, 1977, 1979, 1992; Black and Conroy, 1977). However, in this chapter we have formulated a model of accessibility and sustainability that is introduced for the first time for comment and critique. Before presenting the results of the metrics, we outline NSW Government initiatives with decentralised employment location in metropolitan Sydney since 1948. This is followed by an evaluation of the outcomes of metropolitan employment location policy that aims to promote more equitable and sustainable regional outcomes.

An international collaborative research project on polycentric employment formation and its transport implications in member countries of the East Asian Society for Transportation Studies (EASTS) that includes Australia applied analytical methods that were first tested for robustness and relevance with a case study of Istanbul (Alpkokin et al., 2008). The outcomes expected from this comparative study of 11 Asian and Australian cities include a better understanding of the dynamics of decentralisation of employment, multi-centric formations and associated commuting patterns (Alpkokin et al., 2007). The study would further illuminate policy making on socially, environmentally and economically sustainable urban development (Black, 2006), including land use policies that encourage employment creation in the right places, and the role of public transport serving those centres (Klug et al., 2007).

A Sydney case study (Black et al., 2007) not only applied a common, collaborative methodology, but also stimulated us to introduce innovation with the definition of additional metrics (Doust, 2008). Metrics and indicators are used by planners to describe the direction of social, economic or natural conditions in a metropolitan system. Metrics differ from indicators in that they are measures of performance rather than judgements of performance (Blakely et al., 2006). The topic of employment generation and its urban location is a key issue. Interviews with stakeholders (elected politicians, city government employees, private sector infrastructure providers, and community leaders) in the largest global cities of the world found that 81% of stakeholders cited the economy and employment as the most important issue driving decision-making (Lofthouse, n.d.: p. 6) and that transport was the most serious challenge facing the city's infrastructure (Lofthouse, n.d.: p. 21). The metrics we have developed are based on the three pillars of sustainability: environmental sustainability, social equity, and economic efficiency. Analysis is undertaken for small geographical areas (traffic zones) that entail measurements of accessibility to jobs from residential areas, accessibility from major employment centres to the labour force, and greenhouse gas emissions from motor vehicles in the journey to and from work (plus the embodied greenhouse gas emissions from road construction and maintenance).

Metropolitan employment location policy

There have been strategies in Sydney for the suburbanisation of employment (see Figure 7) into centres since its first spatial plan received the Royal Assent in 1951. The County of Cumberland Planning Scheme was dubbed 'Sydney's great experiment' by Winston (1957: p. 42), who wrote of the transport problems of centralised employment:

'The greatest part of Sydney's traffic problem therefore consists in the movement of workers over comparatively long distances from their homes in the suburbs to and from the centre of Sydney'.

Figure 7: Spatial plans for metropolitan Sydney, 1948–2005

Plan	Published	Base Population	Forecast Population
County of Cumberland Planning Scheme	1948	1,702,000 (1947)	2,297,000 (1980)
Sydney Regional Outline Plan	1968	2,500,000 (1966)	4,750,000 (2000)
Sydney into its Third Century	1988	3,364 ,858 (1986)	4,467,500 (2011)
City of Cities: A Plan for Sydney's Future	2005	3,825,000 (2005)	5,000,000 (2031)

When endorsing the decentralised employment strategy of this plan, the Sydney Region Outline Plan (State Planning Authority, 1968: p. 17) confirmed the biggest single urban problem was 'the great and increasing concentration of employment in the metropolitan city centre'.

Major employment nodes in the suburbs have been key characteristics of all spatial and strategic plans. (For details of the first three plans, see Spearritt and DeMarco, 1988: pp. 55–57). The current metropolitan plan – City of Cities: A Plan for Sydney's Future (2005) – is a whole of government document endorsed by the Cabinet (NSW Government, 2005). It envisages five major 'harbour and river' cities, 10 specialised centres plus 11 major centres with employment by the year 2031. The cities designated as major centres are: the CBD, North Sydney, Parramatta, Penrith and Liverpool.

The Metropolitan Strategy is significant because it embodies real and significant policy decisions by the government, including the implementation mechanisms to translate the Plan with 231 actions that are intended to meet sustainability targets for social, economic and physical land uses. These mechanisms include the Metropolitan CEO's group and the linkage between the Metropolitan Strategy, the State Infrastructure Strategy and the State Budget process. It is a whole of government strategy, adopted by cabinet as the planning and development framework for the next 25 years.

The Employment Lands Task Force looks at policy, demand for and supply of land, analysing trends across industry sectors, and reports annually to ministers. The NSW Government Centre's Policy aims to:

- Establish employment capacity targets for strategic centres.

- Cluster business and knowledge-based activities in strategic centres.

- Establish a Stronger Centres Initiative and strengthen management.

- Use government assets and investment to support centres.

- Ensure sufficient sites for commercial offices in strategic centres.

- Concentrate activities near public transport.

- Support centres with transport infrastructure and services.

- Protect and strengthen the primary role of economic corridors.

Evaluation of metropolitan employment location policy

The current NSW Government believes that the centres policy has been successful. According to the government, centres policies have reduced pressure on central Sydney, created a second CBD at Parramatta, upgraded the public transport network serving those centres, and concentrated major retail developments in subregional centres. As noted by Bob Meyer in an article outlining the success of the centres policy in the *Sydney Morning Herald* (2nd November, 2007), concentration of employment in centres served by rail encourages a greater use of public transport and will serve the future metropolitan region in a more sustainable way. Intuitively, this is a highly defensible strategy to overcome the well-articulated problems of suburban sprawl and car-dependency (Newman and Kenworthy, 1999). Parramatta was nominated as Sydney's second Central Business District (CBD). Through centres policy support since the late 1960s, Parramatta has grown from around 10,000 jobs to around 40,000 jobs. Around 35% of work trips to Parramatta centre are by public transport – the highest share for centres outside those in and around central Sydney.

The County of Cumberland Planning Scheme nominated 16 'District' centres for a future population of 2.3 million. *The Sydney Region Outline Plan* was preoccupied with organising peripheral and corridor growth with the CBD, two subregional centres – Parramatta and Campbelltown town centres – and Blacktown, Chatswood, Mount Druitt, Penrith and Camden as other key centres. *Sydney into its Third Century*, for a population of 4.5 million, had 3 regional centres (CBD, North Sydney, and Parramatta) and 16 subregional centres (Wyong, Gosford, Hornsby, Rouse Hill, Blacktown, Mount Druitt, Penrith, Liverpool, Campbelltown, Bringelly, Wollongong, Sutherland, Hurstville, Bankstown, Burwood, and Bondi Junction).

Only about one quarter of the regional employment share was located in these major centres in 1981 (NSW Department of Planning, 1988: p. 48). Therefore, it is instructive to examine where changes in jobs density have taken place from 1981 to 2001 (the most recent census data at the small geographical scale of a traffic zone). If the spatial plans have been effective, we would anticipate that substantial jobs might be created in the designated employment centres and in the outer suburbs.

Figure 8: Employment density changes by traffic zone, 1981–2001

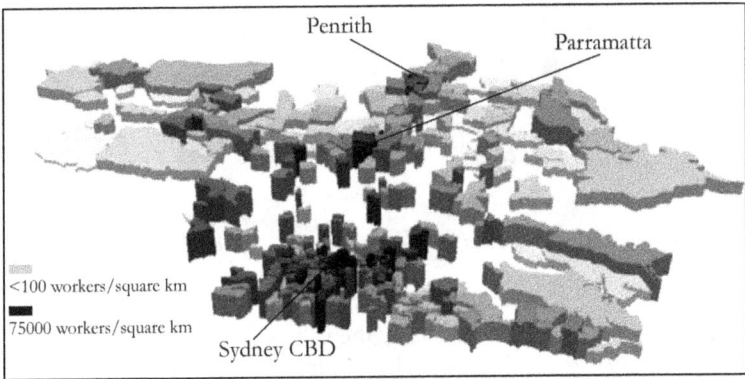

Source: Black et al. (2007): p. 1318

Another way to track the employment change across a region over time is to make a rank-size plot of the logarithm of the number of jobs in each zone of the metropolitan area, or employment density in each zone. As shown in Figure 9, rank-size distributions are plotted from census data for 1981, 1991 and 2001, where the spatial unit of analysis is the traffic zone. An estimate is made for its shape in 2031 according to planning targets in the Metropolitan Strategy and various assumptions. The assumption is that the travel zone forecasts for 2031 can be extrapolated from the 2001 census travel zone employment densities in proportion to the NSW Government forecast for change in respective SLA employment densities from 2001 to 2031. For the Sydney wide data of Figure 9, this is considered an appropriate estimate.

Figure 9: Distribution of employment in traffic zones, 1981–2031

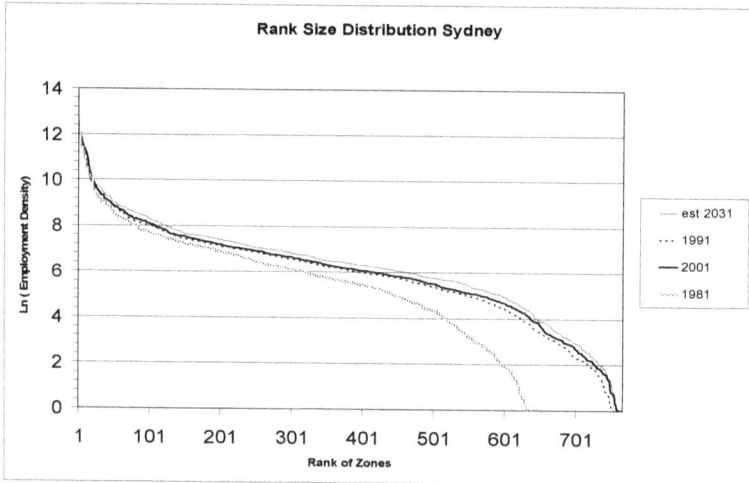

Rank Size Distribution Sydney

Source: Black et al. (2007: p. 1317) using census journey to work surveys

In the 20 years from 1981 to 2001, there has been an increase in the employment density in all zones. Higher density zones have shown the least change over this period, whilst the biggest change has occurred in lower density zones between 1981 and 1991. Relatively little change has occurred between 1991 and 2001. The rank-size distribution estimated from government plans show a continuance of the current trend with slight increases in employment density.

The deterioration in environmental sustainability in the outer suburbs is of major concern especially since 40% of new housing will be in these outer urban release areas by 2031. Jobs have lagged behind residential expansion at the metropolitan fringe. This can be demonstrated by considering the ratio of resident workers to locally available jobs within selected outer Statistical Local Areas (SLAs) of metropolitan Sydney from 1961 to 1996 (Suthanaya and Black, 2001). A ratio of unity (one) is a home-work balance. All areas have a deficit of locally available jobs. For example, Penrith (SLA 6350) – one of the designated major centres in successive metropolitan strategies – shows a continuously deteriorating balance over time with a value of 1.7 at the 2001 Census of Population and Housing.

These imbalances between the spatial, residential and employment markets result in increasingly long commuting distances for outer suburban workers. For example, the mean journey-to-work trip length of workers living in Penrith (55 km from CBD) in 2001 was 26 km (the metropolitan mean distance was about 18 km). This can be compared with a mean of 6 km for residents of the City of Sydney, and 8 km for residents of North Sydney. To complete the comparative picture for the other two major employment centres designated under the metropolitan strategy: Parramatta (23 km from the CBD) has a mean trip length of 16 km, and Liverpool (32 km from the CBD) a mean trip length of 19 km. Are these empirical results a function of outer suburban workers preferring to travel longer distances to get to work?; or, is it a function of poorer accessibility to job opportunities?

Selecting the example of Penrith, Figure 10 shows how the degree of 'self containment' of local labour markets has been reduced, especially in the period 1961 to 1981. The table shows for three census years – 1961, 1981 and 2001 – the percentage of workers who live in Penrith who complete their journey to work (find a place of employment) on reaching the specified proportion of all metropolitan job opportunities (accessibility to jobs). In 1961, Penrith was a largely independent town serving its predominantly rural and agricultural hinterland. Almost three-quarters of the workers worked locally within the Penrith SLA (on reaching 5% of metropolitan jobs). By 1981, this percentage had dropped to 50% on reaching 5% of metropolitan jobs. In 1981 and 2001, the change was slight: there was a minor increase in those working 'locally'. For instance, on reaching half of the metropolitan job opportunities in 1981 and in 2001, 90% had found a workplace in 2001, 6% more than in 1981. Similar patterns have been identified for other outer western suburbs and a full interpretation of changes in commuter travel will be undertaken in future work.

Figure 10: Employment in Penrith, 1961–2001

Year	5% jobs*	10% jobs	20% jobs	30% jobs	50% jobs	75% jobs
1961	70%	77%	82%	85%	86%	95%
1981	50%	60%	70%	75%	84%	97%
2001	54%	58%	68%	78%	90%	97%

*Shows percentage of workers living in Penrith and finding a job given the specified percentage of metropolitan jobs reached, 1961–2001. * cumulative % of metropolitan jobs reached from Penrith. Source: Analysis of Census of Population and Housing, journey to work tabulations based on Ton (1989) and Cheung and Black (2005)*

Equity, sustainability and economic efficiency

Urban policy directs public resources and therefore policy can influence urban development in certain directions. In the case of pursuing the policy objective of centres employment formation, urban policy is about defining and promoting suitable locations for major employment relocation and growth, and the transport links and services to those locations. Three locational variables are at work – jobs, housing and transport – which together determine the type and level of a person's employment opportunities. Equity has been one dimension of the spatial planning of Australian cities (Alexander, 1981). The Federal Australian Labor Party has also been concerned with equity issues in general, and the belief that many inequities in urban areas could be alleviated by the public sector and by urban planning measures (Whitlam, 1975; Alexander, 1981: p. 145). The Hawke Federal Labor Government was also interested in redressing problems of 'locational disadvantage' in Australian cities (Black, 1992).

Contemporary urban policy in Australia is now concerned with the problems of the sustainability of cities (for example, House of Representatives Standing Committee on Environment and Heritage, 2005; Black, 2006) with the 'triple bottom line' outputs from proposed developments in terms of economic efficiency, inter- and intra-generational equity, and environmental sustainability. National and international research in urban transport has aimed to define sustainability in more operational terms (see, for European cities, Minken et al., 2002; Spiekermann and Wegener, 2003; for Japanese cities, Kachi et al., 2005; and for Australia, Lennox and Turner, 2005) and to recommend to policy makers appropriate metrics that measure progress towards sustainability (Hidas and Black, 2001; Black et al., 2002; European Commission, 2004, 2007).

Research by Doust (2008) has formulated two novel relationships that involve the three pillars of urban sustainability: a link between equity (accessibility to employment) and environmental sustainability (greenhouse gas emissions in travel to work); and a link between economic efficiency (accessibility to labour markets from employment centres) and environmental sustainability (greenhouse gas emissions in travel from place of employment to home). Thus, we are concerned with accessibility and commuter travel from discrete locations (traffic zones), either as residential areas or as employment centres. Calculations of accessibility (equity and efficiency) are made for specific zone to zone pairs, where the census journey to work travel data identifies the home-work or work-home desire lines, and TRANSCAD (commercially available GIS software widely used by transport planners) allows this traffic to be assigned to a representation of the transport network. In this chapter, as we only present the findings for all commuters by private transport, only the road network is used for the analysis. Greenhouse gas emissions by private transport per unit distance is estimated from authentic data on emissions rates plus the embodied energy (and emissions) in road construction and maintenance.

Employment location efficiency

Figure 11 provides a series of visualisations of the environmental sustainability and accessibility to workforce for the centre employment travel zones in the Penrith 'River City' precinct. Figure 12 provides the same visualisations of the Sydney 'global city' for comparison. The visualisations are for car-based trips to all travel zones with worker residences right across the Sydney Metropolitan Area. Each travel zone pair is represented by a metric point. The census year data sets for 1981 and 2001 are plotted in these figures, to allow interpretation of the spread and distribution in environmental sustainability – accessibility space and the changes across a twenty-year timeframe. The plot scale is logarithmic for both the environmental sustainability and the relative accessibility measures.

Each scatter plot visualisation in Figures 11 and 12 represents the relative accessibility measure plotted with an urban environmental sustainability measure $(1/CO^2\text{-e})$ for each travel zone pair. Over the 20-year timeframe from 1981 to 2001, a reduction in environmental sustainability is noticeable for both centres. However, a greater reduction in the Penrith environmental sustainability is evident. This is consistent with a larger increase in vehicle kilometres for the journey to work travelled in the outer areas of Sydney over the same timeframe (see Suthanaya and Black, 2001). In comparison to the Sydney centre employment zones, the Penrith scatter plot displays a similar degree of spread (left to right) in relative accessibility, at least four orders of magnitude.

These visualisations confirm that the Sydney Centre employers have a wide choice of workforce zones with comparable accessibility. The Penrith Centre, however, is at a disadvantage by comparison with only a third of the number. Industry and business at Penrith may be less than optimally efficient as a result of a less accessible workforce and difficulties in attracting and retaining labour.

Figure 11: Visualisations of centre sustainability, Penrith

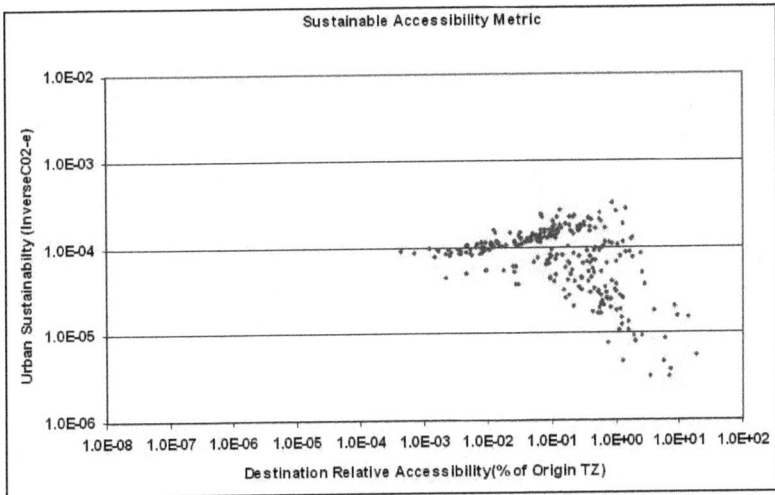

Sustainable Accessibility Metric

y-axis: Urban Sustainability (InverseCO2-e)
1.0E-02, 1.0E-03, 1.0E-04, 1.0E-05, 1.0E-06

x-axis: Destination Relative Accessibility(% of Origin TZ)
1.0E-08 1.0E-07 1.0E-06 1.0E-05 1.0E-04 1.0E-03 1.0E-02 1.0E-01 1.0E+00 1.0E+01 1.0E+02

1981

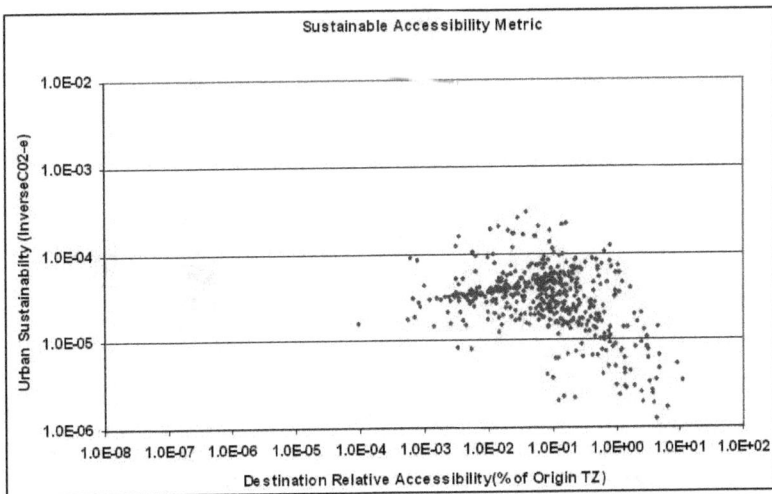

Sustainable Accessibility Metric

y-axis: Urban Sustainability (InverseCO2-e)
1.0E-02, 1.0E-03, 1.0E-04, 1.0E-05, 1.0E-06

x-axis: Destination Relative Accessibility(% of Origin TZ)
1.0E-08 1.0E-07 1.0E-06 1.0E-05 1.0E-04 1.0E-03 1.0E-02 1.0E-01 1.0E+00 1.0E+01 1.0E+02

2001

Figure 12: Visualisations of centre sustainability, Sydney

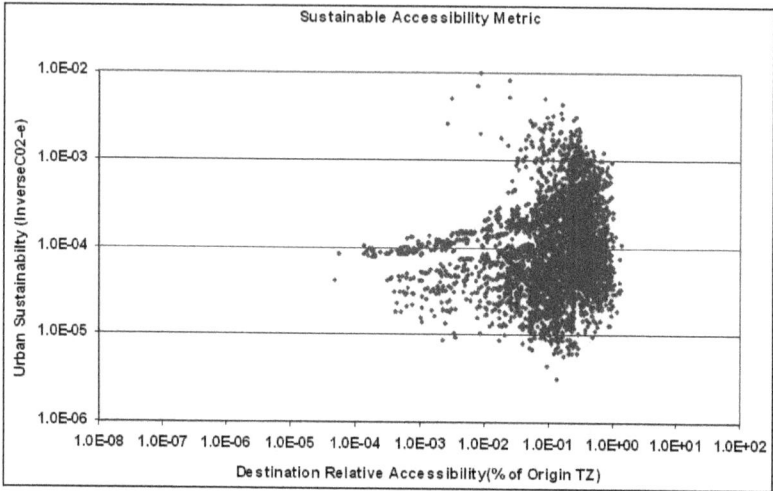

1981

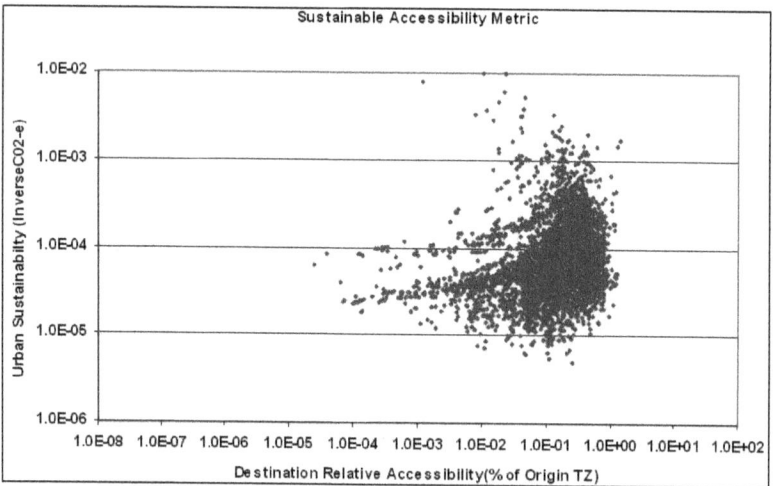

2001

Conclusions

Metrics are an objective measure of truly sustainable performance outcomes, which, when applied with visualisation tools, make it easier to see if policy objectives have been met. As part of a larger study funded by EASTS-IRCA from 2005–2007, we have examined some of the changes that have taken place in metropolitan Sydney since 1945 and have commented on plans for employment centres in 2031. We have applied rank-size distributions over time for employment density across zones of Sydney, and three-dimensional plots using TRANSCAD GIS software for a visualisation of job growth from 1981 to 2001.

New metrics of sustainability have been introduced in this chapter and illustrated with particular reference to the outer metropolitan suburbs of Sydney. These metrics are based on accessibility from home to job opportunities (equity); accessibility to labour markets from major employment centres (economic efficiency); and greenhouse gas emissions in the journey-to-work travel by car (environmental sustainability). These metrics allow an assessment of past trends in urban development and those projected under various planning scenarios, which will be the topic of ongoing research. Further research will aim to undertake a stratified analysis by occupation type or industry category so as to identify 'where the spatial mismatch of jobs and housing will be least for workers with the lowest ability to pay for transport' (Maher et al., 1981: p. 131).

NSW Government policies and strategies have been an integral component of the Sydney metropolitan region's spatial plans from 1948 to 2005 to encourage a suburbanisation and clustering of employment formation in Sydney. The government claims that the centres policy has been successful but careful analyses of data from 1961 to 2001 from the Census of Population and Housing and from the NSW Transport Data Centre presented in this chapter suggest a more cautious interpretation of the success of the centres policy in Sydney. Land use policies that encourage employment creation in the right places in major centres, and policies for public transport technologies serving those centres and parking control, can contribute to more sustainable urban areas. Mean trip lengths for the journeys to work can be contained to polycentric employment centres and there are greater prospects for more of those journeys being made by public transport, cycling and walking.

The CBD and North Sydney continue to be major employment centres and are likely to increase their importance as globalisation continues and more future jobs in the new economy will be located in the 'global arc'. Parramatta, as the second CBD, has grown relatively slowly following the County of Cumberland Planning scheme and subsequent plans. As major centres designated under the 2005 metropolitan strategy, both Liverpool and Penrith have been modest performers as polycentric nodes in a suburban landscape increasingly characterised by low-density sprawling employment.

Notes

The authors are members of ICRA-003 supported by the Eastern Asia Society for Transportation Studies International Collaborative Research Activity. The principal researchers are Professors Yoshitsugu Hayashi (Nagoya University) and John Black. The authors thank: Dr Pelin Alpkokin, Technical University of Istanbul, and colleagues at Nagoya University, for the collaboration on the development of some of the analytical computer software used in preparing this paper; Karl Ikaunieks for assistance with the scatter plot algorithm; the NSW Ministry of Transport, Transport Data Centre for providing the Census of Population and Housing Journey to Work Tabulations; and Dr Bruno Parolin, Faculty of the Built Environment, University of NSW, for access to the TRANSCAD 4.5 licence.

References

Alexander, I. (1981) 'Post-war metropolitan planning: goals and realities,' in P. Troy (ed.) *Equity in the city*. Sydney: George Allen & Unwin, pp. 145–171.

Alpkokin, P., Black, J., Kato, H. and Vichiensan, V. (2007) 'Poly-centric employment formation in mega-cities: analysis from APEC-TR collaborative research.' *Journal of the East Asia Society for Transportation Studies*. vol. 7: pp. 1446–1459.

Alpkokin, P., Cheung, C., Black, J. and Hayashi, Y. (2008) 'Dynamics of clustered employment growth and its impacts on commuting patterns in rapidly developing cities.' *Transportation Research Part A: Policy and Practice*. 42(3): pp. 427–462.

Black, J. (1975) *Some equity aspects of urban development: abstract of key concepts*. Abstract of paper to Urban Biology Group, Australian National University, Canberra, May 1st 1975.

Black, J. (1977) *Public inconvenience: access and travel in seven Sydney suburbs*. Canberra: Australian National University.

Black, J. (1979) 'Changes to employment accessibility in Sydney,' in K. O'Connor (ed.), *Proceedings: third annual meeting of the regional science association (Australian and New Zealand Section)*, pp. 118–129.

Black, J. (1992) 'Journey to work and access to transport with particular reference to locational disadvantage on the outer fringes of major Australian cities,' in *Transport disadvantage: trends and issues, discussion papers prepared for the Department of Prime Minister and Cabinet*, vol. 1(31).

Black, J. (2006) 'Sustainable urban transport technologies and policies: a research perspective,' in *Dialogues in Urban Planning, Sydney*. The Planning Research Centre at the University of Sydney, pp. 4–20.

Black, J., Cheung, C., Doust, K., Shabtay, O. (2007) 'Metrics of changes to major employment centres: analyses of spatial plans for Sydney 1948–2031.' *Journal of East Asia Society for Transportation Studies*. vol. 7: pp. 1311–1325.

Black, J. A. and Conroy, M. M. (1977) 'Accessibility measures and the social evaluation of urban structure.' *Environment and Planning, A.*, vol. 9: pp. 1013–1031.

Black, J., Páez, A. and Suthanaya, P. (2002) 'Sustainable urban transportation: performance indicators and some analytical approaches.' *Journal of Urban Planning and Development, American Society of Civil Engineers*. 128(4): pp. 184–209.

Blakely, E. J., Bista, S., Leng, E., Khan, A., Woodcock, S., Raskall, P., Searle, G., Maganov, P., Deeming, S., Bliss, J., Gardiner, W., Morrison, K., Southall, L. and Richardson, R. (2006) *Essential Sydney: benchmarking our city*. Published by the *Sydney Morning Herald*, July 2006.

Cheung C. and Black J. (2005) 'Spatial interaction models for the journey to work: a reappraisal of the intervening opportunities model applied in the 1960 Chicago Area Transportation Study based on developments in computing technologies', *Proceedings of the 9th International Conference on Computers in Urban Planning and Urban Management, presented at the University College London, 29 June to 1 July, 2005* (Conference CD-Rom).

Doust, K. (2008) 'Metrics of environmental sustainability, social equity, and economic efficiency in cities'. Unpublished PhD thesis, University of New South Wales (submitted).

European Commission (2004) *Expert group on sustainable urban transport plans: final report deliverable D4*. Brussels: European Commission.

European Commission (2007) *Sustainable development indicators*. Brussels: European Commission.

Hidas, P. and Black, J. (2001) 'SMART targets for sustainable transport: a review of international and local (NSW) practice.' *Transport Engineering in Australia*. 7(1&2): pp. 77–92.

House of Representatives Standing Committee on Environment and Heritage, Parliament of Australia (2005) *Sustainable cities*. Canberra: House of Representatives.

Kachi, N., Hayashi, Y., Kato, H. and Black, J. (2005) 'Making cities more compact by improving transport and amenity and reducing hazard risk.' *Journal of the Eastern Asia Society for Transportation Studies*. vol. 6: pp. 3819–3834.

Klug, S., Alpkokin, P., Black, J. and Hayashi, Y. (2007) 'Policies for employment centers in metropolitan regions.' *Journal of Eastern Asia Society for Transportation Studies*. vol. 7: pp. 1417–1432.

Lennox, J. and Turner, L. (2005) *State of the environment report on human settlements: stocks and flows indicators*. Canberra: CSIRO Sustainable Ecosystems for Department of the Environment and Heritage.

Lofthouse, G. (ed.) (n.d.) *Megacity challenges: a research project conducted by GlobeScan and MRC McLean Hazel Sponsored by Siemens*. Munich: Siemens A G.

Maher, C., O'Connor, K. and Logan, M. (1981) 'Employment opportunities,' in P. Troy (ed.) *Equity in the city*. Sydney: George Allen & Unwin, pp. 123–144.

May, A. D., Matthews, B. and Jarvi-Nykanen, T. (2001) 'Decision making requirements for the formulation of sustainable urban land use: transport strategies'. Unpublished paper. 9th World Conference on Transport Research, Seoul, 22–27 July, Conference CD-Rom.

Minken, H., Jonsson, D., Shepherd, S. P., Järvi, T., May, T., Page, M., Pearman, A., Pfaffenbichler, P., Timms, P., and Vold, A. (2002) *Procedures for recommending optimal sustainable planning of European city transport systems – deliverable No.2 evaluation tools*, January 2002.

Newman, P. and Kenworthy, J. (1999) *Sustainability and cities: overcoming automobile dependency*. Washington DC: Island Press.

NSW Department of Planning (1988) *Centres policy*. Unpublished paper.

NSW Government (2005) *NSW Government's metropolitan strategy – city of cities: a plan for Sydney's future* (CD-Rom).

Spearritt, P. and DeMarco, C. (1988) *Planning Sydney's future*. Allen & Unwin, in conjunction with NSW Department of Planning, Sydney.

Spiekermann, K., and Wegener, M. (2003) 'Modelling urban sustainability'. Proceedings of the 8th Conference on Computers in Urban Planning and Urban Management (CUPUM'03), Sendai. (CD-Rom).

State Planning Authority (1968) *Sydney Region Outline Plan*. Sydney: State Planning Authority.

Suthanaya, P. and Black, J. (2001) 'Urban form and journey to work travel behaviour using census data for 1961–1996.' *Journal of the East Asia Society for Transportation Studies: Environment and Safety*. 4(5): pp. 27–42.

Ton, T. T. (1989) *Dynamics of Journey-to-Work Travel Response in Local Government Areas of Sydney*. Unpublished MEngSc Project, School of Civil Engineering, University of New South Wales.

Whitlam, E. G. (1975) *Chifley Memorial Lecture*, University of Melbourne, 14th August 1975.

Winston, D. (1957) *Sydney's great experiment: the progress of the County of Cumberland Plan*. Sydney: Angus and Robertson.

Chapter 3

COLLABORATIVE PLANNING & SUSTAINABILITY: EXPLORING ECOSYSTEMS AS COMMON-POOL RESOURCES IN THE LOCKYER CATCHMENT

Krishna K. Shrestha and Ashutosh Sarker

Conventional approaches to planning and management of natural resources based on rational, top-down thinking remains dominant, despite a large body of empirical evidence suggesting that such an approach has compromised sustainability, often delivering outcomes that are ecologically damaging and socially inappropriate. This chapter examines the current planning and management of natural resources in the Lockyer Catchment in Queensland, Australia, and explores potentials for planning and management informed by the concept of 'commons' or 'common-pool resources' (CPR), which emphasise bottom-up, collaborative planning and management by community groups.

It is found that the making and implementation of plans by the government agencies have simplified the complex interdependence between natural and social systems. The implementation of the current management plans has led to deterioration of ecological health and integrity. Despite an enormous interest in collaborative action by stakeholders, the planning and management of ecosystems is inherently a political process where government line agencies control the processes while other stakeholders are effectively excluded. The CPR approach offers theoretical and practical insights to inform collaborative planning and management of ecosystems where stakeholders could work together as equal partners to identify issues, negotiate solutions, devise plans and implement agreed institutional arrangements to enhance sustainability.

Introduction

Sustainable planning and management of natural resources has become one of the key goals for many government agencies, non-government organisations and community groups around the world today. However, conventional approaches for planning and management of natural resources, either based on a rational, top-down system or market-based privatised approach remains largely dominant in many contemporary government policies and practices. A large body of empirical evidence, however, suggests that conventional planning and management by government agencies or private organisations has often delivered unsustainable management outcomes that are ecologically damaging and socially inappropriate (Blaikie and Brookfield, 1987; Ostrom, 1990; Sarin et al., 2003; Turner, 2004). Frequent calls for rethinking government-controlled or privatised planning and management are not new, but their persistence in policy and practices demonstrates a great deal of defiance. A critical analysis of the centralised and privatised natural resource planning and management is therefore required.

A growing body of literature on collaborative planning has heavily criticised the top-down, rational comprehensive planning model. Advocates of collaborative planning emphasise that two or more stakeholders can communicate and learn from each other, and negotiate and build consensus to solve problems neither of them can do individually (e.g., Forester, 1989; Healey, 2003; Innes, 2004). Collaborative planning is increasingly popular in contemporary planning theory and practice mainly because of its appeal to enhance democratic decision-making and to bring together a range of stakeholders fragmented by varying degrees of power and responsibility to solve critical problems. Yet, a collaborative approach to decision-making has been questioned for its ability to engage with a range of issues relating to unequal power relations, and to sufficiently account for a wide range of social, economic and political contexts in which planning decisions are made (Flyvbjerg, 2002; Hiller, 2003).

Literature on collaborative planning is surprisingly silent on the linkage between collaborative planning and its allied concept of commons or common-pool resources (CPR). Moreover, this approach is yet to be explored for its relevance and possibility for ecosystem planning and management. It is therefore useful to examine the planning and management of ecosystems, and explore the potential for sustainable planning and management of such ecosystems informed by the concept of commons or CPR.

Ecosystems have become one of the core elements in the shifting debates in natural resource planning and management. An ecosystem is usually defined as a natural system consisting of biotic factors (all plants, animals and microorganisms) and abiotic factors (all non-living components of the environment) which function together in area(s) of the physical world. The concept has evolved from referring to a relatively simple, closed and static system involving linear relationships between biotic and abiotic factors, to sets of complex, open and dynamic systems (Nantel et al., 2003). In debates over how to plan and manage ecosystems, two common themes emerge – a) that planning and management should maintain or improve ecosystems, and b) that ecosystems should provide a range of goods and services to a variety of stakeholders (Christensen et al., 1996).

The ecosystem services, which are generated through the complex interaction between the environment and living organisms, include a range of goods and services that are useful for humans such as purification of air, reduction of sediment flow and maintenance of water quality (Daily, 1997; MEA, 2005). In the past, understanding of the complex and dynamic nature of relationships between biotic and abiotic factors was limited, leading to decisions that resulted in unregulated access and use of ecosystem services almost as abundant free gifts of nature. Over time, this led to a systematic degrading of the quality and quantity of ecosystems (such as in the Himalayas, see Ives 1987) due to intense population growth (Ehrlich, 1968) and lack of a sustainable management approach (Hardin, 1968).

Three broad approaches have been recommended for the planning and management of natural resources. Some scholars argue that the market-based approach (i.e., privatisation) is the most efficient form of ownership, planning and management (e.g., Demsetz, 1967), while others argue for a centralised approach (i.e., government ownership and control) (e.g., Ophuls, 1973). Yet many other scholars cite examples of failed state-planning and management of natural resources to call for a return to local, collectively organised planning and management approaches (Berkes, 1989; Ostrom, 1990; Li, 1996; Ostrom, 2003). Their research indicates that centralised or privatised systems fail to account for factors which encourage collective action and self-regulating capabilities of user groups (Runge, 1986), and that centralised and privatised systems often confuse common property with open access, failing to distinguish between common property and no property (Ciriacy-Wantrup and Bishop, 1975; McKean, 2000).

Hence the tragedy of the planning and management of resources results not from the sharing of the rights, but the absence of rights. Many geographers, political scientists and anthropologists argue that societies have devised, maintained or adapted collective arrangements to manage CPRs, and therefore, planning and management of natural resources by their users can be an appropriate system (Blaikie and Brookfield, 1987; Ostrom, 1990; Baland and Platteau, 1996; Gibson, et al., 2000; Menzies, 2003; Ostrom et al., 2007). However, the planning and management of ecosystems has yet to be considered through the lens of CPRs. Our aim, therefore, is to explore potentials for CPR as an alternative approach for planning and management of ecosystems to address issues related to market failure arising from externalities by examining the centralised and privatised planning and management of natural resources. This chapter raises three interrelated questions – a) What is the ecosystem health in the case study catchment? b) How are ecosystems being planned and managed, and why has the centralised system persisted? and c) How do stakeholders view collaborative ecosystem planning and management of natural resources?

The chapter is structured as follows. Firstly, an overview of the concepts of CPR and externality will be provided, followed by a description of qualitative and quantitative methods that we have employed to collect and analyse direct and indirect data and briefly outline the background for the case study – the Lockyer Catchment in Southeast Queensland, Australia. The third section presents the findings, focusing on the three questions set out above, followed by a critical discussion on why centralised planning and management has persisted, and how a collaborative approach informed by the concept of CPR could be applied to planning and management of natural resources to internalise externalities and improve social and ecological outcomes. Finally, we conclude by highlighting the potential for the CPR approach to establish and foster collaborative planning and management.

Common-pool resources (CPR) and externality

A CPR is defined as a natural resource system, often characterised by two attributes: a) excludability – it is very difficult to exclude a beneficiary from deriving a benefit from the resource, and b) subtractability – once the beneficiary derives the benefit, it becomes unavailable to other potential beneficiaries (Ostrom, 1990; Ostrom et al., 1999; Ostrom, 2005). The attributes of CPRs are summarised in Figure 13, which shows the attributes of CPRs such as irrigation and fisheries that generate water and fish as resource units respectively. Once a certain amount of the resource unit is subtracted, it is no longer available to others (i.e., subtractability). It is also difficult to exclude the potential users from appropriating the resource units (i.e., excludability).

Figure 13: Key attributes of common-pool resources

Attributes of a resource	Low subtractability of benefits	High subtractability of benefits
Difficult to exclude beneficiaries	Public goods (e.g. defence, national radio)	Common-pool resources (CPR) (e.g. irrigation systems, forests)
Easy to exclude the beneficiaries	Toll goods (e.g. swimming pool)	Private goods (e.g. private farming land)

Source: Ostrom et al. (1994) p. 7

In a similar way, an ecosystem used by many users tends to share these two attributes. The resource unit of an ecosystem is an ecosystem service which can be subtracted by the activities that users undertake. One example is land clearing by a landholder who subtracts the level of ecosystem services (as a result, soil erosion and salinity problems occur) for the other landholders. Ecosystem services such as improved water quality are utilised by one individual leading to low level of water quality available to other users. It is also difficult for some individuals to exclude others to restrict access of water quality, since the nature of water quality, particularly rivers, creeks or ocean cannot be trapped or fenced within a fixed boundary.

Ecosystem services are unique because the nature of services is complex and the services can generate far reaching cross-boundary consequences in both temporal and spatial terms. These two characteristics are also the source of problems for the planning and management of ecosystems as CPRs. For instance, the difficulty of exclusion can result in over-exploitation of resources, while the subtractability of resources can lead to the degradation or destruction of ecosystems. Two assumptions underlie the solutions proposed by CPR theorists. First, societies have devised, maintained or adapted collective arrangements to manage CPRs (e.g., Gibson et al., 2000). Second, local users are interdependent, and are willing and capable of communication, collective action and institutional development to solve CPR problems. Yet, CPR solutions tend to focus on a group of people who manage natural resources on-site and fail to attend to the indirect and off-site effects.

Such failure may be overcome by employing the concept of externality in ecosystem planning and management as CPR. An externality issue arises, for instance, when an individual or group undertakes an activity that creates costs or benefits for others, but the sufferers are compensated and the beneficiaries are not required to pay any extra for the increased benefits (Samuelson and Nordhaus, 1998; Pindyck and Rubinfeld, 2001). This means a market may not necessarily take the externalities into account. In neoclassical economics, failure to internalise such external benefits (or losses) is believed to create 'market failure'. Such failures are inherent in ecosystem planning and management. In any typical CPR situation, for instance, individuals, groups and societies are interdependent, and actions by an individual or group to access, use and benefit from ecosystem services affect one another, both in temporal and spatial terms. Similarly, physical resources such as land, vegetation and water are interdependent: the loss of biodiversity in certain parts of ecosystems, for example, will adversely affect not only the particular ecosystem and where the loss occurs, but also the other parts of the ecosystem. Issues of direct and indirect as well as on-site and off-site effects are often termed by economists as 'externality issues'.

Externalities can be classified into two types: within-boundary and cross-boundary externalities (cf. Quiggin, 2001). A within-boundary externality occurs within the periphery of a particular CPR. In the case of the groundwater CPR, for example, one user's water appropriation affects the level of appropriation for other users within the specific CPR boundary. On the other hand, an externality can be cross-boundary when users of one CPR can impose externalities on another CPR. In other words, the effects can cross CPR boundaries. For instance, when a large amount of water is withdrawn from a river (surface water CPR) or intercepted in the landscape by farm dams, this affects the amount of water draining underground to replenish a groundwater CPR, creating a cross-boundary externality. The surface water CPR imposes cross-boundary externalities on the groundwater CPR.

In the case of a within-boundary externality, however, the action of individuals (or groups) affects the other, but it does not always happen in a cross-boundary externality. For example, when trees, which have some CPR attributes through the ecological benefits they confer to other natural resources, are cleared away from hill slopes or river banks, soil erosion and unwanted nutrient flow occur and deteriorate the water quality of streams and rivers. This type of cross-boundary externality is uni-directional in that the decreasing water quality does not in turn enhance soil erosion and nutrient flows. The uni-directional, cross-boundary externality within one catchment may even cross the catchment boundary to impose further externalities downstream. It is therefore important to carefully account for externalities as well as relationships between different externalities so as to understand the effects on planning and management of ecosystems as CPR.

Research method

This study employs a mixed method using an in-depth case study as a research strategy. The case study offers a method of learning about a complex instance through extensive description and contextual analysis (Yin, 2002). It is a valuable method for identifying, linking and comparing issues of resource management (Howitt, 2001). Primary data were collected by combining qualitative and quantitative methods. Qualitative methods include field visits and observation of various sites, as well as interviews, discussions and participant observation involving government officials (state and local council levels), landholders, community groups and researchers from universities and Healthy Waterways. Quantitative method involves the analysis of survey data collected from published materials. Qualitative and quantitative methods and analysis were employed in such a way that they complemented each other in that the data collected from one method were checked and verified by the data collected from another method so as to increase research validity and rigour. Secondary data were collected from various publications, and were also checked with research participants. In the Brisbane River and Moreton Bay area, participation focused on the activities of the Healthy Waterways Partnership because of its long-term involvement in previous studies in environmental management.

The Lockyer Catchment

The case study area is the Lockyer Catchment in South East Queensland (SEQ) Australia. The catchment is characterised by extensive historical land clearing which has significantly affected the capacity of ecosystems to provide important ecosystem services such as the prevention of soil erosion and maintenance of water quality in the creeks and rivers. The Lockyer Catchment is located 90 km west of Brisbane, Queensland's capital, and comprises an area of 2,954 square kilometres, an average annual rainfall of 700–1200 mm and population of around 33,000. The Lockyer Catchment has a total length of streams of 2,062 kilometres and population of 33,331 (SEQRWQMST, 2001). It has a dry tropical climate with an average annual rainfall of 800 millimetres recorded between 1895 and 1995 (Rajbhandari, 2003). The catchment is composed of fertile farming land and is often referred to as the 'salad bowl of South-East Queensland'. It is the key supplier of vegetables in Queensland and vegetable-growing contributes significantly to the economic base of the catchment (Boyes, 2001).

The study area is a nested set of catchments which includes the Lockyer Catchment, Brisbane River and Moreton Bay Marine Area in South Eastern Queensland (Figure 14). The Lockyer Creek drains into the Brisbane River, and is thus part of the much larger Brisbane River Catchment. This in turn drains to Moreton Bay, a marine area semi-enclosed by islands, which has other contributing rivers besides the Brisbane. This nested set of catchments is of interest because of the significance of on-site and off-site externality issues associated with ecosystem services, the ecological significance of the Moreton Bay and the Brisbane residents' high value of environmental quality.

Figure 14: Lockyer, Brisbane River and Moreton Bay catchments

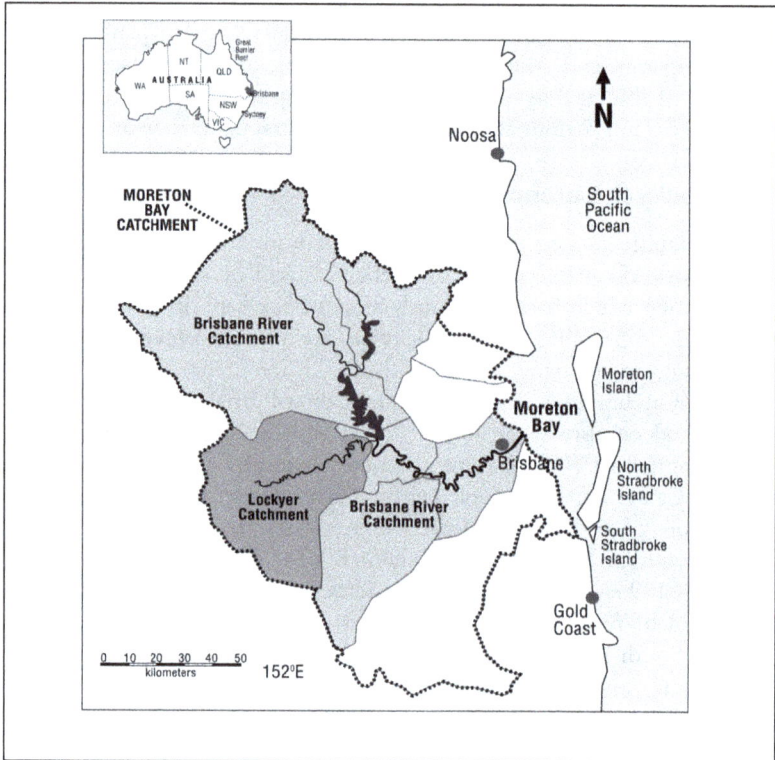

Source: Sarker et al. (2008)

Results

Ecosystem health of the Lockyer Catchment

The ecosystem health of the Lockyer Catchment is poor. It exhibits a low vegetation cover particularly along the riparian zone in combination with heavy soil erosion. Apan et al. (2002) describe the low vegetation cover in the Lockyer Catchment and demonstrate that within the period from 1973 to 1997, about 16,470 hectares of riparian woody vegetation was converted to pasture and the catchment currently has disconnected patches of vegetation. Before settlers came in the early to mid 1800s, the catchment was rich with native vegetation and the riparian vegetation played an important role in trapping sediments during floods and rains (SEQRWQMST, 2001; Apan et al., 2002; Abal et al., 2005). At present, land clearing and land use practices have allowed sediments and nutrients to flow from the catchment into its creeks and adjacent water resources such as Brisbane River and Moreton Bay. Consequently, this has reduced biodiversity in the catchment and the health of aquatic ecosystems in the water resources.

The water quality of the Brisbane River was viewed by many respondents as very low and the water quality of Moreton Bay unsatisfactory. One respondent said, '... water [in Brisbane River] is extremely polluted, nowhere can we see anything under the surface, it's worrying'. The Ecosystem Health Report Cards released by Healthy Waterways (a collaborative organisation between the Queensland government, industry, researchers and the community) confirms the poor health of the ecosystem in the catchment, highlighting that the streams are in very poor condition, channel and gully erosion is widespread and sediment loads are significant during flood times in the catchment (MBWCP, 2006; 2005; 2004; 2003; 2001). The Report Cards also indicate that the catchment received extremely poor evaluations – ranging from F in 2001–2003 and D or D- in 2004–2006 (where D refers to 'poor' and F refers to 'fail'). These findings suggest that regulations and control mechanisms employed by government agencies have had little success in preventing or solving the ecological problems in the catchment.

The planning and management of ecosystems in the Lockyer Catchment

The planning and management of ecosystems in the Lockyer Catchment is largely a political process, controlled by the Queensland Government and the Brisbane City Council, with issues entrenched within their bureaucratic structures and functions. One respondent said: 'environmental planning decisions are controlled by the Queensland Government and Brisbane council, with minimal consultation with community'. Another respondent added that '[community] consultations are fake, decisions are pre-determined ... they only come to get support [of communities] for their decisions'. A number of discussions revealed that most government staff members are not interested in listening to community voices, as they need to work according to the bureaucratic policy and targets set at higher levels. The diverse and often conflicting community voices are likely to delay their delivery of required performance according to their job description. One respondent said: 'it is the system of bureaucracy where decisions are made by senior officials and politicians usually informed by science'. Another respondent added: 'if there is a problem, it is the problem of the system of bureaucracy'.

The current approach to planning and management is simplistic. The complex interdependent relationships within and between different ecological and social systems have been simplified for technical and administrative convenience. Many respondents shared a belief that the planning and management approach of the government has overlooked the connections between a set of CPRs (such as groundwater and vegetation) that constitute the ecological richness of the catchment. The decisions that are made by the government experts are, as one respondent asserted, 'driven by fixed resources, targets and predetermined policies, not according to the severity of the problems and the concerns of stakeholders'.

Respondents from landholders, Healthy Waterways, officials of the Brisbane River and Moreton Bay, and private organisations are concerned about soil erosion, salinity and water quality issues perceived to have emerged from the damaging activities as mentioned above in the surrounding Lockyer Catchment. The approach adopted by the government is seen to be focussing on a single resource system in order to address on-site issues, ignoring the connection between different resources. Government interventions have mainly focussed on on-site problems identified by their staff, and if there are resources, they implement specific plans to solve them. One respondent claimed: 'resource management is much more complex as ecological and social processes overlap, but government approach has consistently failed to recognise this connection'. The simplified government approach has failed to tackle the issues of externalities of social and ecological interdependence.

The current planning and management of resources has significantly damaged the environment and disengaged most community groups. For example, as one landholder said: 'initially governments encouraged people to clear land and convert lands into agricultural fields, now we face unsustainable situations'. The government has granted individual property rights to landholders as an approach to maximise the use of lands, with few restrictions on use. Although the land was cleared many years ago, one respondent said, 'the current generation is suffering, most likely the future generation will suffer'. A common theme to emerge from the discussions and interviews was that land clearing has considerably worsened the problem not only in the area where the land was cleared but also in areas far from the cleared land. This is perhaps 'one of the most damaging policy interventions that the government has ever made', one respondent highlighted. Soil erosion problems have reduced the level of ecosystem services and reduced the water quality for downstream users. Many respondents said that government has now started to restore ecosystems but the landholders are required to pay for correcting past government mistakes. The government is trying to manage the riparian buffer zone, but with limited consultation with the community groups. Many respondents remain discontented with the government's exclusionary approach to the planning and management of the restored riparian zone.

Regulating authorities have also employed market-based approaches to creating a market for ecosystem services. They attempted to divert payments for ecosystem services (PES) to the landholders so as to induce them to set aside productive farming lands to build up riparian buffer strips for producing the ecosystem services to improve water quality. While landholders are positive about this initiative, they doubt that the regulating authorities will be able to successfully execute the PES scheme because of the lack of collaboration among landholders and between landholders and other stakeholders to forego the lands to create a facilitating market framework where transactions for the payment for ecosystem services will occur.

Stakeholders' interests in collaborative planning and management

All respondents shared a similar view that they are interested in collaborative work. As one respondent said: 'natural resource planning and management is not possible by the governments or communities alone'. This was also the common answer to the question of why the government and stakeholders need to work together. Many respondent landholders, particularly from downstream Brisbane, had keen interests in the management of resources in the upstream because they saw resource exploitation and agriculture activities in the catchment as the main sources of the downstream problems. Most respondents, including members from government agencies, private organisations and landholders, are now aware of the problems as well as the collaborative approach that could potentially solve them. International examples of success in collaborative resource management have also set examples for Lockyer stakeholders; as one respondent pointed out: 'we have international examples of success in collaborative natural resource management, we can minimise mistakes and maximise success by learning from others'. International agreements that Australia has signed have also required collaborative approaches to natural resource governance, reflected in one respondent's claim that 'it is not the matter of choice, it is the requirement as Australia has already signed various agreements'. A common theme to emerge was that collaborative planning and management is not only possible, but is essential to improve social and ecological outcomes.

A well-defined common space or a 'collaborative platform' is lacking. As one respondent said: 'we are keen to work together, the difficulty is that there is no suitable platform to work together'. Another respondent highlighted the issues of equality, saying that 'any collaborative decisions must be based on equality principles, everyone's needs and voices are equally important'. Issues of power and resources vested in government officials were frequently raised by many stakeholders and as one respondent maintained: 'the government agencies are current managers, they have the power and resources, they are well-situated to initiate collaborative work'. However, another respondent questioned such a critical role for the government: 'the power and resources held with government agencies is also a risk for collaborative work, their role must change from decision makers to supporters for collaborative work'. Many respondents drew attention to the need for change in the expert attitude of the government agencies, and emphasised the need for a new participatory, flexible and inclusive culture to make collaborative planning a reality. A respondent also highlighted a critical need for community groups and businesses to prioritise the communal needs and problems, rather than individual benefits and losses in the process of consensus building through collaborative engagement. In general, respondents were keen to become part of a collaborative process in ecosystem planning and management.

Discussion

The government has adopted an exclusionary, top-down and centralised approach together with some elements of a privatised/market-based approach in ecosystem planning and management practices which has had little success in delivering ecologically sustainable and socially desired outcomes. As demonstrated by the above findings, the ecosystem health has degraded due mostly to simplified, rational and exclusionary policy prescriptions that have led to adverse impacts on ecological processes and systems in the Lockyer Catchment. The regulating authorities have also neglected the complex interdependence between social and ecological processes. Despite enormous interest from all stakeholders to work towards the collaborative planning and management of natural resources, it has yet to be considered in the policy and practices. The questions to emerge then are: Why has the centralised approach persisted, despite delivering such negative ecological and social outcomes? And, how could collaborative planning and management be initiated and fostered?

Why has centralised planning and management persisted?

The finding from the case study demonstrates that there is little change in the way government agencies have conventionally planned and managed natural resources. Downs (1967) argues that the bureaucracy generally encourages bureaucrats to behave as avoiders of change. The centralised bureaucratic system of planning and management has avoided change and persisted over time due to its political, financial, technical and other backings. The centralised approach ensures that it is easy for the government agencies to make decisions unilaterally. The institutional efficiency of the government agencies is still being judged in terms of rational decision-making and protection of natural resources, rather than the management of collaborative actions. After the endorsement of various international agreements, however, the bureaucracy is now obliged to meet a range of social, economic and environmental objectives. For this, the agencies need to retain some key authority in which there is flexibility for community consultation and some inclusions of community views, while more important decisions are made by the politicians and bureaucrats at the higher levels. This practice is also reflected in the maintenance of a culture supported by a controlling bureaucratic structure. As Ribot (2004) argues, the bureaucracy fears losing economic benefit from the control over natural resources and the power that defines and supports its political and administrative role. Institutional reform of the state agencies is often called institutional strengthening when much of the problem is that the institutions are already too strong (Fisher, 1994). The possibility of collaborative approaches does not appeal to the agencies because its assumptions for inclusive decision-making require the shift in functional assumptions underlying the government and bureaucracy as controller. Instead, custodial ideas about the government and bureaucracy making decisions for the people (often covertly) is a simple model for delivering quick results according to preset targets.

The underlying reasons for the persistence of a centralised approach may also be due to bureaucratic norms and ideology. Weber (1958) argues that in a modern bureaucracy, the relationship between bureaucrats and clients are supposed to be functionally specific and impersonal. There is an existence of a *bossy* tradition in state bureaucracy in which subordinate staff must follow their boss' order and the orders are hierarchically transmitted from top to the bottom. The order at the top is informed by an ideology for the maintenance of the bureaucracy to impose standards of social and environmental wellbeing. These vague concerns are often misguided from knowledge of orthodox science that identifies problems and devises solutions based on scientific methods which ignore social, economic, political and ecological contexts. Therefore, the problem is essentially ideological about how the bureaucracy is organised and operated.

The analysis of findings from the Lockyer Catchment suggests that the decision-making is driven by the restricted thinking about resource planning and management that focuses on a single resource and the simple definition of relationships. This restricted thinking is linked to orthodox science which provides knowledge and skills to facilitate narrow understanding of problems and solutions. The knowledge produced by science has traditionally focussed on collecting politically neutral and accurate facts through quantitative and economic analyses of problems. This knowledge informs policies because they are widely accepted in the policy circle. The historic practices of sampling and inference do not fully account for the social, political and ecological connections in which socio-ecological problems are experienced. The planning and policies were poorly informed; they could not address the issues situated in wider social, economic and political processes. And even when the policy has attempted to solve problems, it has been implemented through a universal and target-oriented model of the agencies which practically neglects the complex interdependence. The conventional power relations remain unchanged and the traditional bureaucratic planning and management maintains the status quo.

Towards sustainability: collaborative planning and management of ecosystems

Our findings suggest that stakeholders are keen to work together. This can be taken as a foundation for a collaborative approach to the planning and management of natural resources. Herein, we propose a relatively new CPR approach in establishing and fostering collaborative planning and management of ecosystems as CPR which, we believe, can enhance sustainability. Collaboration between various stakeholders for the Lockyer Catchment, Brisbane River and Moreton Bay can resolve various externality issues that arise in the catchment and marine areas. This is consistent with the vision of the Healthy Waterways Partnership, which notes: 'By 2020, our waterways and catchments will be healthy ecosystems supporting the livelihoods and lifestyles of people in South East Queensland, and will be managed through collaboration between community, government and industry' (Healthy Waterways, 2007: p. 13). This is also reflected in the view of integrated catchment management in Australia. As Syme et al. (1994) recommend, collaboration involving both the government and the community is crucial to develop and implement catchment planning and management. The importance of collaborative management is also supported by international experiences (e.g., Wittmer, 2005; Swallow et al., 2005; Kandel and Rosa, 2005). In addition, legal frameworks are vital for regulating and institutionalising the planning and management approach, and in Queensland a strong legal framework for catchment management needs to be established (Ewing, 2003).

The idea of collaborative management among users, which is also consistent with the literature on nested multiple use CPRs (e.g., Steins and Edwards, 1999), integrated catchment management (Syme et al., 1994), and with the vision of the Healthy Waterways Partnership (Healthy Waterways 2007), is useful for understanding the issues of the wider socio-ecological interdependencies in which CPRs are embedded. A huge body of empirical literature on collaborative action provides examples for effective collaborative approaches that have addressed the issues emerging from social and ecological research to improve planning and management of CPRs (Cleaver, 2000; Ostrom, 2004; Shrestha, 2005). The idea of collaborative planning and management is also useful for addressing management issues of natural systems, including catchments (German et al., 2006; Kerr, 2007). Other studies demonstrate that a collaborative management and planning approach is critically important in enhancing the collective action among different groups of stakeholders, especially for complex landscapes (Selin and Chavez, 1995; Lubell et al., 2002; Marshall, 2005).

Figure 15: Collaborative planning and management of ecosystems

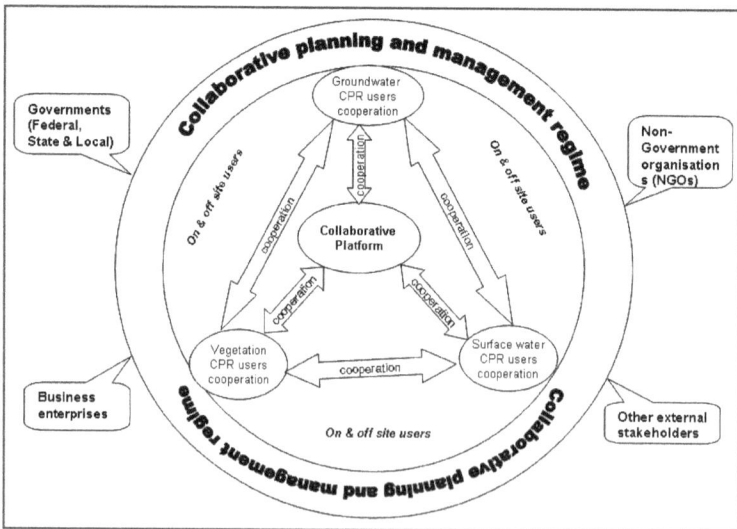

Source: Authors

We propose a framework for planning and management of ecosystems in a catchment, as shown in Figure 15. It is proposed that both on-site and off-site users from the Lockyer Catchment, Brisbane and Moreton Bay can work together within an open and equal platform – i.e., a 'collaborative platform' – coordinated by relevant government line agencies with non-government organisations, environmental groups, businesses enterprises and other stakeholders such as universities. Stakeholders could work together to identify issues, negotiate solutions, devise plans, and implement agreed-upon institutional arrangements to improve social and ecological outcomes and to internalise externalities rooted in socio-ecological interdependence. It is a multi-layered, multi-stakeholder framework, adaptable to the needs of stakeholders and based on open, respectful communication and negotiation.

In this framework, it is expected that stakeholders will be able to cooperate on multiple levels to correct issues of within-boundary and cross-boundary externalities and market failure. On-site users refer to those who are using groundwater and surface water in the catchment, while offsite users are downstream stakeholders including the authorities and managers of the Brisbane River and Moreton Bay, Healthy Waterways and private organisations. Cooperation among the on-site users of different CPRs addresses the externalities that occur within the catchment, while the cooperation between on-site and off-site users deals with the cross-boundary externalities that occur beyond the boundary of the catchment. In particular, cooperation between landholders and offsite beneficiaries can address cross-boundary externalities arising from land clearing and soil erosion in the Lockyer Catchment, affecting the water quality of the off-catchment water resources such as the Brisbane River and Moreton Bay.

The framework is for CPR-based collaborative planning and management of ecosystems which can capture the merits of government and market-based approaches, bringing the technical and professional experiences into practice with those of other stakeholders. The process enhances the participation of stakeholders to improve ecosystem health, institutional development, community revitalisation and capacity strengthening. For instance, one initiative that the government is attempting to implement through top-down regulation and a market-based instrument (PES scheme) for water quality improvement is the construction of riparian buffer strips to prevent sediment flows from the catchment into the Brisbane River and Moreton Bay. The idea is useful, but since it requires landholders along the river to agree to forgo land and plant riparian vegetation, a high degree of collaboration among the stakeholders is essential. Furthermore, financing required for a PES scheme could also be arranged and structured through the collaboration between the buyers and sellers of ecosystem services. The beneficiaries would buy ecosystem services from the landholders, with the landholders acting as sellers.

Although collaborative planning and management approaches have become popular in many countries to address various natural resource problems, and as we have argued, have the potential to do well compared to centralised or privatised systems in the specific context of our case study, we do not claim that this is the best framework to guarantee success in all areas. We cannot emphasise enough the need to refine this framework. We also recognise that effective collaboration is not easy. The critical role that we have recommended for the government agencies, as agreeing with one of our research participants, does pose a degree of risk because letting their power go within the collaborative approach is not what they are accustomed to.

We are very much aware of the uncertainty involved in making decisions in a collaborative platform as we are still learning about how society and ecological systems work and interact. Therefore, our idea for a collaborative platform is that of a flexible, open and evolving forum for discussion and communication within the context of stakeholders' own perceptions of conditions, problems and possible solutions for the present and future. The platform is about understanding, reflecting and synthesising ideas, problems and experiences to bring about change – the change that can only be possible with genuine interest, commitment and passion by involving stakeholders towards a common, concerted action for a better future. We agree with Ostrom et al. (2007) who asserted in relation to the CPR analysis that collaborative approaches are not a panacea. The approaches may, however, be applied as diagnostic tools for exploring natural resource problems and solutions for a sustainable future.

Conclusions

The centralised and privatised planning and management of natural resources, which is still dominant in the Lockyer Catchment, has failed to internalise externalities that are inherent in the complex social and ecological interdependence. The centralised approach has delivered outcomes that are ecologically damaging and socially inappropriate and thus unsustainable. In addition, while the current planning and management approach attempts to improve ecological and social outcomes, the actual practice fails to do so. This failure necessitates the exploration of an alternative approach that has a potential to do better than the current one. A collaborative planning and management approach does have potential in the Lockyer Catchment, given that all stakeholders are interested in and willing to work together to improve social and ecological outcomes. An open, inclusive and equal 'collaborative platform' has been proposed, with a critical role assigned to government agencies. It will be the task of these agencies to initiate, establish and foster an active and equitable collaborative platform where stakeholders can work together as equal partners – a major shift from what is currently happening.

The centralised approach of planning and management of natural resources has persisted for a long time. A real shift from the centralised approach towards the collaborative approach can therefore be a slow and challenging process. A degree of resistance from the government agencies may prevent the platform from work effectively. A collaborative approach may not appeal to the agencies because its assumptions for inclusive decision-making require a fundamental shift in functional assumptions underlying the government and bureaucracy as controller. The centralised approach is also deeply embedded within a long tradition of bureaucratic culture, norms and ideology supported by strong, established and well-resourced structures, which encourage bureaucrats to behave as avoiders of change. A dominant discourse is informed by an ideology of the bureaucracy that must maintain standard and social and environmental wellbeing. These vague concerns are often misguided from knowledge of orthodox science that identifies problems and devises solutions based on scientific methods which ignore complex social, economic, political and ecological interdependence.

The possibility of a collaborative approach to originate and advance practice therefore depends heavily on understanding and addressing issues entrenched in the bureaucracy and how it has been established, organised and operated, as well as how it makes rational decisions based on scientific knowledge. Major rethinking is needed on the ideological and functional underpinnings of bureaucracy, and on modifying the role of governments as rational decision makers to political facilitators in order to initiate, maintain and institutionalise an effective collaborative platform in the planning and management of natural resources, one that can improve social and ecological outcomes and enhance sustainability.

Notes

The authors are indebted to Professor Helen Ross from the School of Natural and Rural Systems Management at the University of Queensland for her valuable insights, comments and suggestions. We also acknowledge several works by Sarker et al. and K. K. Shrestha which provided a solid ground for initiating this chapter. The authors are grateful for the time and information given during interviews and open discussions by community members and government officials. We also thank the government offices for providing access to their documents. We are grateful for useful comments provided by our colleagues at the University of Queensland, and by the audiences in the Urban and Regional Planning and Policy Seminar at the University of Sydney.

References

Abal, E. G., Bunn, S. E., Dennison, W. C. (eds.) (2005) *Healthy waterways healthy catchments: making the connection in South East Queensland, Australia.* Brisbane: Moreton Bay Waterways and Catchment Partnership.

Apan, A. A., Raine, S. R. and Paterson, M. S. (2002) 'Mapping and analysis of changes in the riparian landscape structure of the Lockyer Valley Catchment, Queensland, Australia.' *Landscape and Urban Planning.* 59(1): pp. 43–57.

Baland, J. M. and Platteau, J. P. (1996) *Halting degradation of natural resources: is there a role for rural communities?* Oxford: FAO and Clarendon Press.

Berkes, F. (1989) 'Cooperation from the perspectives of human ecology,' in F. Berkes (ed.), *Common Property Resources: Ecology and Community-based Sustainable Development.* London: Belhaven Press. pp. 70–88.

Blaikie, P. and Brookfield, H. (1987) *Land degradation and society.* London and New York: Methuen.

Boyes, B. (2001) *Land use planning handbook for the Lockyer Catchment.* Forest Hill, Gatton, Queensland: Lockyer Catchment Association.

Christensen, N. L., Bartuska, A., Brown, J., Carpenter, S., D'Antonio, C., Francis, R., MacMohan, J., Noss, R., Parsons, D., Peterson, C., Turner, M. and Woodmansee, R. (1996) 'The report of the Ecological Society of America committee on the scientific basis for ecosystem management.' *Ecological Applications.* 6(3): pp. 665–691.

Ciriacy-Wantrup, S. V. and Bishop, R. C. (1975) 'Common property as a concept in natural resources policy.' *Natural Resources Journal.* 15(1): pp. 713–727.

Cleaver, F. (2000) 'Moral ecological rationality, institutions and the management of common property resources.' *Development and Change.* 28(3): pp. 61–383.

Daily, G. (ed.) (1997) *Nature's services: societal dependence on natural ecosystems.* Washington DC: Island Press.

Demsetz, H. (1967) 'Toward a theory of property rights.' *The American Economic Review.* 57(2): pp. 347–359.

Downs, A. (1967) *Inside bureaucracy.* Boston: Little Brown.

Ehrlich, P. R. (1968) *The population bomb.* New York: Ballantine Books.

Ewing, S. (2003) 'Catchment management arrangements,' in S. Dovers and S. Wild-River (eds.), *Managing Australia's environment*. Sydney: The Federation Press. pp.393–412.

Fisher, R. J. (1994) 'Indigenous forest management in Nepal: why common property is not a problem,' in M. Allen (ed.), *Anthropology of Nepal: peoples, problems and processes*. Kathmandu: Mandala Book Point, pp. 64–81.

Flyvbjerg, B. (2002) 'Bringing power to planning research: one researcher's praxis story.' *Journal of Planning Education and Research*. 21(4): pp. 353–366.

Forester, J. (1989) *Planning in the Face of Power*. Berkeley: University of California Press.

German, L., Taye, H., Charamila, S., Tolera, T. and Tanui, J. (2006) *The many meanings of collective action: lessons on enhancing gender inclusion and equity in watershed management*. CAPRi Working Paper 52. Washington DC: International Food Policy Research Institute.

Gibson, C. C., McKean, M. and Ostrom, E. (eds.) (2000) *People and forests: communities, institutions, and governance*. Cambridge, Massachusetts: MIT Press.

Hardin, G. (1968) 'The tragedy of the commons.' *Science*. vol. 162: pp. 1243–1248.

Healey, P. (2003) 'Collaborative planning in perspective.' *Planning Theory*. 2(2): pp. 101–123.

Healthy Waterways (2007) *Recognition and reward for efforts to protect and restore the waterways, catchments and bays of South East Queensland*. Brisbane: Healthy Waterways.

Hiller, J. (2003) 'Agonizing over consensus: why Habermasian ideals cannot be real.' *Planning Theory*. 2(1): pp. 37–59.

Howitt, R. (2001). *Rethinking resource management: justice, sustainability and indigenous peoples*. London and New York: Routledge.

Innes, J. (2004) 'Consensus Building: Clarifications for the Critics.' *Planning Theory*. 3(1), pp. 5–20.

Ives, J. D. (1987) 'The theory of Himalayan environmental degradation: its validity and application challenged by recent research.' *Mountain Research and development*. 7(3): pp. 189–199.

Kandel, S. and Rosa, H. (2005) 'Managing the commons: payment for environmental services: emerging issues, conclusions and recommendations,' in L. Merino and J. Robson (eds.), *Managing the commons: payment for environmental services.* Mexico City: Instituto de Ecologia (INE).

Kerr, J. (2007) 'Watershed management: lessons from common property theory.' *International Journal of the Commons.* 1(1): pp. 89–109.

Li, T.M. (1996) 'Images of community: discourse and strategy in property relations.' *Development and Change.* 27(3): pp. 265–283.

Lubell, M., Schneider, M., Scholz, J. T. and Mete, M. (2002) 'Watershed partnerships and the emergence of collective action institutions.' *American Journal of Political Science.* 46(1): pp. 148–163.

Marshall, G. R. (2005) *Economics for collaborative environmental management: renegotiating the commons.* London: Earthscan.

McCarthy, N., Dutilly-Diane, C. and Drabo, B. (2004) 'Cooperation, collective action and natural resource management in Burkina Faso.' *Agricultural Systems.* 82(3): pp. 233–255.

McKean, M. (2000) 'Common property: what is it, what is it good for, and what makes it work?' in C. C. Gibson, M. McKean and E. Ostrom, *People and forests: communities, institutions, and governance.* Cambridge, Massachusetts: MIT Press, pp. 27–56.

Menzies, N. (2003) *Partners in governing the forests: reviewing community-based forest management,* in 'Forests, Source of Life', XII World Forestry Congress, Quebec City.

Millennium Ecosystem Assessment (MEA) (2005) *Ecosystems and human well-being: synthesis.* Washington DC: Island Press.

Moreton Bay Waterways and Catchments Partnership (MBWCP) (2006; 2005; 2004; 2003; 2001). *Report card. Ecosystem health monitoring program.* Brisbane, Queensland.

Nantel, P., Moreau, A., Sougavginski, S. and Doyon, F. (2003) *Ecosystem management of forest resources in Canada: an overview of concepts and current experiences,* in 'Forests, Source of Life', XII World Forestry Congress, Quebec City.

National Research Council (2002) *The drama of the commons.* Washington DC: National Academy Press.

Ophuls, W. (1973) *Leviathan or oblivion? towards a steady state economy.* San Francisco: Freeman.

Ostrom, E. (1990) *Governing the commons: the evolution of institutions for collective action.* Cambridge: Cambridge University Press.

Ostrom, E. (2003) 'How types of goods and property rights jointly affect collective action.' *Journal of Theoretical Politics.* 15(3): pp. 239–270.

Ostrom, E. (2004) 'Understanding collective action,' in R. Meinzen-Dick and M. D. Gregorio (eds.), *Collective action and property rights for sustainable development*. New York: International Food Policy Research Institute.

Ostrom, E. (2005) *Understanding institutional diversity*. New Jersey: Princeton University Press.

Ostrom, E., Burger, J., Field, C. B., Norgaard, R. B. and Policansky, D. (1999) 'Revisiting the commons: local lessons, global challenges.' *Science* vol. 284 (April 9th): pp. 278–282.

Ostrom, E., Gardner, R. and Walker, J. (1994) *Rules, games and common-pool resources*. Ann Arbor: University of Michigan Press.

Ostrom, E., Janssen, M. A. and Anderies, J. M. (2007) 'Going beyond panaceas.' *Proceedings of the National Academy of Sciences of the United States of America*. 104(39): pp. 15176–15178.

Pindyck, R. S. and Rubinfeld, D. L. (2001) *Microeconomics*. New Jersey: Prentice Hall.

Quiggin, J. (2001) 'Environmental economics and the Murray-Darling river system.' *Australian Journal of Agricultural and Resource Economics*. 45(1): pp. 67–94.

Rajbhandari, B. (2003) 'The role of riparian buffer in water quality improvement: an economic perspective'. Masters Thesis, School of Natural and Rural Systems Management, University of Queensland, Australia.

Ribot, J. C. (2004) *Waiting for democracy: the politics of choice in natural resource decentralisation*. Washington, DC: World Resource Institute.

Runge, C. F. (1986) 'Common property and collective action in economic development.' *World Development*. 14(5): pp. 623–635.

Samuelson, P. A. and Nordhaus, W. D. (1998) *Economics*. New York: McGraw-Hill.

Sarin, M., Singh N., Sundar, N. and Bhogal, R. (2003) *Devolution as a threat to democratic decision-making in forestry: findings from three states in India*. London: Overseas Development Institute.

Sarker, A., Ross, H. and Shrestha, K. K. (2008). 'A common-pool resource approach for water quality management: an Australian case study.' *Ecological Economics*. (*In Press*).

Selin, S. and Chavez, D. (1995) 'Developing a collaborative model for environmental planning and management.' *Environmental Management*. 19(2): pp. 189–195.

Shrestha, K. K. (2005) 'Collective action and equity in Nepalese community forestry'. Unpublished PhD Thesis. University of Sydney, Australia.

South East Queensland Regional Water Quality Management Strategy Team (SEQRWQMST) (2001) *Discover the waterways of South-east Queensland: waterways health and catchment management in South-east Australia.* Brisbane, Queensland: Moreton Bay Waterways & Catchments Partnership.

Steins, N. A. and Edwards, V. M. (1999) 'Platforms for collective action in multiple-use common-pool resources.' *Agriculture and Human Values.* 16(3): pp. 241–255.

Swallow, B., Meinzen-Dick, R. and van Noordwijk, M. (2005) 'Localizing demand and supply of environmental services: interactions with property rights, collective action and the welfare of smallholders,' in L. Merino and J. Robson (eds.), *Managing the commons: payment for environmental services.* Mexico City: Instituto de Ecologia (INE).

Syme, G. J., Butterworth, J. E. and Nancarrow, B. E. (1994) *National whole catchment management: a review and analysis of processes.* Canberra: Land and Water Resources Research and Development Corporation.

Turner, M. D. (2004) 'Political ecology and the moral dimensions of "resource conflicts": the case of farmer-herder conflicts in the Sahel.' *Political Geography.* 23(7): pp. 863–889.

Weber, M. (1958) *The religion of India: the sociology of Hinduism and Buddhism.* New York: The Free Press.

Wittmer, H. (2005) 'Managing the commons: payment for environmental services: thematic introduction,' in L. Merino and J. Robson (eds.), *Managing the commons: payment for environmental services.* Mexico City: Instituto de Ecologia (INE).

Yin, R. K. (2002) *Case study research, design and methods.* Newbury Park: Sage Publications.

Chapter 4

CRAFTING ECONOMIC DRIVERS FOR SUSTAINABLE LOCAL AREAS IN A GLOBALISING REGIONAL ECONOMY: SYDNEY AS A CASE STUDY

Edward J. Blakely, Santosh Bista and Godfrey Lubulwa

Sydney is facing its future. It is the largest city and one of the fastest growing metropolitan areas of Australia. Like many newly emerging global cities, Sydney is dealing with its past economy while it shapes its future economic scenarios. Spatially uneven outcomes seem inevitable as metropolitan regions globalise. But for Sydney, this transition is especially painful when the nation bases its socio-political fabric on equal outcomes – 'a fair go' for all citizens. In response to change, Sydney has adopted a new approach to metropolitan planning that has moved from a traditional land use system to one that comes to grips with socioeconomic issues.

Using tools of small area analysis of the internal spatial economies of the Sydney metropolitan region, this chapter looks at how the region could reach new strategic goals with a more equitable metropolitan economic pattern. The analytical template for this approach is a new form of metropolitan suburban district analysis of a greater metropolitan system. This research uses city/suburban data to explore patterns of spatial drivers in the metropolitan system. These are tracked internally their implications for the performance of a regional spatial economy are assessed. The research offers explanations and a mechanism to identify the causes and consequences of unequal metropolitan economic performance. Furthermore, it provides an alternative for crafting economic drivers for sustainable local area development in a globalising regional economy in a more equitable and stronger performing region.

Introduction

One of the more troubling aspects of the new global regional economics is spatial inequality (Goldsmith and Blakely, 1992). In crafting a future economic scenario for a large globalised region, there are locational winners and losers. For decades, central city and older suburban areas have declined in the wake of globalisation. This process of unevenness is now a central issue in regional plan making (Hill and Wolman, 1997; Ledebur and Barnes, 1992). The reason for this fascination with unequal subregional development can be traced to studies of US inequalities between central cities and the growing suburban areas. Much of the US work in regional economic inequality reflects the racial and spatial outcomes of metropolitan areas (Kasarda and Parnell, 1993), the latter represented as a spatial economic apartheid and the central thesis of recent American regional scholarship. Douglas Massey and Nancy Denton's classic work, *American apartheid: segregation and the making of the American underclass* (1993) details the deep division of resources between haves and have-nots occupying the same regional economic geography.

But space and race are not the only reasons for differential economic outcomes between suburbs and central cities in the United States. Myron Orfield (1997) provides a different analysis of the regional suburbanised economy in the Minneapolis St. Paul region to show how underlying policy and economic migration factors undermine city economies and generate suburban advantages as a region globalises creating inter and intra-city disparities (p. 67). The consequences, as Orfield (1997) has noted are sprawl and uneven wealth distribution among suburbs. Essentially, the new economy is not just about suburbs and the inner city but also and most importantly about the specific economies of suburbs and specific parts of the inner city.

Moreover, in some parts of the world, including Sydney, it is the outer suburbs, rather than the central city, where emerging inequality is pronounced and more deeply embedded in the socioeconomic structure. While race may be a prime factor for unequal allocations in the US, this is not the case in Sydney where recent immigration patterns and other factors, as is the case in many European cities, are at work that create uneven spatial economies. Michael Stoll (1999), a researcher specialising in poverty, race and space, suggests that being near work does not guarantee that residents in a global region are able to gain work irrespective of race. As this research shows, spatial economic drivers in different parts of a region can have profound effects on the nature and course of globalisation. This chapter looks at uneven regional performance in Sydney, Australia to find the economic drivers that generate economic disparities across a region. It suggests the keys to intervening that might help make underperforming places more competitive as the region's economy is transformed by global economic forces. Sydney is an ideal case of spatial redistributions as a result of international forces since it is isolated from border incursions or easy access by migrants and has a long history of national economic management aimed at even distribution of wealth (Stimson et al., 2002).

Sydney metropolitan region

The Sydney economy has grown for the last three decades adding jobs and people. Sydney grew 707,075 jobs over 25 years and increased its population by 1,113,601 over the same period — a ratio of 0.63. Sydney is the largest recipient of international immigration and internal emigration within the nation. The new immigrant human resources added to Sydney are an economic dimension since many come with high skills or come seeking tertiary education opportunities and remain in Sydney adding to the regional skill pool, which attracts new firms and enhances existing firms' competitiveness (O'Connor, 1999).

Sydney is undergoing a new metropolitan regional strategic planning process (Searle, 1996). Unlike former regional plans that focused almost solely on allocating land for housing estates, this puts a greater emphasis on using tools to affect spatial economic outcomes. The new Sydney Strategic Plan is designed to influence spatial allocation of job creation opportunities and to improve spatial economic wellbeing across the entire metropolitan area (DIPNR, 2005). Sydney is not alone in seeking to use planning tools for a more just socioeconomic outcome. The new London Plan has the same goals with only a slightly different emphasis. Similar ideas are expressed in regional plans for Long Island in New York, Seattle, San Francisco and Paris. The theme of spatial inequality is central to regional science. However, most regional science tools are aimed at addressing smaller grained problems in the regional economic network for Sydney or other similar regions.

Sydney and Australia are characterised as a homogenous national spatial economy. For over half a century, Australian wages have been set through national wager tribunals and working conditions organised to present uniform entitlements. Moreover, public investments such as schools, roads and the like have been more evenly provided through state institutions. Yet as Sydney embarks on its fourth major metropolitan plan the central issue is job and income fragmentation. In essence, Sydney and Australia have joined the global market place. Despite more even public infrastructure endowments, Sydney is becoming increasingly economically segregated with different economic drivers altering the socioeconomic outcomes across the region. In this research we look for the subregional drivers of local city jurisdictional areas as micro-regional spaces vs. the macro-region of Sydney's metropolitan system of nearly 5 million people to see how regional science can help identify and correct the gaps in regional economic outcomes as the region and the nation globalise. Unless the pattern of local economic drivers in spatial areas below the large metro-region are understood, it is difficult to apply spatially sensitive actions through planning schemes that generate more equal outcomes for areas that are socially and spatially disadvantaged by the globalisation processes. We do not have the space to present the history of Sydney's economy here but there is substantial data on how spatial inequalities arose over time (Searle, 1996). We therefore focus on spatial economic drivers across the Sydney region through the lens of city jurisdictional nodes to provide better guidance for local suburban and regional policymakers as they craft regional economic policies.

Study scope

This study uses regional economic analysis tools to look at the structure of Sydney's subregions or districts (Illawarra, Hunter, Western Sydney etc.), the statistical local areas that cover the Sydney Greater Metropolitan Region (GMR) (see Figure 16). It undertakes a comprehensive analysis using income and population growth as proxies for socioeconomic prosperity in the localities studied. We select these key variables because in combination they illustrate socioeconomic health. While population loss can be an indicator in a mature economy of community decline, rising incomes are a strong measure of wealth. However, there are circumstances where these variables might be false signals. For example, an old community might have high incomes but is ageing with a declining population. Or, a fast growing place with new lower socioeconomic immigrant residents might seem like it is doing well, but the human resources and skill levels base might not produce a strong economy despite apparent population growth. Therefore, in this study, we look at population and income from various analytical perspectives to determine the drivers of growth and the decline in the statistical local jurisdiction and aggregated subregional districts of the economy of the Sydney GMR as a whole. Statistical Local Areas (SLAs), which are city sized jurisdictional areas, were used as the basis of the analysis. We note that regional areas the size of US style Standard Metropolitan Statistical Areas (SMSAs) are convenient for firm based economic analysis, but fail to reveal the difference in social demographic spatial outcomes at a lower city sized level. For example, while Orange County or Long Island may look at wealth in aggregate, there are well known pockets of poverty lying in the larger spatial system. In this work, we look at the differential drivers at the micro-city spaces of fast growing economies in a robust region to see where and why differential patterns emerge and what might be done about them. An essential question is: do some places perform better or worse than their neighbours in the same economic space? If so, what are the economic drivers for these divergences in performance?

This research uses Australian Bureau of Statistics (ABS) data for 1990–2001, data sets developed by the Bureau of Transport and Regional Economics (BTRE, 2003b, 2004 and 2005), and specific ABS data for the local areas. Much of the data are four years old, and in a rapidly changing dynamic economy, it may be a better illustration of past performance than an indicator of future directions or barriers. However, it is the best data available and the trend lines are clear and deepening.

Research approach

In this study, we base our examination of the smallest unit for analysis on the statistical local area (SLA), an ABS geographic collection approximating suburbs or closely related groups of small city-suburbs. Our fine grain analysis based on SLAs is richer than is possible in most regions in the United States, where the data available for counties or larger units mask more finely grained spatial differences.

SLAs are small and imperfect proxies for subregional economies. We group the statistical local areas in the Sydney GMR into nine natural economic units or districts. These districts are: East Central Sydney, West Central Sydney, North Sydney, South Sydney, North West Sydney, South West Sydney, Illawarra, Newcastle, and Central Coast. Some of these districts remain known for their old economic base while others are clearly influenced by new information industries and new technology. So we look at SLAs across the larger Sydney GMR to see what the drivers of growth are.

Figure 16: Districts in the Sydney Greater Metropolitan Region

	District	Name of Statistical Local Areas Covered
1	Eastern Core	Ashfield, Burwood, Canterbury, Concord, Drummoyne, Leichhardt, Marrickville, Strathfield, Botany Bay, Randwick, South Sydney, Sydney Inner, Sydney Remainder, Waverley, Woollahra, Ryde, Hunters Hill, Lane Cove, Mosman, North Sydney, Willoughby (N=21)
2	Western Core	Auburn, Bankstown, Fairfield, Holroyd, Parramatta (N=5)
3	North	Hornsby, Ku-ring-gai, Manly, Pittwater, Warringah (N=4)
4	South	Hurstville, Kogarah, Rockdale, Sutherland E, Sutherland W (N=4)
5	Northwest	Baulkham Hills, Blacktown – North, Blacktown – SE, Blacktown – SW, Blue Mountains, Hawkesbury, Penrith (N=5)
6	Southwest	Camden, Campbelltown, Liverpool, Wollondilly (N=4)
7	Central Coast	Gosford, Wyong (N=2)
8	Illawarra	Kiama, Shellharbour, Wollongong (N=3)
9	Newcastle	Cessnock, Lake Macquarie, Maitland, Newcastle – inner, Newcastle – remainder, Port Stephens (N=6)
	Total	(N =54)

Source: Authors

Analytical methods

The analytical framework of this chapter examines two variables to ascertain regional economic growth – total population and aggregate taxable income. It assesses the *drivers* or forces that produce either or both. The target or dependent variables are growth in total population (human resources) and growth in aggregate taxable income. These two variables were selected because in combination they are a measure of socioeconomic health. Changes in population size of an area are often associated with changes in a region's economic activity. In the past, because of a lack of better indicators, population change has often been used as an indicator of regional growth. Rising incomes in a region are strongly related to rising wealth. Nonetheless, there are circumstances where these variables might give false signals because of the rapid growth of new immigrants, lower skilled people, or low income retirees on fixed incomes who relocate to less expensive housing environments such as mobile home parks in Sunbelt areas.

The analysis of this research is threefold. First, location quotients are used to measure the performance of each statistical local area. Location quotients are ideal for ascertaining the performance of places and variables over the same period and using the same base. However, they measure the outcomes, not the inputs that generate relative performance. So, the second stage examines key economic growth activities using economic base analysis methods and correlation analysis. These methods show the relationships between factors associated with economic growth in a SLA to determine which of these factors are significant. Finally, the third stage takes the results of the first two measures and filters them through regressions (multivariate analysis) to see the influences of the significant economic drivers spatially within SLAs in the Sydney GMR. This analytical approach is similar to the work done by Toft and Stough (1986), who look at economic spatial shifts and use shift share with location quotients to measure the rates of growth among regions by comparing regional competitiveness in selected industries (Stimson et al., 2002: p. 87). A similar strategy to that in Stimson et al. (2002) was used in Blakely (1994: p. 113) to establish economic development pathways in the subregions of the Brisbane/Southeast Queensland economy. The analytical approach is outlined in Figure 17.

Figure 17: Approach to determining regional economic growth

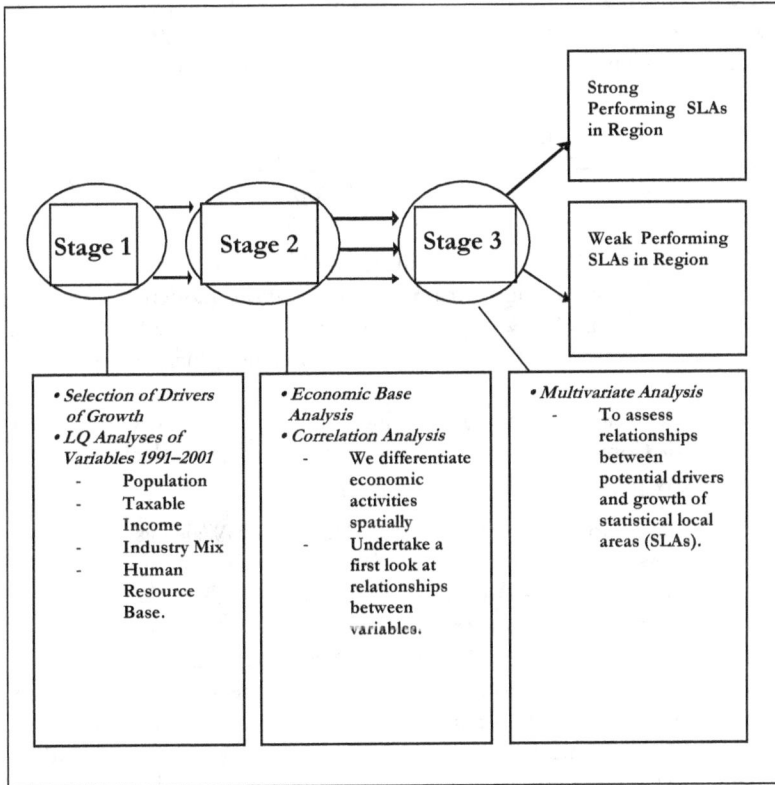

Source: Authors

Location analysis and results

The locational analysis technique is applied to the following variables: population in a region, taxable income in a region, and employment in industries located in the SLAs in the Sydney GMR. This technique was employed to identify the change in selected variables for SLAs between 1991 and 2001. We use the state of NSW as the reference region as has been done in earlier studies (for example, Stimson et al., 2002). The location quotient contains a notion of competition by considering a

77

location's share of the NSW population. The location quotient is used in the same manner as Mikelbank (2005) did to assess the performance of suburbs in the United States. In the case of population for a SLA, the location quotient (LQ) of population for SLA i, is calculated as:

$$LQ_i = (\sum_{1991}^{2001} \frac{Population_{i,t} / Population_{NSW,t}}{Population_{i,t-1} / Population_{NSW,t-1}}) / N$$

where N denote number of years in the study period. The top term (the numerator) in the equation for population location quotients represents SLA $i's$ share in the NSW population in time period t. The bottom term (the denominator) in the equation for population location quotients represents SLA $i's$ share in the NSW population in time period $t-1$. Thus, any SLA with a population LQ>1 increased its population share over the period. Conversely, a population LQ<1 indicates a decline in that SLA's NSW population share.

The population location quotients with New South Wales as a reference region show whether a given region grew faster than the overall NSW population (i.e. its LQ>1) or slower than the overall NSW population (i.e. its LQ<1). The LQ analyses, taking the 1991 and the 2001 population, shows that out of 54 SLAs, 24 had LQ values greater than 1, as shown in Figure 18 below. This indicates that the statistical local areas in the following districts – namely, North West of Sydney, South West of Sydney, the Central Coast and the Illawarra regions (i.e. the urban fringe) – stand out as attracting population. On the other hand, the Eastern core of Sydney, the Western core, North and South Sydney (referred to as the global arc) all have at least two-thirds of their statistical local areas with LQ>1. Over the period covered by this study, the global arc lost population share.

Figure 18: SLAs with high population location quotient, 1991–2001

District Name	Number of SLAs with LQ>1	% of SLAs in the district which have Population LQ>1	Name of the SLAs	Total SLAs in the Districts
Eastern Core	11	52%	Botany Bay, Burwood, Concord, Hunters Hill, Lane Cove, Mosman, Strathfield, Sydney Inner, Sydney Remainder, North Sydney, Woollahra	21
Western Core	2	40%	Auburn, Bankstown	5
North	1	25%	Hornsby	4
South	0	0%		4
North West	1	20%	Hawkesbury	5
South West	3	75%	Camden, Liverpool, Wollondilly	4
Central Coast	2	100%	Gosford, Wyong	2
Illawarra	1	33%	Kiama	3
Newcastle	3	50%	Cessnock, Maitland, Newcastle Inner	6
Total	24	44%		54

Source: Derived by the Planning Research Centre, the University of Sydney and BTRE based on an analysis of Australian Bureau of Statistics Estimated Resident Population, 1991–2001

Location quotients – taxable income

Income is a mark of economic strength. The Bureau of Transport and Regional Economics (BTRE, 2005) has argued that aggregate real taxable income in an area can serve as a proxy not only for wealth but also productivity. We look at taxable income changes over the study decade 1991–2001. To generate the results for location quotient analysis of aggregate taxable income for statistical local areas in the Sydney GMR, we used the following equation:

$$LQ_i = (\sum_{1991}^{2001} \frac{Taxable\ income_{i,t} /\ Taxable\ income_{NSW,t}}{Taxable\ income_{i,t-1} /\ Taxable\ income_{NSW,t-1}}) / N$$

The interpretations of the results for taxable income are similar to those for population. The taxable income location quotients with NSW as a reference region show whether a given SLA's taxable income grew faster than NSW (i.e., LQ>1) or slower than NSW (i.e., LQ<1). There is a relationship between places that had population growth and those with income growth as shown in Figure 19. The statistical local areas in the Eastern core of Sydney and in North Sydney perform more strongly with respect to income than they do for population. In contrast, statistical local areas on the Central Coast, the Illawarra, and the Southwest of Sydney do well with regard to both population and income growth.

Employment specialisation

This research employed an additional level of analysis to ascertain what industries had impacts on local and subregional economic areas. The data used to determine employment specialisation by statistical local area is from the ABS Census Journey to Work data. Information about journey to work has been collected from the Australian Census of Population and Housing since 1971 (Robertson, 2000). Klosterman et al. (1993) proposed a technique which we use in this section to further look at the statistical local areas by dividing employment in selected industries into two categories: basic and non-basic sector jobs. This technique will enable the identification of which sectors in a statistical local area serve the local market, and which sectors serve a national or international market. The non-local employment is also referred to as basic employment. The results from the application of this technique for the statistical local areas in the Sydney GMR are as follows. For each statistical local area, a positive entry indicates the number of non-local jobs in the statistical local areas. A negative entry shows that for that industry, there are no basic (i.e. non-local) jobs in the area.

Figure 19: SLAs with high taxable income quotient, 1991–2001

District Name	Number of SLAs with LQ>1	% of SLAs in the district with taxable income LQ>1	Name of the SLAs
Eastern Core	11	67%	Leichhardt, South Sydney, Sydney Inner, Sydney Remainder, Randwick, Waverley, Woollahra, Concord, Drummoyne, Hunter's Hill, Lane Cove, Mosman, North Sydney, Willoughby
Western Core	2	0%	-
North	1	100%	Hornsby, Ku-ring-gai, Manly, Pittwater/ Warringah
South	0	25%	Sutherland Shire
North West	1	60%	Baulkham Hills, Blacktown, Hawkesbury
South West	3	75%	Camden, Wollondilly, Liverpool
Central Coast	2	100%	Gosford, Wyong
Illawarra	1	67%	Kiama, Shellharbour
Newcastle	3	17%	Newcastle Inner
Total	24	44%	

Source: Derived by the Planning Research Centre, the University of Sydney and BTRE based on analysis of aggregate SLA taxable income, 1990–1 to 2000–1 from Bureau of Transport & Regional Economics (2005)

Strengthening and growing the local economy is often related to enhancing the basic sector employment. It also assumes that the basic sector is the engine for the growth of local economies (Klosterman, 1990: p. 115). The employment location quotient (ELQ) of employment for SLA i is calculated as:

$$ELQ_i = \frac{e_i / e_t}{E_i / E_t} \quad \text{where, } ELQ_i = \text{location quotient for industry } (i),$$

e_i = SLA's employment in industry (i),

e_t = SLA's total employment (t),

E_i = NSW's employment in industry (i), and

E_t = NSW's total employment (t).

The above tool was employed to identify which industries each district/SLA specialised in, as against the reference region (NSW). The technique measures the extent to which the study district or SLA is specialised relative to the reference region (Klosterman, 1990: p. 129).

If for a given industry, for example manufacturing, the ELQ is greater than one for a SLA, the share of people employed in manufacturing jobs in that SLA's total employment is larger than the share of NSW people employed in manufacturing jobs in NSW's total employment. If employment in manufacturing is more important than it is (on average) for the state of New South Wales, the SLA is considered to specialise in manufacturing. Manufacturing for this SLA would be a non-local sector. The SLA would be a net-exporter (to other SLAs) of manufacturing jobs. That is, the supply of manufacturing jobs in the SLA is likely to exceed the demand (capacity to fill) for such jobs in the SLA.

Similarly, if for a given industry the ELQ is less than 1 for a SLA, this means the share of manufacturing jobs in an area's total employment is less than the share of total employment in NSW manufacturing jobs. This therefore indicates that manufacturing sector jobs are less important in that SLA compared to NSW and that SLA would be a net-importer (from other SLAs) of manufacturing products. Results from the employment specialisation analysis show that in Sydney, the retail sector is performing better than retailing in NSW as a whole. However, the ELQ for the retailing sector is for 19 regions (out of 54) less than 1.

From this analysis the anchors of Sydney's economy are finance, trade and knowledge sector jobs. Sydney's Western SLAs are home to manufacturing jobs, while Sydney's South looks like a 'construction industry' core, and Newcastle is specialising in health related jobs.

Multivariate analysis of potential drivers of growth

Growth in population and aggregate taxable income

Sydney's population is growing with most of the GMR's growth being from natural increase. The remainder comes from Sydney's attractiveness to people from other parts of Australia and overseas. Population forecasts suggest that about half a million new jobs will be needed over the next 25 years to meet the demands of the ever growing population.

Based on taxable income, the ten fastest growing statistical local areas in the period 1990 to 2001 were: Sydney Remainder, Sydney Inner, Camden, Hunter's Hill, Mosman, Blacktown, South Sydney, Liverpool, Woollahra, and Leichhardt. Three out of the 10 SLAs with the fastest growth in taxable income are outer fringe SLAs. These are Blacktown, Camden and Liverpool.

However, based on resident population, the ten fastest growing regions in the period from 1991 to 2001 are: Newcastle Inner, Kiama, Sydney Remainder, Sydney Inner, Mosman, Cessnock, Concord, Auburn, Hawkesbury and Maitland. One possible explanation for the fast growth in outer/fringe areas of the Sydney GMR is the high prices of houses in areas closer to the Sydney commercial business district (CBD).

Explanatory variables: factors affecting population growth

The previous section identified the independent or explained variable. This section discusses factors that previous empirical and/or theoretical studies have identified to affect growth of an area. The aim is to identify factors or variables that are associated with growth of total population and/or of aggregate taxable income in a statistical local area. These explanatory variables fall into the following main groups: socioeconomic variables, proxies for human capital in a statistical local area, and industry related variables. These are discussed below.

Socioeconomic variables

The regional research literature suggests that the size of a region influences regional growth in two diametrically opposite ways (see for example, Bradley and Gans, 1998). First, regions with a large population may grow slower because of diseconomies of regional size. A region with a large population tends to experience rising housing costs and commuting costs. These factors exacerbate socioeconomic differences across the region and may lead to perceived changes in quality of life in a region and may contribute to lower growth rates. On the other hand, regions with large populations can grow faster because of agglomeration effects (Feser, 2001) including productivity because of a larger labour pool, and because of inter-industry knowledge spill overs between co-located industries which can lead to product variety and diversity and an overall better quality of life.

The justification for including a SLA's initial period income per taxpayer amongst explanatory variables of growth can be found in the Bureau of Transport and Regional Economics (2005). The research expects a similar negative relationship between income per taxpayer in 1991 and growth in the Sydney GMR from 1991 and 2001.

The Australian Bureau of Statistics (2002) suggests that there may be a relationship between the population density and the population growth of an area. This research hypothesises that population growth will be higher in statistical local areas which in 1991 had lower population densities.

SLA's human capital

Recent international studies (OECD, 2001a, b, c) of the role of education in relation to skills and qualifications in regional economic performance suggest that human capital has a favourable impact. In this study, we also explore the relationship between the growth of a statistical local area and the following proxies for human capital in a SLA: (a) the percentage of a SLA's population who had a degree or higher (Ed1) in 1991; and (b) the percentage of a SLA's population who have completed skilled vocational training (Ed3) in 1991. In this study two variables are used as proxies for a SLA's human capital. They are: Ed1 – the share of a region's population with a Bachelor's degree or higher, and Ed3 – the share of a SLA's population who have a skilled vocational qualification. Exploratory analyses ruled out the use of other possible proxies (which were often insignificant).

Industry-related variables in a SLA

Various theoretical studies have predicted that industry agglomeration has positive impacts on growth of a given area (Marshall, 1920; Hoover, 1937). Bostic et al. (1997) proposed a way to construct a measure of industry-based agglomeration. This measure proxies the degree to which an industry's economic activity takes place in one or a small number of geographical areas. The effect of industry-based agglomeration depends on the number and the size (in terms of employment) of industry agglomerations in a given statistical area. This research uses the approach of Bostic et al. (1997) for defining agglomeration.

The interpretation for estimating the value of industry-based agglomeration is as follows. If a SLA had 1% more industry-based agglomeration in 1991, then the SLA's taxable income would, on average, have grown by 1.1% faster (than the rest of NSW) in the period 1991 to 2001. The same SLA would have had its population growth reduced by about 5% over the same period as shown in Figure 16 above. Figure 19 lists the SLAs in Sydney GMR arranged in descending order of degree of industry-based agglomeration effects. SLAs with low industry-based agglomeration effects tend to attract fewer industries to the area, or low employment industries.

Bradley and Gans (1998) and Bostic et al. (1997) suggest that specialisation for a statistical local area is a possible explanatory variable in a regression equation for growth. When specialisation is zero, this shows a SLA that is diversified (with employment spread evenly across all industries, and zero specialisation), while a value of 1 indicates a region's employment is concentrated in a single industry. We use the formula from Bradley and Gans (1998). Bradley and Gans (1988, p. 269) concluded that industry specialisation does have negative risk implications but can also have higher productivity due to an encumbered exploitation of comparative advantage.

This research used the share of basic (non-local) jobs in SLAs as a proxy for openness of the SLA. The distinction between local versus the non-

85

local jobs in a SLA is important because it is usually assumed that the non-local (basic) jobs are a prime cause of small area growth (see for example, Klosterman, 1990). This research is based on the hypothesis that SLAs that have larger shares of the more diverse set of industries with non-local jobs are likely to grow faster than those that do not have such industries. It postulates a positive relationship between a region's openness and a SLA's growth. It used the following where: SLA openness at time t = (Number of basic jobs in SLA)/ (All jobs in SLA); Basic (i.e. non-local) jobs in industry $'j'$ in SLA $'r'$ = $(Cjr-Dr)*Ej$, where: Cjr = (Number of jobs in industry j in SLA r)/ (Total NSW jobs in industry j); Dr = (Number of jobs in SLA r)/ (Total number of jobs in NSW), and Ej = (Total NSW jobs in industry j).

Figure 20 summarises the pathways leading to this variable impacting differently on aggregate real taxable income growth compared to its impact on estimated resident population growth.

Degree of openness is a significant variable in explaining growth of taxable income of a SLA. SLAs which were more open in 1991 had their taxable income grow faster in the period from 1991 to 2001. The variable was insignificant in the population growth regression equation.

The central part of Sydney and the areas stretching north from the North Sydney area through the CBD form a global arc of communities with strong human resources. Places like Botany Bay are attractive to people but have other factors inhibiting development related to past settlement patterns, ethnicity, and related issues.

This research used employment in the government sector as a proxy for the role of government in an area. Bradley and Gans (1998) suggest that government plays a role in any region. The variable that Bradley and Gans (1998) used as a proxy for the role of government was significant but had a negative value in the regression equation. They recommend caution in interpreting the negative sign associated with this variable.

Much regional literature, suggests that industry structure affects the rate of growth in a region (Bradley and Gans, 1998; Blakely and Bradshaw, 2003: p. 67). To test this hypothesis, data on the share of employment in Australian and New Zealand Standard Industrial Classification (ANZSIC) sectors are used. In the multivariate analysis we focus on the 16 industries (at the one-digit level in the Australian New Zealand

Standard Industry Classification, ANZSIC). For each SLA, the research computes the number of people employed in each of the 16 industries as a percentage of the total number of people employed in a SLA. The count of people employed in each SLA by employment per industry sector is derived from the ABS Census journey to work data discussed in section 3. The share of employment in the different industries defines the 'industry structure' of a SLA.

Figure 20 : Industry agglomeration, taxable income and population

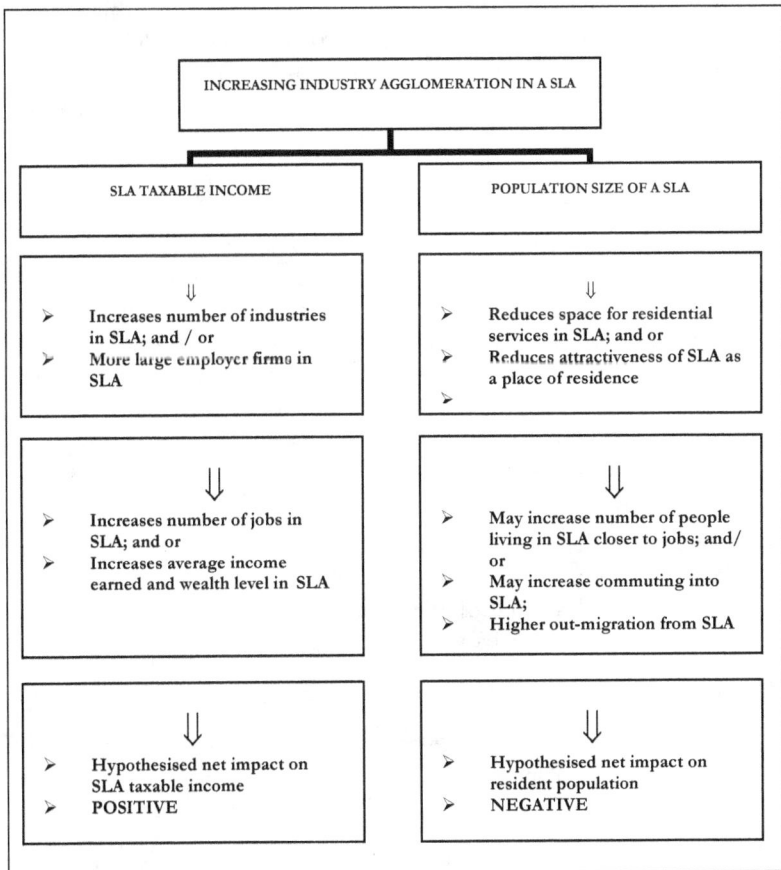

District indicator variables

A common way to explore differences between regions in a multivariate analysis of regional growth is to introduce region-indicator variables. For example, Bradley and Gans (1998) in a model which covers 104 cities in Australia, introduce state indicator variables which are used to investigate whether cities in one Australian state diverge from the average. District indicator variables take on values of one (1) if a place falls in that region, and zero (0) if it does not. To explore possible differences in the growth of districts in the Sydney GMR, this research introduces three district indicator variables: (a) Core Sydney which is '1' if a SLA falls in core Sydney districts, and '0' if it does not; (b) Newcastle which is '1' if a SLA falls in the Newcastle district, and '0' if it does not; and (c) Central Coast which is '1' if a SLA falls in the Central Coast district, and '0' if it does not .

Statistical basis of excluding certain variables

The previous section has outlined the theoretical basis for considering variables as possible explanatory variables in regression models on SLA growth. But not all of these possible explanatory variables are in the regression models because of technical constraints, we briefly explain here. A key statistical requirement for the models we construct is that the explanatory variables should not be highly correlated. If the variables are highly correlated the regression coefficients have large standard errors and they cannot be estimated with great precision or accuracy (Gujarati, 1995).

To ascertain whether our possible explanatory variable is highly correlated or not, we undertook exploratory pair-wise correlation analyses of variables. One of the variables in such a pair is excluded from the analysis. On this basis, this research excluded the following:

- Ed2 – the % of population (15 years of age and over) who have a Diploma or an Advanced Diploma;

- Ed4 – the % of population (15 years of age and over) who have basic vocational qualifications and/or left school age 15 or higher;

- A SLA's connectivity – the % of the population resident in a SLA who commute to other SLAs for work; and

- Four industry structure variables – the % of population (15 years of age and over) who in 1991 were employed in the following industries: accommodation, cafés & restaurants, finance & insurance, communication services; and personal & other services.

This research expresses the growth (relative to NSW) of a SLA between 1991 and 2001 as a linear function of the remaining explanatory variables with two regression models. One model has as the dependent variable the average *population* location quotient values (with NSW as the reference region) for all SLAs in the Sydney GMR – averaged over the period 1991 to 2001. Another equation has as the dependent variable the *aggregate real taxable income location* quotient values (with NSW as the reference) for all SLAs in the Sydney GMR – averaged over the period 1991 to 2001.

Results from multivariate analyses

Figure 21 presents the results of the two regression analyses. It discusses these results at two levels. Firstly, it assesses the quality of the regression models by answering three basic questions: (a) How much of the variance in the data does the model explain? (b) What is the goodness of fit of the model? (c) What is the strength or significance of the relationship between the explained and explanatory variables? Secondly, it discusses in more detail the individual estimates. This detailed discussion is limited to those variables which are statistically significant. In Figure 21 the variables which are significant are underlined. No weight or meaning can be given to the variables that are not statistically significant in the interpretation of results. The standard errors associated with these estimates tend to be large making the estimates themselves unreliable.

Strongly and weakly performing areas

A major question in this study is, what is the difference between strongly performing and weakly performing SLAs in the Sydney GMR? There are different methods one can adopt to explore this question (see for example Barreto and Hughes, 2004). This chapter used an alternative (non-econometric) approach to supplement the analysis in earlier sections of the chapter to find the possible sources of divergence between SLAs in the Sydney GMR. Mikelbank (2005) recently applied this approach.

Figure 21: Taxable income, population and growth, 1991–2001

	Taxable income			Population		
Variables (1991)	Est (a)	SE (b)	T (c)	Est (a)	SE (b)	T (c)
Adjusted R-squared	0.783			0.671		
Socioeconomic variables						
Log of SLA population	-0.018	0.003	-5.64	NS	NS	NS
Population density	NS	NS	NS	-0.029	0.010	-2.76
Log (Income per taxpayer)	NS	NS	NS	NS	NS	NS
Proxies for a SLA's human capital - % of SLA population with:						
University degree or higher	0.128	0.050	2.54	NS	NS	NS
Skilled vocational training	NS	NS	NS	-1.139	0.536	-2.12
Agglomeration of industries, specialisation & degree of openness in a SLA						
Industry agglomeration	1.129	0.302	3.73	-5.118	1.666	-3.07
Specialisation, 1991	-0.579	0.239	-2.42	2.177	1.320	1.65
Openness of SLA	0.052	0.0251	2.11	NS	NS	NS
SLA's industry structure - % of SLA population employed in:						
Government & defence	0.353	0.105	3.36	NS	NS	NS
Education, cultural etc.	0.307	0.082	3.74	-1.257	0.452	-2.78
Construction	0.427	0.137	3.11	-3.175	0.755	-4.20
Health & community	0.286	0.093	3.08	NS	NS	NS
Transport & storage	0.288	0.094	3.06	-1.141	0.519	-2.20
Manufacturing	0.196	0.064	3.06	NS	NS	NS
Property & business	0.329	0.137	2.39	NS	NS	NS
Mining	0.353	0.129	2.73	-2.563	0.714	-3.59
Agriculture, forestry etc.	NS	NS	NS	2.799	0.938	2.29
Electricity, gas & water	NS	NS	NS	NS	NS	NS
Retail	0.346	0.124	2.78	NS	NS	NS
Wholesale	0.176	0.086	2.05	NS	NS	NS
Accommodation, cafés etc.	Highly correlated with Manufacturing & Wholesale					
Finance & insurance	Highly correlated with Construction & Agglomeration					
Personal & other	Highly correlated with Retail & Accommodation					
Communication services	Dropped 16th industry because all shares add to 1					
District indicator variables						
SLA is in Core Sydney	NS	NS	NS	NS	NS	NS
SLA is in Central Coast	NS	NS	NS	NS	NS	NS
SLA is in Newcastle	NS	NS	NS	NS	NS	NS
Constant	0.542	0.246	3.59	NS	NS	NS

Notes: (a) The regression equations were estimated using STATA linear regression procedure (b) SE stands for standard error of the estimate (c) This column gives T-values computed by dividing the estimate of a coefficient by the standard error of the estimate (NS) Not statistically significant at the 5 % level of significance. Source: Derived by Planning Research Centre, University of Sydney and Bureau of Transport and Regional Economics (BTRE, 2005).

Figure 22 is based on a scatter plot of data on taxable income location quotients (with NSW as the reference region) and data on population income location quotients (with NSW as the reference region) for the SLAs in the Sydney GMR.

Figure 22: Scatter plot of strong and weak performing SLAs

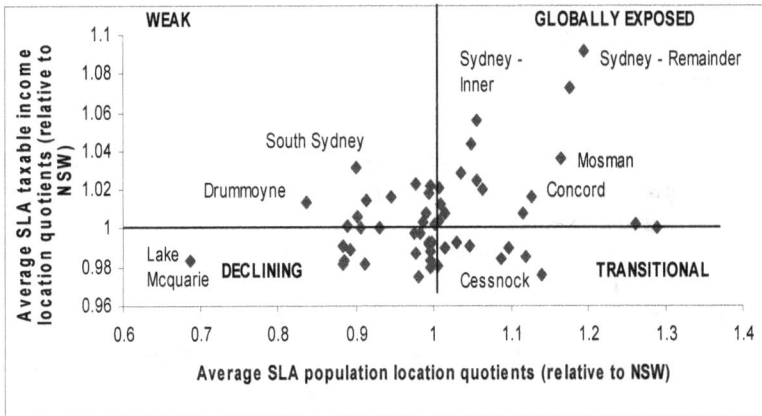

The matrix in Figure 22 provides a summary of current performance and economic options in the Sydney GMR. It shows that strongly-performing SLAs have higher growth in population and taxable income than weakly-performing SLAs. It further groups SLAs into four categories:

- Globally exposed strongly-performing SLAs (based on population and income growth) – these SLAs are listed in the upper right quadrant. They are places which are globally exposed and able to forge a new destiny because they have population and globally oriented specialisation.

- Transitional, modest-performing SLAs (based on population and income growth) – these SLAs are listed in the upper left quadrant. They are places that are getting new people but not yet specialising, usually commuter communities that have not galvanised an economic base.

- Static, weak-performing SLAs (based on population and income growth) – this group of SLAs is in the lower right corner. They consist of SLAs with the strongest income bases but that are static in human resources capital. They will need to improve their human capital base to forge a new economic destiny.

- Declining weak-performing SLAs (based on population and income growth) – The lower left quadrant of Figure 21 lists the poorest performers across most dimensions in our study and they are characterised as declining SLAs.

One significant difference between strong-performing and weak-performing regions is in industrial diversity and openness. The average share of manufacturing jobs in total employment in strongly performing SLAs is found to be negative, but the share in knowledge intensive and finance sectors are positively correlated with regional growth. This means SLAs with high values for human capital variables are likely to grow faster. Government employment is an inducer of better economic activity but it does not in itself stimulate a strong economy.

Conclusions

Lang and Blakely (2005) concluded that small suburban areas can be heterogeneous even when they occupy the same regional economic geography. Each small area has endowments from the past (such as industries, natural resources etc.), and each can grow or languish depending on how they capitalise on the past and view the future.

As the techniques we employed show, not all factors are equally important for the economic growth of a small area. Some small areas have human resource assets, while others have manufacturing or retail attributes as building blocks. So, each small area has in essence a recipe for success that differs in some degree with others nearby. Small areas within a greater economic whole such as the Sydney Greater Metropolitan Region can compliment each other and compensate for weaknesses such as human resource capacity, using other assets in fields that represent economic growth (for example, occupations in computer or other technology).

Sydney has a strategic advantage in the global economy with its access to sophisticated technology, highly skilled and multilingual labour force. All SLAs in the Sydney GMR, including those with high unemployment, can capitalise on these opportunities through innovative and productive partnerships that build on alliances.

The job market in Sydney GMR is changing rapidly. Manufacturing employment has largely given way to 'technology & knowledge intensive' and 'finance, insurance, property & business services' jobs that are at the heart of Sydney as a global city – a financial hub linked to all corners of the world. Sydney's jobs will need to be innovation-related and knowledge-based to support its aging population and compete internationally. Employment is an important factor in determining macroeconomic policy settings.

Although the Sydney GMR as a whole has experienced strong employment growth in the period 1996–2001 (1.6%), there have been some emerging sectoral and spatial imbalances confirmed by this study. The industries of the future in the Sydney GMR need a more educated workforce and the ability to quickly develop and adapt technology. Creativity as a new growth theory is the most important factor of production today. Not surprisingly, it improves labour and capital and extends older resources such as manufacturing, agriculture and engineering as well. What is more, creativity increases the quantity and quality of final goods and services and the latter in turn can enlarge creativity. Finally, creativity tends to increase productivity across all sectors of the local economy.

What a community needs to do is list the strongly and weakly performing sectors in its local economy. Then it can build an economic development strategy, as Blakely and Bradshaw (2003) suggest. Such a strategy would attempt to optimise each area's attributes and focus on reducing its deficiencies. Thus, a community may need to bolster its industrial diversity even though it has excellent human resources. This brings more science to the process versus the imitation approaches that are frequently used, based on the latest economic development fad.

Figure 18 reinforces the story of small area change within a larger globalising region. Regions, like Sydney, do not globalise evenly across all space. Some areas lag behind because of their historic drags from previous industrial structures like mining and steel production. In some cases, previous success in a sector such as Wollongong as a successful steel city will retard the transition to a new economic order. In some respects, having an old economic engine that is highly productive will influence the potential future economic scenarios dramatically as we have shown. So the 1991 economic engine, as our data show, is a predictor of post-1991 success for SLAs in the Sydney GMR. Thus, a community like Newcastle, that underwent a more rapid decline, is able to rebound faster than one that slowly declines. But areas with endowed human capital institutions like hospitals, universities and well positioned land with good housing stocks are better off today and have more options for their economic futures.

Finally, this chapter looked at the regional economy at a fine spatial grain. It used techniques that are simple but powerful for determining economic development. It applied the techniques in a tiered fashion so the vagaries of one analytical template do not give false response or easy answers to complex problems. These techniques can be fashioned to the region changing or shaping its future so that all subareas can be analysed in-depth allowing each of the localities to play a role in the future of the region. The same techniques are useable in monitoring interventions at a micro/suburban area scale overcoming current technical difficulties for assessing differential performance over time to find drivers and alter the performance of lagging areas. In this way, all communities across a metropolitan area can meet the same equitable goals from different economic drivers and economic roots.

References

Australian Bureau of Statistics (2002) *Sydney: a social atlas based on 2001 Census of Population and Housing.* Canberra: ABS.

Barreto, R. A. and Hughes, A. W. (2004) 'Under performers and over achievers: a quintile regression analysis of growth.' *The Economic Record.* 80(248): pp. 17–35.

Blakely, E. J. (1994) *Planning local economic development: theory and practice.* California: Sage Publications.

Blakely, E. J. (2004) *Regional science Cyclops: from a one eye to two eyed view of a changing regional science world.* Keynote address to the 2004 ANZRSAI Conference, Wollongong, New South Wales, September 2004.

Blakely, E. J. and Bradshaw, T. K. (2003) *Planning local economic development: theory and practice.* California: Sage Publications.

Bostic, R. W., Gans, J. S. and Stern, S. (1997) 'Urban Productivity and factor growth in the late nineteenth century.' *Journal of Urban Economics.* 41(1): pp. 38–55.

Bradley, R. and Gans, J. S. (1998) 'Growth in Australian cities.' *The Economic Record.* 74(226): pp. 266–278.

BTRE (2003) *Focus on regions no.1: industry structure information.* Canberra: Bureau of Transport and Regional Economics.

BTRE (2004) *Focus on regions no.2: education, skills and qualifications.* Canberra: Bureau of Transport and Regional Economics.

BTRE (2005) *Focus on regions no.3: taxable income.* Canberra: Bureau of Transport and Regional Economics.

Department of Infrastructure, Planning and Natural Resources (DIPNR) (2005) *Sydney metropolitan strategy.* Sydney: DIPNR.

Feser, E. J. (2001) 'Agglomeration, enterprise size and productivity' in B. Johansson, C. Karlssson and R. Stough (eds.), *Theories of endogenous growth.* Heidelberg: Springer-Verlag. pp. 231–251.

Goldsmith, W. and Blakely, E. J. (1992) *Separate societies: poverty and inequality in US cities.* Philadelphia: Temple University Press.

Gujarati, D. N. (1995) *Basic econometrics.* Singapore: McGraw-Hill.

Hill, E. W. and Wolman, H. L. (1997) 'City-suburban income disparities and metropolitan area employment: can tightening labour markets reduce the gaps?' *Urban Affairs Review.* 32(4): pp. 558–582.

Hoover, E. M. (1937) *Location theory and the shoe and leather industries.* Cambridge: Harvard University Press.

Kasarda, J. D. and Parnell, A. M (eds.) (1993) *Third World cities: problems, policies, and prospects.* Newbury Park: Sage.

Klosterman, R. E. (1990) *Community and analysis planning techniques.* Maryland: Rowland and Littlefield Publishers.

Klosterman, R. E., Brail, R. K. and Bossard, E. G. (1993) *Spreadsheet models for urban and regional analysis.* New Jersey: Centre for Urban Policy Research.

Lang, R. and Blakely, E. J. (2005) 'Keys to the new metropolis.' *Journal of the American Planning Association.* 71(4): pp. 1–11.

Ledebur, L., and Barnes, W. (1992) *City distress, metropolitan disparities and economic growth.* Washington DC: National Language of Cities.

Marshall, A. (1920) *Principles of economics.* London: Macmillan.

Massey, D. and Denton, N. (1993) *American apartheid: segregation and the making of the American underclass.* Cambridge: Harvard University Press.

Mikelbank, B. A. (2005) 'Local growth suburbs: investigating suburban change in the metropolitan context.' *Opolis: International Journal of Suburban and Metropolitan Studies.* 2(1): pp. 1–5.

O'Connor, K. R. (1999) 'Economic and social change and the futures of Australian metropolitan areas,' in B*enchmarking 99: future cities research conference.* Conference Papers, Melbourne City Council, pp. 59–66.

Orfield, M. (1997) *Metropolitics.* Washington DC: Brookings Institute.

Organization for Economic Co-operation and Development (OECD) (2001a) *The well-being of nations: the role of human and social capital.* Paris: OECD.

Organization for Economic Co-operation and Development (2001b) *Cities and regions in the new learning economy.* Paris: OECD.

Organization for Economic Co-operation and Development (2001c) *Does human capital matter for growth in OECD countries? Evidence from pooled mean-group estimates.* Paris: OECD.

Robertson, E. (2000) *Population census evaluation 1996 census data quality: journey to work.* Canberra: Australian Bureau of Statistics.

Searle, G. (1996) *Sydney as a global city.* Discussion Paper: Department of Urban Affairs and Planning and the Department of State and Regional Development.

Stimson, R. J., Stough, R. R. and Roberts, B. H. (2002) *Regional economic development: analysis and planning strategy.* New York: Springer.

Stoll, M. (1999) *Race, space, and youth labour market.* New York: Garland Publishing.

Toft, G. S. and Stough, R. R. (1986) *Transportation employment as a source of regional economic growth: a shift share approach, transportation.* Washington DC: Research Board, National Research Council.

Part Two

PLANNING PRACTICE

Chapter 5

THE IMPORTANCE OF ORGANISATIONAL STRUCTURE IN BUILDING A SUSTAINABLE NON-PROFIT HOUSING SECTOR

Tony Gilmour

Affordable housing is considered one of the main pillars of sustainable urban development, providing shelter close to the place of employment of key support workers on modest incomes. With the recent announcement of the National Rental Affordability Scheme to build 100,000 affordable homes over the next decade, there is a concerted effort to increase housing supply (Australian Government, 2008a, 2008b). Many of these new rental units will be built and managed by non-profit housing organisations. The sector covers a wide range of institutions, from small community-based welfare charities to large professionally managed non-profit developers and arms-length branches of government. To its supporters, non-profit managed housing is responsive to tenants' needs, locally grounded, preserves affordable housing stock in the long term and can 'contribute to wider social policy outcomes, like building stronger communities, enhancing employment opportunities and contributing to social cohesion' (CHFA, 2001: p. 3). Less supportive commentators tend not to criticise non-profit housing's social outcomes but doubt whether the sector will be sustainable in the medium term due to a shortage of robust organisations and skilled staff.

This chapter reviews the limited research on organisational typologies in countries with similar liberal welfare regimes, focusing on examples from England and Australia. It provides an understanding of the emerging types of non-profit housing organisations using the management theories of new institutionalism, networks, and global convergence. Finally, the chapter proposes a new typology for non-profit housing organisations and suggests how this might assist policy makers create a sustainable non-profit housing sector. Strong non-profit organisations have the ability to produce more sustainable outcomes than private developers by improving social cohesion and reducing commute times.

Introduction

The recent growth of the non-profit housing sector in Europe and North America has been spectacular. In England, the Housing Corporation claims housing associations complete one new affordable home every three minutes (Housing Corporation, 2007). After a decade of hesitant and patchy progress in Australia, 2007 appeared to mark a watershed year for non-profit housing providers. New South Wales (NSW) issued a consultation paper in March calling for a ten-year increase of community housing from 13,000 to 30,000 (NSW Department of Housing, 2007). This will be achieved by innovations in asset ownership, stock transfers, commercial financing, public-private partnerships and an initial $120m state grant. On the 1st May 2007 Western Australia announced that out of $376m spending over four years on social housing, $210m would be for non-profit providers – a five-fold increase (Government of Western Australia, 2007). Continuing the largesse, the next day Victoria announced a $510m housing budget with non-profits allocated $300m to build 1550 affordable homes (State Government of Victoria, 2007).

Additional public funding for the non-profit sector is only the first step towards increasing affordable housing supply. Delivery of new homes relies on the skills of the myriad non-profit organisations that manage specific building projects. These organisations have been described in Australia as 'eclectic and diverse' (National Community Housing Forum, 2004: p. 10) and in England as 'extremely complex' (Mullins and Murie, 2006: p. 207). Given the importance of understanding the types and capacities of non-profit housing providers, this chapter follows new institutional theory (Powell and DiMaggio, 1991) by bringing *organisations* rather than policy to the centre of the affordable housing debate.

This chapter seeks to provide a clearer though not definitive approach to categorising non-profit housing providers to help track and conceptualise organisational developments in the sector. Building on frameworks developed in organisational theory, a heuristic typology is developed for conceptualising the wide range of institutional vehicles used to deliver affordable housing. Using examples from the non-profit housing sector in England and Australia, four typological questions are addressed. These are: what range of organisations operate in the sector? Where are the sector boundaries and how permeable are they? Are non-profit housing providers becoming more similar? Finally, what typologies have previously been used to describe the sector and could a new model provide helpful insights? The chapter aims to stimulate debate in Australia and encourage further cross-national comparison.

Context

The rise of the non-profit housing sector has been at a time when market mechanisms have been used to increase the supply and the range of housing, particularly in countries characterised by Esping-Andersen (1999) as liberal welfare regimes. Expansion of public housing is uncommon and responsibility for supplying new affordable housing has shifted in varying degrees towards non-profit providers. The sector is characterised by 'innovation and dynamism, the spread of business perspectives, the emergence of hybrid organisations and inter-sectoral partnerships' (Paton, 2003: p. 1). However, there is a feeling that 'housing research has not yet critically addressed this changing world' (Mullins et al., 2001a: p. 621). In particular at the organisational level there has been limited analysis of housing non-profits, restricted to a few countries: England (Mullins and Riseborough, 2000), the Netherlands (van Bortel and Elsinga, 2007), Australia (Milligan et al., 2004; Bissett and Milligan, 2004; NSW Department of Housing, 2007), and Ireland (Mullins et al., 2001b; Rhodes, 2007).

There are a number of drivers for the growth of the non-profit housing sector. Public sector reform has accelerated in many countries since the early 1980s based on the popularity of 'new public management' bringing competition and commercialisation within the public sector (Pollitt and Bouckaert, 2004). This led to a move from formal structures such as public housing towards greater public funding of non-profit and for-profit organisations which are coordinated with less hierarchical relationships. Described as a move from *government* to *governance*, the new policies are 'characterised by inter-dependence, resource exchange, rule of the game and significant autonomy from the state' (Rhodes, 1997: p. 15). Non-profits are considered good at catering for groups with specific housing needs such as the elderly, disabled and immigrants. Their properties, constructed over the last two decades, tend to be more spatially and socially dispersed in neighbourhoods, unlike traditionally clustered single-tenure public housing estates (Wood, 2003). By involving tenants and local people in decision making, it is claimed that non-profits can better respond to neighbourhood needs and build social capital through strong community networks. Non-profit housing organisations often enjoy wide support across the political spectrum.

While there are certain common trends in affordable housing provision between England and Australia, four important differences need highlighting. First, England continues to have a considerably larger social housing sector with around 2,000 housing associations managing 1.8m homes, some 8% of the total housing stock in 2004 (Hills, 2007: p. 43). In Australia, the community housing sector managed 44,000 properties in 2003, equivalent to 9% of all houses (National Community Housing Forum, 2004: p. 10). Second, the transformation of housing non-profits has been more rapid and started earlier in England, from the Housing Act of 1974 which introduced public funding to the 1988 Act which tilted the balance away from local councils (Malpass, 2000; Cope, 1999). In Australia, the major impetus was the *National Housing Strategy of 1991– 2* endorsing community housing as a valid social housing delivery model and funding sector capacity building (Bissett and Milligan, 2004). Third, Australia's housing non-profits are more dependent on direct government assistance than in England as many do not own the properties they manage, and there is a lower level of rent subsidy. Finally, England is a unitary state with a centrally coordinated housing policy even if implementation is localised and shared between local councils and non-profits (Berry et al., 2006). In contrast, there was no Australian Housing Minister from 1996–2007.

Organisational types

The range of affordable housing organisations is broad in terms of their legal constitution, size, date formed, historical development, charitable status, group structure, clients served, property types managed, delegation of decision making, diversification of activities, management style, finance sources, use of volunteers, institutional capacity, religious affiliation, social mission, urban/rural location and involvement of tenants. Several housing non-profits are run like commercial companies although most remain modest in ambition, size and capacity (Light, 2002). *Figure 23* provides a broad comparison of non-profit housing organisation types in England and Australia:

Figure 23: English and Australian housing non-profit types

Type	England	Australia
[1] Traditional charitable	■ Date back to 12th century providing charity for the poor. Sometimes religious links. Most are now in category [2] by having become more commercial and/or merging.	■■■■ Most important category in Australia by number of organisations. Generally small, tenancy management rather than new property development. Some 17% managed by church groups.
[2] Commercial charitable	■■■■ Most important category in England by number of organisations. Normally retain charitable/community status but can raise private finance for new development after the *Housing Act 1988*.	■ Fewer have shifted from category [1] than in England. Some such as *City Housing Perth* and *Port Phillip Housing Association* have raised external private finance. *Port Phillip* retains strong local government links.
[3] Government established	- No examples of establishing new companies for building new homes although government instrumental in establishing categories [4]-[6].	■■ Popular for new schemes. Similar to [2] but with more government control (board members or shares). E.g., *City West*, Sydney (1994); *Brisbane Housing Co.* (2002)
[4] Stock transfer	■■■■ Large scale voluntary transfer (LSVT) of public housing estates after *Housing Act 1988*. Over one million homes transferred, mainly to category [2]. Refurbishment may involve PPP.	- Under development: e.g., NSW agreed in 2006 to transfer 2,500 properties by 2008. Bonnyrigg (see [5]) will be both a stock transfer and PPP. Stock transfers part of NSW Community Housing Strategy 2007–2012.
[5] Public-private partnership (PPP)	■■ Some use for student and key-worker housing. Main use is with councils for public housing refurbishment to meet 'Decent Homes' standard by 2010 using Private Finance Initiative (PFI).	■ Have been used for break-up/refurbishment of larger public housing estates, e.g., Westwood in Adelaide and a large $500m scheme at Bonnyrigg in NSW. Category [2] normally used for longer term asset holding.

Type	England	Australia
[6] Arms-length management (ALMOs)	■■■ Transfer of public housing from direct council control permitted from 2001. Greater tenant involvement and usually funding refurbishment through PFI. 52 ALMOs with 800,000 homes to 2006.	- No examples.
[7] Cooperative and tenant union	■ Mainly 19th century growth. Still some existing but generally not expanded as fast as [2] so remain relatively small.	■■■ Tenant managed cooperatives are relatively important although rarely own properties and small (average 9 properties each in NSW).
[8] For-profit companies	■ Private companies allowed to bid for £137m Housing Corporation funds (*Housing Act 2004*): first award to *Barrett Homes* in Jun-06. First private company *Pinnacle* accredited as a housing manager in Jan-07.	- No direct examples except involvement in PPPs in category [5], as in England. Occasional joint working with private developers, e.g., Community House Canberra. CSHA 2003 called for greater role for the private sector.

Source: Housing Corporation (2008); Clough et al. (2002); Milligan et al. (2004); National Community Housing Forum (2004); NSW Department of Housing (2007).

■ *indicates relative importance of organisation type in each country.*

There are two tentative conclusions from *Figure 23*. First, government decisions on the future of public housing will have a major impact on the growth of the non-profit housing sector. While England has a wider range of affordable housing providers than Australia, most organisational innovation over the last two decades has resulted from changes to the boundary between public housing and non-profits/commercial companies. Direct property transfers from the public to non-profit sector of nearly 900,000 homes between 1990 and

2006 (Housing Corporation, 2007: p. 27) allowed the sector to achieve critical mass and source cheap bank finance (Berry et al., 2004). Unlike the stock transfers and semi-independence of much of what remains of public housing in England, Australia's public housing has remained largely under state control. However, the modest pace of transfers may be set to accelerate, especially in NSW where they form a major component in expanding the non-profit sector to 2017 (NSW Department of Housing, 2006; 2007).

Second, England spent nearly two decades commercialising its traditional housing charities by allowing private finance, encouraging mergers, governance reforms and leveraging developer contributions through the planning system. The English housing non-profit sector therefore grew in size by a combination of stock transfers and organic growth (Bissett and Milligan, 2004). In comparison, the pace of Australian non-profit commercialisation has been modest and traditional charities and cooperatives, with a few important exceptions, continue to concentrate on tenancy management (Barbato et al., 2003). The exceptions include a small number of traditional organisations favoured by state governments for growth such as St George Community Housing, formed in 1986 and part of a consortium awarded the A$500m public-private partnership to redevelop the Bonnyrigg public housing estate in western Sydney in 2006 (St. George Community Housing, 2007). Whilst the 2003–2008 Commonwealth State Housing Agreement (CSHA) called for 'innovative approaches to leverage additional resources into Social Housing through community, private sector and other partnerships' (Commonwealth of Australia, 2003: p. 4), much commercialisation bypassed traditional non-profits altogether. New non-profit companies established by governments, such as Brisbane Housing Company, resemble housing non-profits in organisational structure but have often adopted more entrepreneurial business models.

More detailed analysis is available for England's non-profit sector due to the rich data collected by the Housing Corporation. Figure 24 shows organisational diversity in 2005:

Figure 24: England's housing associations, 2005

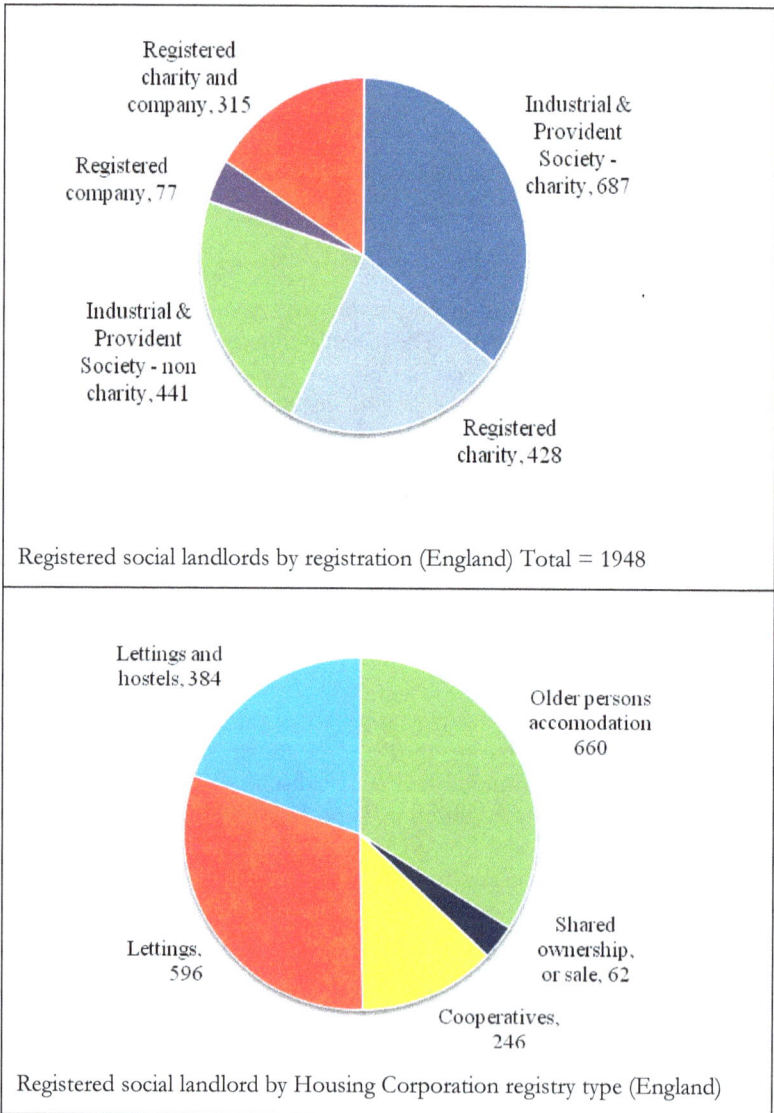

Registered social landlords by registration (England) Total = 1948

Pie chart 1 labels:
- Registered charity and company, 315
- Registered company, 77
- Industrial & Provident Society - non charity, 441
- Industrial & Provident Society - charity, 687
- Registered charity, 428

Registered social landlord by Housing Corporation registry type (England)

Pie chart 2 labels:
- Lettings and hostels, 384
- Older persons accomodation 660
- Lettings, 596
- Shared ownership, or sale, 62
- Cooperatives, 246

Source: Data from Housing Corporation (2006: p. 33) as at 31ˢᵗ March 2005

108

The most popular legal form in Figure 24 is as an Industrial and Provident Society (58%) followed by registration under the Companies Act (20%). Only three quarters of the 1948 registered social landlords have charitable status, with the remainder presumably paying tax on profits. Just under 67% of organisations managed fewer than 250 properties with 92% managing fewer than 5,000 properties. Using Housing Corporation categories, there are a number of niche organisations: 34% cater for older people, 20% provide some hostel accommodation and 3% assist low to moderate income earners to buy affordable homes. The figure for housing cooperatives (13%) is higher than expected given their relatively low profile. During the previous twelve months, there had been a modest net decrease of 36 housing associations, or 1.8% of the total (Housing Corporation, 2006: p. 34).

Australian housing non-profit statistics are in short supply, hard to benchmark across states and problematic to compare with the larger, more mature English housing associations. A survey in 2002–3 documented 1229 CHSA funded community housing organisations in Australia, with most in Queensland (28%), followed by Western Australia, Victoria and NSW (16%). The average dwellings per organisation ranged from under six in the Northern Territory to around 48 in NSW and the ACT although this data excludes organisations unfunded by CHSA which would reduce average size (Bissett and Milligan, 2004: p. 16). The difference in size distribution of housing non-profits between England and Australia is due to a tail-end of very small organisations in Australia and the absence of very large organisations with over 2500 properties. However, Australia may be more comparable with other countries: there are fewer differences if NSW (population 6.7m, 2006 Census) is compared to Ireland (population 4.2m, 2006 official data). Both states have 10% of their social housing managed by non-profits and average organisation size is 33 properties in NSW compared to 35–40 in Ireland (NSW Department of Housing, 2007; Mullins et al., 2003).

Is the diversity of non-profit housing providers described in this chapter so great it renders meaningless an international comparison of organisational types? From *Figure 23*, there is evidence of policy convergence, for example the diffusion of stock transfer ideas from England to Australia and the expansion of affordable housing through a favoured commercialised housing association model rather than tenant cooperatives. The recent NSW draft plan acknowledges 'Europe, North America and the UK ... [and] other Australian states and territories are considering a broader role for community housing ... [and the NSW policy] reflects these national and international directions' (NSW Department of Housing, 2007: p. 6). The state will grow the non-profit sector by an expansion of 'a limited number of providers – those who are high performing' (NSW Department of Housing, 2007: p. 5). These are the 'growth housing providers' (Bissett and Milligan, 2004: p. 50), comparable in relative size to the 'super league' which Mullins and Murie (2006: p. 194) observed in England from the 1990s. In Australia these growth providers are set to take an increasing proportion of properties controlled by the sector. The next section looks at how organisational theory can shed light on these changes.

Understanding boundaries

In this chapter, there is an assumption that there is validity in the social construct of a 'housing non-profit sector' and that it has determinable boundaries with other sectors into which housing organisations could be grouped. Constructivist writers argue that housing sector definitions will be deeply embedded in power relationships such as the emergence of housing managers as a profession, the expansion of university and private sector housing research and the political legitimation of the move to market-based housing systems (Jacobs et al., 2004). The housing non-profit sector can also be seen through the perspective of organisational theory which is dynamic, moving from Weber's rational-bureaucratic 'iron cage' through the 1960s behavioural science vogue to contemporary 'new institutionalism' (DiMaggio and Powell, 1983). New institutional writers have brought back the importance of organisations as it is through them that broader political and global economic forces are mediated (Pollitt and Bouckaert, 2004; Ingram and Silverman, 2002). However, unlike with Weber, they place organisations in a broader, more complex and connected setting: 'the core institutionalist contribution is to see environments and organisational settings as highly interpenetrated' (Jefferson and Meyer, 1991: p. 205).

In organisational and network theory, the term 'sector' has given way to the more nuanced 'organisational field', described as comprising 'those organisations that, in the aggregate, constitute a recognisable area of institutional life' (DiMaggio and Powell, 1983: p. 148). Sectors can be defined by economic or social outputs, whereas organisational fields are understood by the strength of networks and the forces of institutionalisation. For example, a 'housing supply sector' could be defined, comprising public, private and non-profit organisations that build homes. However, the lack of networks sharing information and an absence of common professional associations spanning private and social house builders suggest the 'housing supply sector' does not constitute an organisational field. Sectors are often defined by government statistics and organisations are either 'in' or 'out': fields can be more or less institutionalised depending on the extent of interaction and information flow between organisations, and the awareness of organisations and the media that the organisations are involved in a common set of activities. Common regulation, funding, legal structures and professional accreditation can all contribute towards building organisational fields in housing (Mullins, 2002).

In England, there have been moves to define a broader 'social housing field' encompassing the variety of housing associations, ALMOs etc. shown in *Figure 23* together with the remaining public housing providers and occasional private companies receiving subsidies. English government policy has defined a 'social housing sector' by legislation, data collection, deliberate network support, and careful language management such as the use of 'social housing' and building local 'partnerships' (ODPM, 2005). Mullins (2001a) agrees that there is an emerging social housing *field* in England but notes that it is relatively weak, whereas the subfield comprising housing associations has become stronger and more institutionalised. Therefore, in England 'cross-sectoral policy communities and networks operate best at subsectoral, rather than at sectoral, level' (Mullins et al., 2001a: p. 610).

In contrast, Australia does not have a well defined social housing sector or social housing field. There are modest signs of change, for example a Housing Institute founded in 2001 describes itself as 'the professional association of people working and volunteering in the multi-disciplinary social housing industry' (Australasian Housing Institute, 2006: p. 6). Broader field definition is not helped by legislative fragmentation and lack of staff transfer between the public and non-profit sector. Greater institutionalisation has been occurring at the field (or subfield) of Australian community housing with the emergence of peak bodies: the NSW Federation of Housing Associations in 1993 and the Community Housing Federation of Australia in 1996. National Community Housing Conferences were first held in 1990 and 1994 (Bissett and Milligan, 2004), and since 2004 there have been calls for a National Affordable Housing Agreement to be delivered through the community housing and private sectors (National Affordable Housing Forum, 2006).

If the previous section of this chapter gave a snapshot of the diversity of non-profit housing providers, the idea of organisational fields has made the process dynamic by highlighting how boundary definition is deeply contested, and changes over time and location (Mullins and Rhodes, 2007). This complexity is a strong argument in favour of a typological approach which will be discussed after first addressing the issue of whether non-profit organisations are become more or less similar in structure and delivery systems.

Same or different?

An important tenet of new institutional theory is 'institutional isomorphism', the tendency of organisations operating in the same organisational field to adopt similar business practices, and not just for efficiency benefits: 'organisations compete not just for resources and customers, but for political power and institutional legitimacy, for social as well as economic fitness' (DiMaggio and Powell, 1983). Isomorphism will only take place once an organisational field has become sufficiently established, therefore the arguments about field definition in the last section are crucial to understanding which organisations could be expected to become more similar, and when.

The three mechanisms contributing to isomorphism identified by DiMaggio and Powell (1983) are shown in Figure 25, illustrated with examples from the non-profit housing sector. Countries such as England and Australia have a regulated non-profit housing sector and coercive isomorphism is important, more so in Australia where there is greater reliance on public funding. Mimetic isomorphism is encouraged in Australia where state governments use limited resources to develop a small number of well publicised demonstration projects.

Figure 25: Mechanisms of isomorphism for non-profit organisations

	Description	Examples
Coercive	Dependency on resources (such as funding) from a small number of actors prompts organisations to behave in a way seen as appropriate by the resource provider. Hence the need to seek legitimacy. Coercive isomorphism can be both by force (e.g., legal sanctions) and by persuasion.	State funding will require organisations to have skilled board members, submit regulatory returns etc. In England a non-performing housing association can be taken over by the Housing Corporation. Bank lenders will require management accounts, a financial controller, outside auditors etc.
Mimetic	Emergence of organisations seen to be leaders in their field which other organisations seek to emulate. Role model organisations are particularly valued at times of uncertainty and sectoral change (Jefferson and Meyer, 1991). Knowledge can be transmitted through staff movements.	Bridge Housing in California and Brisbane Housing Company in Australia are seen to be 'leaders'. Executives of both organisations are asked to present at housing conferences. Through the Internet, other organisations can mimic their mission statements, board structures and tenancy management policies.
Normative	Common set of assumptions established through professional training, career structure and networking. It is important to know how complete the 'professionalisation process' is within a field (i.e. proportion of total staff who belong to a professional institute).	Professional associations, university housing researchers (including AHURI in Australia), conferences, job secondments and trade magazines are all important. Staff have moved into affordable housing (including as non-exec directors) from the private sector, bringing a more commercial/less welfare outlook.

There are limits to isomorphism, both in theory and practice. With coercive isomorphism, organisations are not simply passive actors unquestioningly absorbing influences from the wider environment. For example, Greer and Hoggett (1999) described a housing association that manipulated its regulatory returns to avoid Housing Corporation demands to extend geographical coverage of its housing provision from its core inner-city base. In a study on the introduction of private sector management techniques to American non-profit organisations, Lindenberg (2001) found Michael Porter's 'five forces' business model was thought useful by senior managers but was rejected in the organisation by staff who considered they worked in a social environment. Similarly, when non-profits produce housing data, 'performance indicators have an important ritual quality. Their reverential status implies that the practice is to a large extent a symbolic one' (Jacobs and Manzi, 2000: p. 90). Hence organisations may appear to be isomorphing, but appearances can be deceptive. Erlingsdóttir and Lindberg (2005) coined the term *isonymism* when organisations use the same names but practices remain different. Coercive isomorphism may lead to similar organisational practice but on a superficial level, much weaker than Weber's 'iron cage' of control (Paton, 2003).

Mimetic and normative isomorphism rely on networks to transmit ideas about preferred business practice. Network forms of governance are now common in housing, unlike the hierarchical relationships in the past between governments and housing providers based on a principal/agent relationship with an active/passive power balance (Reid, 1995; Rhodes, 1997; van Bortel and Elsinga, 2007). In England from the late 1980s there was a move away from both local authorities and publicly funded housing associations acting in the integrated roles of direct provider, distributer and manager of social housing: 'the assumption that all of these roles automatically belong together had given way to a widening range of diverse organisational arrangements' (Mullins et al., 2001a: p. 601). Partnerships and collaboration were actively encouraged in English social housing by outsourcing to housing associations, compulsory competitive tendering of council services and the involvement of service users through the 1991 Citizen's Charter and the 1999 Tenant's Compact (Mullins and Rhodes, 2007). Organisational responses to this more networked environment in England have included mergers, shared services, diversification into wider social service provision and partnership agreements with local councils.

It remains unclear whether there is a causal relationship between stronger non-profit housing networks and a trend to organisational isomorphism. Networks have developed further and faster in England than Australia over the last two decades whereas English housing associations have probably become more diverse, and Australian more similar. One explanation is that, despite the increased importance (and knowledge of) networks, they do not fully explain organisational relationships. Reid (1995) identified three types of coordination within a policy field: *hierarchies* involving clear roles and responsibilities, *markets* based on competition, and *networks* of individuals and organisations acting more in cooperation than competition. The three approaches are not mutually exclusive and exist in simultaneously in social housing (Mullins et al., 2001a). For example, the relationship between an English housing association and the Housing Corporation is hierarchical; the association may compete in the market for land yet be part of a network sharing news of best practice tenancy management. Whichever technique works best will be used to achieve particular outcomes. Networks have become part of the governance tool-kit, not replaced it.

In England, housing associations have always been diverse, but their heterogeneity has increased since the early 1990s (Mullins et al., 2001a). Housing associations diversified their social mission into building communities, not just homes, and by raising commercial finance they moved to a new economic mission. Both trends favoured employing staff with general rather than housing skills which weakened the professions, reducing normative isomorphism. The new 'super league' of very large associations with over 10,000 properties contrasts with traditional community non-profits hence 'the trend towards even bigger housing associations driven by development ambitions is diluting commitment by community involvement that was the hallmark of good management. Many smaller organisations perform better on this front, but funding drifts to large scale organisations' (Rogers, 2005: p. 11). The fear is that professionalisation of larger non-profits, coupled with complex group structures, may lead to them becoming more remote to the communities they serve.

The emergence of the English non-profit 'super league' and the Australian 'growth sector' raises an interesting question: do organisations such as these in a number of counties form part of a new housing subfield within which individual non-profits will start isomorphing towards a similar organisational type? There is growing evidence of organisational learning, policy transfer and mimetic isomorphism through international 'ideal type' affordable housing companies such as

Bridge Housing in California. New thinking on housing spreads through networks between countries in a similar way to within countries. Comparative housing research is popular, and often didactic: a survey published in Australia contrasting financing affordable housing noted: 'Australian policy debates could also benefit from the much broader discussions in the UK concerning key worker and employer provided affordable housing ... both countries might usefully look to the United States in relation to use of tax incentives to encourage the greater involvement of institutional investors in affordable housing provision' (Berry et al., 2004: p. 86).

International housing networks are helped by the Internet which allows researchers and policy makers to track success with overseas housing companies and policy innovations. Housing academics form a relatively strong international network transferring ideas through conferences and overseas study: the three key-note speakers at the 2005 National Affordable Housing Conference in Sydney were Christine Whitehead from the UK, Dr Michael Stegman formerly of the US Department of Housing and Urban Development, and Carol Galante of Bridge Housing in California. Network connectivity is strongest where countries are close together geographically, for example the European Network of Housing Researchers and CECODHAS, the European Liaison Committee for Social Housing (Czischke, 2007). Network limitations are from the domestic focus of most professional associations and the framing of housing policy at country level, even in the European Union. If a new housing subfield is emerging, then to date it is relatively weak.

Typologies

The possible emergence of a 'super league' of growth non-profits described in the previous section reinforces the need for a clear framework in which to place and compare individual housing providers which may be located in different countries. Typologies can be useful tools for classifying related items, particularly those existing in complex and fast changing environments. They can help correct misconceptions and organise knowledge by defining organisational field and subfield boundaries (Tiryakian, 1968; Allmendinger, 2002). Typologies are popular in the social sciences, and are used particularly by organisational and management theorists (e.g. Mintzberg, 1979; Porter, 1980). Rather than acting as passive classification systems, typologies assist inductive theory building (Doty and Glick, 1994). With their focus on ideal type organisations, they can allow researchers to identify organisational forms that may be more effective than any currently existing.

Given the strengths of a typological approach, it has been used surprisingly few times to map the non-profit housing sector and studies have concentrated on a single or neighbouring pair of countries. The most comprehensive research to date has suggested size, location, origins and service provision as 'key dimensions for understanding the different subgroups' in Ireland (Mullins et al., 2003: p. 87). The qualitative study used the Delphi Method, but with no mapping of individual organisations within categories, nor suggestion of how 'size' should be delineated. In earlier research using similar methods for English housing associations Mullins and Riseborough (2000) defined organisations as small with under 250 properties, medium with 250–5000, and large with over 5,000. Newcombe (2000) defined medium as 250–2500 properties. For the Housing Corporation, small housing associations manage up to 250 properties and very large over 10,000. However, the main typology used by the Housing Corporation is not based on size but on the distinction between 'traditional' and 'stock transfer' associations (Housing Corporation, 2007).

Figure 26 summarises six possible typologies which could be used to classify non-profit housing organisations. Descriptors [1] to [4] are from the study by Mullins et al. (2003: pp. 84–86) and category [5] is based on the approach used in Figure 23 of this chapter. The least helpful descriptors in Figure 26 are [2], [3] and [4] as they are tied to particular factors which help differentiate organisations in Ireland. They allow an analytical categorisation of organisations by geography, history etc. but were not intended to be a comprehensive typology. Descriptor [1] is a powerful tool to categorise organisations but there are major national variations: a large housing non-profit in England or the Netherlands might have over 10,000 properties, in Scotland or Northern Ireland over 1000, and in Australia or the Republic of Ireland over 250. Traditional descriptors such as legal status [5] are popular but do not capture the organisation's values, nor help identify sector innovators. Therefore, descriptor [6] has been adopted for further testing:

Figure 26: Possible non-profit housing typologies

Criterion	Basis	Strengths	Weaknesses
[1] Size	Rank organisations by properties held, e.g., up to 250; 250–5,000; over 5000	[a] Straightforward, with data easy to obtain [b] Used before in studies and familiar to researchers	[a] Typical organisation size varies markedly between countries [b] Size not a good descriptor of how organisations function
[2] Location	Based on urban or rural location	[a] Worked in survey of Irish housing non-profits	[a] Hard to define urban and rural. Does urban include suburban? [b] Fast growth organisations tend to be urban based
[3] Origins and formation	Date of formation, possibly grouped by decade	[a] Worked in survey of Irish housing non-profits [b] Data easy to obtain	[a] Not possible to compare across countries as timing different [b] Only meaningful if linked to other attribute, eg ethos
[4] Service provision	Differentiate between housing and mixed service providers	[a] Worked in survey of Irish housing non-profits [b] Captures important diversification trend	[a] Country specific, e.g., would work for Ireland but not for England. [b] Hard to measure the degree of diversification
[5] Organisation form	Similar to Figure 23, e.g., cooperative, housing association, ALMOs etc.	[a] Straightforward approach based on legal form [b] Used by England's Housing Corporation	[a] Too much based on national legislation and regulation [b] Legal structure gives no clues about values, functioning etc.
[6] Ethos and values	Community, state or business values – see Figure 27	[a] Designed to work on trans-national case studies [b] Better at capturing growth sector of market	[a] Based on qualitative ideas so hard to classify organisations [b] Not yet tested by research thus still a conceptual model

A typology based more on ethos than organisational characteristics was proposed by Gruis and Nieboer (2004) for a national social housing system categorisation along a spectrum from strategic/market-orientated to operational/task-orientated. This was later developed into a market-orientated versus government-regulation split for the management of social housing assets (Gruis and Nieboer, 2007). Whilst their model is helpful in supporting a qualitative, flexible approach, the typology characteristics proposed in Figure 27 are based on a tripartite model of business, public and third (i.e. non-profit) sector popularised by the Johns Hopkins Comparative Non-profit Sector Project (Salamon, 2002; Salamon et al., 2003). The categories in Figure 27 are orientated towards ethos not organisational form.

Figure 27: Typology characteristics based on ethos and values

	Community-centric	State-centric	Business-centric
Values	Voluntary Local Flexible Participatory	Equitable Bureaucratic Fixed Consultative	Entrepreneurial Strategic Flexible Customer-driven
History	Normally longer-established, social needs-driven in specific local area	Often set up by the state, possibly stock transfer from public housing	More recently established with clear economic and social mission
Finances	Reliant on the state for ongoing funding using supply and demand levers. May receive donations	Often set up with public funding then potentially becoming more self-financing from income	Often cross-subsidy of market/social activities: finances are 'cutting edge'. Debt financing common
Scale	Often small and local, sometimes part of larger group. Slower growth	Often large if based on stock transfers or arms length management.	Varies, sometimes only a demonstration project. Normally fast growing
Example shown in Figure 29	Longer established non-profit, e.g., an English housing association (A)	Stock transfer of public housing to a non-profit organisation (B)	Non-profit with initial public funding then uses market techniques (C)

The typology developed in Figure 27 does not capture the full complexity of the housing non-profit sector with many organisations having a mix of community, state and business attributes. Sector boundaries are becoming less well defined as business becomes more socially responsible and governments and non-profits more commercialised. A conceptual solution, shown below in Figure 28, was developed by Mullins and Riseborough (2000) to show the transformation of English housing associations from 1974–1989 (marked X) to their position after 1989 (marked Y). This helps capture the interrelatedness between the public, private and third sectors and shows change over time:

Figure 28: Locating English housing associations

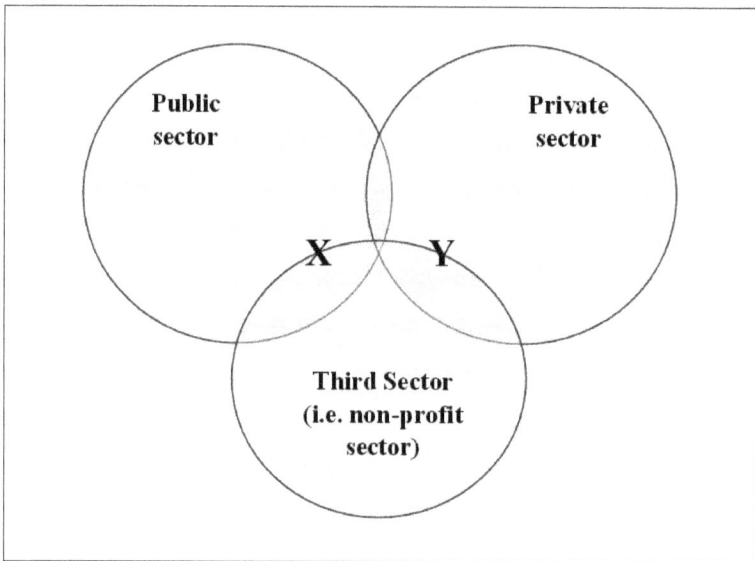

Source: Mullins and Riseborough (2000: p. 5)

The approach shown in Figure 28 provided the conceptual basis for the proposed typological model in Figure 29. Deliberately, there is greater overlap in Figure 29 reflecting the recent convergence of business, public and third sector organisational values:

Figure 29: Proposed non-profit housing typology, with examples

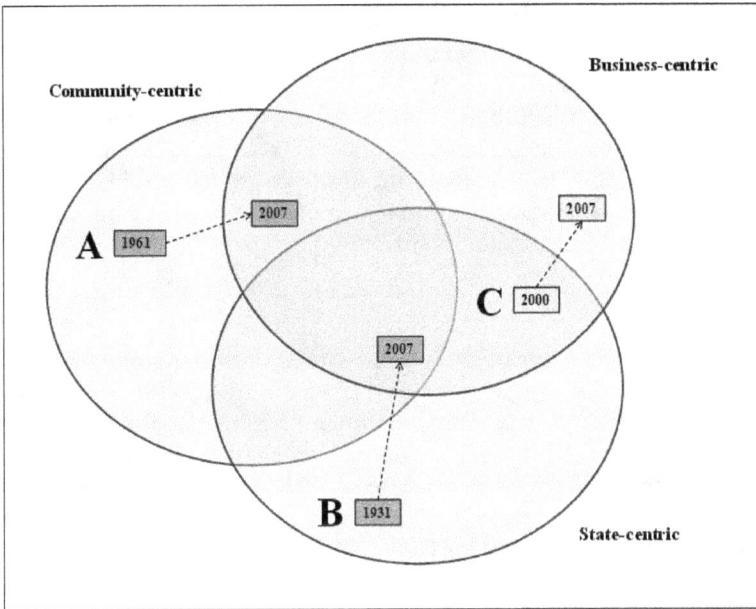

The thinking behind Figure 29 is that whilst an organisation can be summarised as representing a single typological category, it may still have lesser characteristics from other categories. For example, the traditional housing association (A) has moved from being a purely community organisation in 1961 towards adopting business practices but remaining, overall, community-centric. This is shown by it being closer to the centre of the circle representing the 'community-centric' typology than to the centre of the circles representing 'business-centric' or 'state-centric'. Stock-transfer company (B) has changed from being purely state-centric in 1931 when it was in the public sector to a position in 2007 where, whilst its dominant values are state-centric, it has some community values as tenants sit on the board and business characteristics having raised external bank finance. Non-profit organisation (C) was established by the state but has moved to cross-subsidising market rate and affordable housing.

The Venn diagram allows a representation of the rate at which an organisation has changed over time (shown by the length of the dotted arrow) and can also be used to highlight whether organisations are developing in a common direction, for example whether they are all becoming more business-centric. However, at this stage the typology is a tentative hypothesis which needs to be tested by case study research and practitioner discussions. It has been designed as a framework for debate rather than a definitive solution, thereby avoiding the problem where 'the very success and acceptance of a typological classification may ... freeze the level of explanation' (Tiryakian, 1968: p. 179).

Conclusions

The key to building a sustainable non-profit affordable housing sector is to ensure that the organisations in that sector are robustly structured, well managed and have proper governance. Organisational and network theories are important tools in understanding the changes currently taking place, although they often tend to be overlooked in housing policy. On the one hand, there is an increasing diversity of organisational types, affordable housing delivery models, and management value systems. On the other, the commercial and partnership approach is being replicated in a number of countries. A proposal advanced in this chapter is for a convergence amongst a 'super league' of growth affordable housing providers in a number of countries which may mark the emergence of a new housing subfield. This subfield, supported by rich global knowledge networks, has the potential once it becomes more institutionalised to lead to an isomorphing of organisational structure. This may be a necessary precursor to bringing in new forms of institutional investment which, in the case of Australia, are probably necessary to sustain the sector's independence from government.

There remains considerable debate over where field and subfield boundaries should be drawn in the housing sector, and complexity is increasing as new forms of governance make the boundaries more permeable. Despite having traditional legal structures, non-profits are adapting to a changing environment by moving from hierarchical to networked structures and mixing community, public and business values. A tried and tested way to observe these changes is through a typological lens, particularly one that can accommodate both the interrelatedness of the different values systems and the dynamics of change over time. New institutionalism rightly puts organisations back to the centre of the housing debate as it is only through their capabilities that a sustainable non-profit affordable housing sector will be built.

Notes

This chapter is based on a paper *Same or different? Towards a typology of non-profit housing organisations* presented at the 2nd Australasian Housing Researchers Conference, Brisbane Australia, 20th–22nd June 2007.

References

Allmendinger, P. (2002) 'Towards a post-positivist typology of planning theory.' *Planning Theory.* 1(1). March 2002. pp. 77–99.

Australasian Housing Institute (2006) *Supporting our profession: business plan 2006–2009.* Cobargo, NSW: Australasian Housing Institute.

Australian Government (2008a) *Making housing affordable again.* Canberra: Australian Government.

Australian Government (2008b) *National rental affordability scheme: technical discussion paper.* Canberra: Australian Government.

Barbato, C., Clough, R., Farrar, A. and Phibbs, P. (2003) *Stakeholder requirements for enabling regulatory arrangements for community housing in Australia. Final Report.* Sydney: Australian Housing and Urban Research Institute (AHURI), Sydney Research Centre.

Berry, M., Whitehead, C., Williams, P. and Yates, J. (2004) *Financing affordable housing: a critical comparative review of the United Kingdom and Australia.* Sydney: AHURI Royal Melbourne Institute of Technology, National Centre for Social and Economic Modelling and Sydney Research Centre.

Berry, M., Whitehead, C. and Yates, J. (2006) 'Involving the private sector in affordable housing provision: can Australia learn from the United Kingdom?' *Urban Policy and Research.* 24(3). September 2006. pp. 307–323.

Bissett, H. and Milligan, V. (2004) *Risk management in community housing: managing the challenges posed by growth in the provision of affordable housing.* Sydney: National Community Housing Forum.

Clough, R., Barbato, C., Farrar, A. and Phibbs, P. (2002) *Stakeholder requirements for enabling regulatory arrangements for community housing in Australia. Positioning Paper.* Sydney: AHURI Sydney Research Centre.

Commonwealth of Australia (2003) *2003 Commonwealth state housing agreement.* Canberra: Commonwealth of Australia.

Community Housing Federation of Australia (CHFA) (2001) *Community housing: building on success. Policy directions for community housing in Australia.* Canberra: Community Housing Federation of Australia (CHFA).

Cope, H. F. (1999) *Housing associations: the policy and practice of registered social landlords.* Houndsmill, Basingstoke: Palgrave Macmillan.

Czischke, D. (2007) 'A policy network perspective on social housing provision in the European Union: the case of CECODHAS.' *Housing, Theory and Society.* 24(1). March 2007. pp. 63–87.

DiMaggio, P. J. and Powell, W. W. (1983) 'The iron cage revisited: institutional isomorphism and collective rationality in organisational fields.' *American Sociological Review.* 48(2): pp. 147–160.

Doty, D. H. and Glick, W. H. (1994) 'Typologies as a unique form of theory building: toward improved understanding and modelling.' *Academy of Management Review.* 19(2): pp. 230–251.

Erlingsdóttir, G. and Lindberg, K. (2005). 'Isomorphism, isopraxism, and isonymism: complementary or competing processes?' in B. Czarniawska and G. Sévon (eds.) *How ideas, objects and practices travel in the global economy.* Oxford: Oxford University Press.

Esping-Andersen, G. (1999) *Social foundations of postindustrial economies.* Oxford: Oxford University Press.

Government of Western Australia (2007) *Premier announces multi-million dollar package to boost housing affordability. Media statement dated 1st May 2007.* Available at website of Government of Western Australia: www.mediastatements.wa.gov.au.

Greer, A. and Hoggett, P. (1999) 'Public policies, private strategies and local public spending bodies.' *Public Administration.* 77(2): pp. 235–256.

Gruis, V. and Niebocr, N. (eds.) (2004) *Asset management in the social rented sector, policy and practice in Europe and Australia.* Dortrecht, Boston, London: Kluwer Academic Publishers.

Gruis, V. and Nieboer, N. (2007) 'Government regulation and market orientation in the management of social housing assets: limitations and opportunities for European and Australian landlords.' *European Journal of Housing Policy.* 7(1): pp. 45–62.

Hills, J. (2007) *Ends and means: the future roles of social housing in England.* London: London School of Economics – Centre for Analysis of Social Exclusion.

Housing Corporation (2006) *Our stories: Housing Corporation annual report and accounts 2005–06.* London: The Housing Corporation.

Housing Corporation (2007) *Global accounts of housing associations 2006.* London: The Housing Corporation.

Housing Corporation (2008) *Web site, www.housingcorp.gov.uk* (consulted 20th July 2008).

Ingram, P. and Silverman, B. S. (eds.) (2002) *The new institutionalism in strategic management*. Advances in Strategic Management. Volume 19. Amsterdam: JAI.

Jacobs, K., Kemeny, J. and Manzi, T. (eds.) (2004) *Social constructionism in housing research*. Aldershot: Ashgate.

Jacobs, K. and Manzi, T. (2000) 'Performance indicators and social constructivism: conflict and control in housing management.' *Critical Social Policy*. 20(1): pp. 85–103.

Jefferson, R. L. and Meyer, J. W. (1991). 'The public order and the construction of formal organization,' in W. W. Powell and P. J. DiMaggio (eds.), *The new institutionalism in organizational analysis*. Chicago: University of Chicago Press, pp. 204–231.

Light, P. C. (2002) *Pathways to non-profit excellence*. Washington DC: Brookings Institution Press.

Lindenberg, M. (2001) 'Are we at the cutting edge or the blunt edge?' *Non-profit Management & Leadership*. 11(3): pp. 247–271.

Malpass, P. (2000) *Housing associations and housing policy: a historical perspective*. Basingstoke: Macmillan.

Milligan, V. (2003) *How different?: comparing housing policies and housing affordability consequences for low income households in Australia and the Netherlands*. Utrecht: Utrecht University.

Milligan, V., Phibbs, P., Fagan, K. and Gurran, N. (2004) *A practical framework for expanding affordable housing services in Australia: learning from experience*. Sydney: AHURI Sydney Research Centre.

Mintzberg, H. (1979) *The structuring of organizations: a synthesis of the research*. Englewood Cliffs, New Jersey: Prentice Hall.

Mullins, D. (2002) *Organisational fields: towards a framework for comparative analysis of non-profit organisations in social housing systems. Paper presented at ENHR conference in Vienna, 1st–5th July 2002. Workshop on Institutional and Organisational Change in Social Housing Organisations in Europe*. Unpublished. Copy obtained from author.

Mullins, D. and Murie, A. (2006) *Housing policy in the UK*. Houndmills, Basingstoke: Palgrave Macmillan.

Mullins, D., Reid, B. and Walker, R. M. (2001a) 'Modernization and change in social housing: the case for an organisational perspective.' *Public Administration*. 79(3): pp. 599–623.

Mullins, D. and Rhodes, M. L. (2007) 'Special issue on network theory and social housing.' *Housing, Theory and Society*. 24(1): pp. 1–13.

Mullins, D., Rhodes, M. L. and Williamson, A. (2001b) 'Organizational fields and third sector housing in Ireland, North and South.' *Voluntas: International Journal of Voluntary and Non-profit Organizations.* 12(3): pp. 257–278.

Mullins, D., Rhodes, M. L. and Williamson, A. (2003) *Non-profit housing organisations in Ireland, North and South: changing forms and challenging futures.* Belfast: The Northern Ireland Housing Executive.

Mullins, D. and Riseborough, M. (2000) *What are housing associations becoming?* Birmingham: School of Public Policy, University of Birmingham.

National Affordable Housing Forum (2006) *A summary of the forum: achieving a new national affordable housing agreement: 24–25 July, Old Parliament House, Canberra.* Canberra: National Community Housing Forum.

National Community Housing Forum (2004) *National strategic framework for community housing 2004–2008 and community housing snapshot.* Sydney: National Community Housing Forum.

Newcombe, R. (2000). 'Strategies for medium-sized housing associations,' in S. Monk and C. Whitehead (eds.) *Restructuring social housing systems: from social to affordable housing.* York: York Publishing Services, pp. 160–167.

NSW Department of Housing (2006) *Stock transfer program: fact sheet, September 2006.* Ashfield, Sydney: NSW Department of Housing.

NSW Department of Housing (2007) *NSW planning for the future: community housing. Five year strategy for growth and sustainability 2007–2012, consultation draft.* Ashfield, Sydney: NSW Department of Housing.

Office of the Deputy Prime Minister (ODPM) (2005) *Sustainable communities: people, places and prosperity: a five year plan from the Office of the Deputy Prime Minister.* Norwich: HMSO.

Paton, R. (2003) *Managing and measuring social enterprises.* London: Sage Publications.

Pollitt, C. and Bouckaert, G. (2004) *Public management reform: a comparative analysis.* Oxford: Oxford University Press.

Porter, M. E. (1980) *Competitive strategy: techniques for analyzing industries and competitors.* New York: Free Press.

Powell, W. W. and DiMaggio, P. J. (eds.) (1991) *The new institutionalism in organizational analysis.* Chicago: University of Chicago Press.

Reid, B. (1995) 'Inter-organisational networks and the delivery of social housing.' *Housing Studies.* 10(2). September 2001. pp. 133–149.

Rhodes, M. L. (2007) 'Strategic choice in the Irish housing system: taming complexity.' *Housing, Theory and Society.* 24(1): pp. 14–31.

Rhodes, R. A. W. (1997) *Understanding governance: policy networks, governance, reflexivity, and accountability.* Buckingham, Philadelphia: Open University Press.

Rogers, R. (2005) *Towards a strong urban renaissance: an independent report by members of the Urban Task Force.* London: Urban Task Force.

St. George Community Housing (2007) *Website, www.sgch.com.au* (consulted 12th May 2007).

Salamon, L. M. (ed.) (2002) *The State of Non-profit America.* Washington DC: Brookings Institution Press.

Salamon, L. M., Sokolowski, S. W. and List, R. (2003) *Global civil society: an overview.* Baltimore, Maryland: The Johns Hopkins University Institute for Policy Studies, Center for Civil Society Studies.

State Government of Victoria (2007) *Record $510 million for public and social housing. Department of Human Services, press release dated 2nd May 2007.* Available at the website of the State Government of Victoria: www.dhs.vic.gov.

Tiryakian, E. A. (1968). 'Typologies,' in D. L. Sills (ed.) *International encyclopaedia of the social sciences.* New York: Macmillan. pp. 177–186.

van Bortel, G. and Elsinga, M. (2007) 'A network perspective on the organization of social housing in the Netherlands: the case of urban renewal in The Hague.' *Housing, Theory and Society.* 24(1): pp. 32–48.

Wood, M. (2003) 'A balancing act? Tenure diversification in Australia and the UK.' *Urban Policy and Research.* 21(1): pp. 45–56.

Chapter 6

PLANNING FOR SUSTAINABLE CHANGE: A REVIEW OF AUSTRALIAN LOCAL PLANNING SCHEMES

Nicole Gurran and Peter Phibbs

Sustainable development, defined by the World Commission on Environment and Development as 'development that meets the needs of the present without compromising the ability of future generations to meet their own needs', has become a global policy objective with particular resonance for planners (WCED, 1987: p. 43). Many international, national, state and regional policy frameworks emphasise the need to improve the environmental performance of cities and regions and to conserve and renew biodiversity. The increasing prospect of global climatic volatility – hotter temperatures, sea level rise, intense storm events, flooding and bushfires, have added a new urgency for planning and design regulations that build community resilience to withstand impacts of climate change (Hennessy et al., 2007).

Statutory land use plans are the primary instrument for such regulations. Often known as 'planning instruments', 'planning schemes' (many Australian jurisdictions), 'development plans' (the United Kingdom), or 'comprehensive plans' (the United States), statutory land use plans establish the principal policies and controls regulating development within a given area. They are usually prepared by local planning authorities but within the legal and policy framework established by higher jurisdictions (state government authorities in Australia and the United States, national government in the United Kingdom and New Zealand, and provincial or regional bodies in Canada and many European nations). Although prepared under consistent regulatory and policy requirements, land use plans generally differ markedly in terms of scope, policy goals, mechanisms and controls.

Despite the important role played by local plans in implementing higher level environmental and social planning goals, empirical studies of plan content are surprisingly rare. This means that it is difficult to estimate the extent to which local plans contain objectives and provisions relating to sustainability, from environmental design to biodiversity conservation or climate change preparedness. Biodiversity is the 'variety of life forms, the different plants, animals and micro-organisms, the genes they contain and the ecosystems they form' (NPWS, 1999: p. 70).

The Australian Urban Land Use Planning Policy Survey was designed to address such knowledge gaps, examining local approaches to environmental sustainability and housing diversity, choice and affordability. This chapter presents an analysis from the first round of responses to the survey (as at April 2008), focusing on responses relating to sustainability and urban form, environmental protection, and climate change. It firstly explains the spectrum of emerging planning approaches for sustainable urban form (provisions for density, transportation, energy, water and waste management) and biodiversity conservation (protecting important ecological communities and landforms, managing the interface between natural protected and urban areas, and resilience to climate change).

The chapter then presents the initial results of the survey to show the extent to which such approaches are included in local statutory plans across a sample of 129 local authorities from Australian cities and regions. All Australian states and the Australian Capital Territory are included in the initial sample. The Northern Territory, which has a distinctly different planning framework to the other jurisdictions, was excluded from the initial sample but will be represented in the complete database. The chapter concludes by identifying key areas for additional policy work and development in Australian local planning for sustainability and climate change resilience.

Local sustainability planning

All environmental planning legislation of the Australian states and territories refers to sustainability objectives or decision-making criteria, although terminology differs somewhat across the jurisdictions (Gurran, 2007). Under Australia's federalised system of government, the states and territories have the main responsibility for environmental planning and assessment. The Commonwealth Government's limited roles relate to certain defined matters of 'national environmental significance' as defined under the *Commonwealth Environment Protection and Biodiversity*

Conservation Act 1999. At the national level, the terms 'environmentally' or 'ecologically' sustainable development predominate, defined as 'using, conserving and enhancing the community's resources so that ecological processes, on which life depends, are maintained, and the total quality of life, now and in the future, can be increased' (Commonwealth of Australia, 1992). National environmental legislation defines 'principles' of 'environmentally sustainable development' as follows:

- Decision-making processes should effectively integrate both long-term and short-term economic, environmental, social and equitable considerations;

- If there are threats of serious or irreversible environmental damage, lack of full scientific certainty should not be used as a reason for postponing measures to prevent environmental degradation;

- The principle of inter-generational equity: that the present generation should ensure that the health, diversity and productivity of the environment is maintained or enhanced for the benefit of future generations;

- The conservation of biological diversity and ecological integrity should be a fundamental consideration in decision-making;

- Improved valuation, pricing and incentive mechanisms should be promoted (*Commonwealth Environment Protection and Biodiversity Conservation Act 1999*, Part 3A).

While such high level principles establish an important policy framework, translation into specific land use and development regulations is complex. Translating national and international sustainability principles into local land use plans is always a challenge (Dyck, 1998). However, federal divides in nations such as Australia and the United States likely make this process more fragmented and variable than in unitary countries such as England where national planning policy is articulated directly for local implementation. The next section outlines approaches to promoting sustainability through the process of preparing local plans and assessing development proposals against these plans.

The local planning process offers several basic planning mechanisms that can be used to improve the environmental performance of cities and regions and to conserve and renew biodiversity. Allocating land for particular uses and combinations of uses, establishing limits to urban settlements, fixing standards for development and criteria to assess proposals, stipulating conditions of development approval, and refusing development that has unacceptable impacts, are important tools for promoting sustainable urban development (Gurran, 2007). The planning goal in relation to biodiversity is to minimise impacts of urban settlement or activities on natural systems. This means that when land is allocated for new development or for an intensification of existing uses, ecologically sensitive areas like wildlife habitat or water foreshores must be avoided and any likely impact from development within nearby areas must be managed (Beatley and Manning, 1997; Fallding et al., 2001).

Decisions about urban form can improve the environmental performance of cities in terms of energy and water use and the generation of waste, and can also contribute to biodiversity protection. By promoting denser, more compact forms of development, total land and habitat disturbance is minimised. Another important way in which urban form can contribute to sustainability is by reducing the number of trips by motor transport needed to undertake daily activities – going to work, school, childcare, shopping and so on (Newman and Kenworthy, 1999). Advocates of compact urban form argue for better integration of compatible uses and the consolidation or reuse of under-utilised existing urban areas. It is claimed that compact urban forms can reduce carbon dioxide emissions associated with the private motor car and promote an efficient use of the existing urban infrastructure (Newman, 2006). Basic planning mechanisms for achieving these goals are reforming standard zoning patterns that separate residential, commercial and other uses by enabling mixed development in selected urban centres, and promoting higher residential densities near public transport.

There are some analysts who argue against containment on the basis that biodiversity is maximised through detached housing surrounded by domestic trees and gardens (Troy, 1990). However, in the context of large metropolitan areas, the weight of evidence suggests that benefits of dispersed development are outweighed by the loss of rural hinterland or remnant native vegetation and the environmental costs of car dependence as distance to services increases on the urban periphery (Newman, 2006; Williams et al., 2000).

Density is usually achieved in new 'greenfield' areas by permitting smaller lot sizes and a greater diversity of dwellings including villas, townhouses and sometimes apartments. It is important to recognise, however, that higher density forms of housing are not inherently sustainable (Holloway and Bunker, 2006). Concerns relate to the use of 'embodied' energy in building materials (all of the energy that is involved in the construction of the building, including the energy needed to produce and transport construction materials), and the ongoing use of energy and water resources by occupants. In new release areas, a higher density of houses might preserve land, but if the developments remain car dependent or fail to incorporate energy and water efficiency provisions, sustainability gains are modest. Planning policies linking new development to public transport, and urban design configurations and requirements to promote walking and cycling are important tools in ensuring that new developments genuinely contribute to sustainability and reduce greenhouse gas emissions.

Development requirements play an important role in achieving sustainability in building design. Mandatory requirements for climate sensitive building designs to reduce energy demand and for energy efficient domestic appliances provide an example of this approach (Low et al., 2005; Department of Planning, 2007). Other approaches might be the compulsory installation of water collection, and recycling and efficiency measures for individual dwellings or buildings (Kay et al., 2004). The planting of endogenous (locally occurring) species can reduce water demands while also contributing to local biodiversity (Fallding et al., 2001). At the neighbourhood or precinct scale, Water Sensitive Urban Design approaches combine water collection and management approaches to reduce demand and the need for new water supply and treatment facilities (Kay et al., 2004; McManus, 2005).

Specific development controls for waste minimisation and management are an important component of the mix. Plans can articulate objectives and requirements to maximise reuse and recycling of building materials, to minimise waste during construction, as well as requirements for ongoing waste management, such as waste storage and recycling arrangements (McManus, 2005).

There is an international movement towards securing resource requirements (food, water, and other essential products) from within a local or region, while also managing waste within the same catchment (Beatley, 1995; 2004). Regulations that retain spaces for essential production and waste reuse/recycling in new development areas, or seek to preserve areas of agricultural production within and surrounding urban peripheries are examples of concrete planning measures to implement these goals.

Planning for climate change

All of these approaches can help communities include climate change considerations in plan making when specific developments are assessed (ODPM, 2004; Department for Communities and Local Government, 2007). The main issues relate to 'mitigating' contributions to climate change arising from carbon emissions (Rogner et al., 2007). Planning provisions designed to reduce reliance on non-renewable sources of energy and decrease car dependency are examples of approaches that can mitigate climate change contributions (Ewing et al., 2007). Sometimes more specific assessment criteria are needed to help evaluate the potential impact of major development that could have a considerable impact on carbon emissions either within the local area or 'downstream'.

Planning provisions may also be needed to strengthen the capacity of communities to 'adapt' to the consequences of climate change that are already underway (Holper et al., 2006; Hennessy et al., 2007). For instance, design and building standards may be inadequate for the hotter temperatures, increased likelihood of bushfires, and more frequent or intense storms and floods that are anticipated under medium-term climate change scenarios (NSW Greenhouse Office, 2005).

Meaningful community involvement in decision-making is a fundamental tenet of sustainability (WCED, 1990). In addition to engaging local stakeholders in decisions, it is also important to consider Indigenous input to land use planning and environmental management, respecting any ongoing custodian obligations and traditional resource access rights (Baker et al., 2001).

This section has outlined the basic tools for promoting sustainability through land use planning including objectives, land use control, development standards, conditions of planning approval, and, of course, refusal of inappropriate developments. Despite growing awareness of the importance of improving the environmental performance of cities and regions through biodiversity conservation, sustainable urban form and design, and climate change preparedness, little is known about the extent to which Australian land use plans address such issues. The following section outlines a methodology for unlocking this information.

The Australian Urban Land Use Planning Policy Survey

Interest in the extent to which local authorities are planning for emerging global policy concerns, particularly environmental issues and climate change, has inspired exploratory internet based survey research both within Australia and in the United Kingdom (ALGA, 2005; TCPA, 2006). The Australian Land Use Planning Policy Survey was developed by researchers at the Universities of Sydney and Western Sydney, with reference to these studies, although jurisdictional differences necessitated different approaches to question design and content. Administration of the survey was through a questionnaire for online self completion by professional planners. The questionnaire is based on statutory plan content, so can also be completed by research assistants with planning qualifications, ultimately enabling a complete database to be constructed. In contrast to previous plan surveys, the Australian Land Use Planning Policy Survey has been designed to enable continual updating of base data and periodic enhancement to gather new data on additional areas of planning policy.

It is intended that all of the 670 plus local government areas in Australia will ultimately be included in a database known as the Australian Land Use Planning Policy Monitor. Local government amalgamations and differences in the planning responsibilities of local governments in the Australian Territories means that the total number of local jurisdictions needed for completion of the data set will change over time. The database combines both local planner respondent and research assistant survey return. A comprehensive approach is important because of the need to establish a deep reservoir of data on Australian land use planning policy, given the current absence of any such information.

The development of the Australian Land Use Planning Policy Survey required a valid questionnaire able to capture the various planning approaches employed across the diversity of state and territory jurisdictions and local authorities in Australia. A tight focus was needed for the first application of the survey to avoid it becoming too lengthy.

The questionnaire (which can be viewed at: http//:ppm .arch.usyd.edu.au) uses a matrix design to group planning techniques and policy areas. It enables detailed data collection within a relatively short (six screen) internet survey taking between 10–20 minutes to complete for planners familiar with the controls within their own planning jurisdictions. Most questions enabled simple radio button check box responses, and there are two optional opportunities for open-ended responses. Principles of internet survey design (including appearance, format and question order, restricted access to avoid multiple responses or responses from those beyond the target sample, and testing across different browsers) were employed (Burkey and Kuechler, 2003).

After a pilot in late April 2007, the first round of the survey was administered online between May and August 2007, with one follow-up email. University ethics requirements dictated a specific sampling protocol which required an initial approach to be made to General Managers by mail, with a request that they pass on the information about the survey to the relevant planning officers. Following this, we sent two follow-up emails to council staff although we were unable to directly initiate communication with the professional planners, the intended survey participants. Publicity about the survey was achieved through notices in planning institute and local government newsletters, and it appears that many participants learned about the survey in this way. General Managers were encouraged to seek staff participation in the survey by offering free customised access to the database, featuring their local government area responses in relation to other councils.

This approach has yielded 76 local government area participants to date, a response rate of approximately 11 per cent. Response rates for internet administered surveys have not yet been established with assurance (Burkey and Kuechler, 2003; Iraguen and Ortuzar, 2003). In this case, non-response is hypothesised to relate to the difficulty of directly targeting the relevant planning officer within council and a current climate of planning scheme reform across the jurisdictions (although it was emphasised that the survey will be updated biannually to track changes to planning control). Of the respondents, 32 were from metropolitan areas and 44 from regional cities and towns. It might be hypothesised that local government areas with stronger sustainability agendas and records of innovation would be over-represented amongst respondents. However, an analysis of actual respondents did not necessarily support this assumption, particularly given the higher number of respondents from non-metropolitan locations, where resources and capacity for innovation is often limited.

An additional 53 questionnaires were undertaken by research assistants, to reach a target of 20% coverage of Australian local government areas for initial analysis. Both the primary survey and the survey completed by research assistants are administered online, enabling automatic data collation. The overall interim sample size of 129 local government areas is associated with confidence rating of results at +/- 10%. This limits the extent to which wider generalisations can be made in analysing the survey results, particularly where results are equivocal. However, as demonstrated below, clear trends are apparent in relation to most questions, improving confidence in broad findings and trends.

The survey instrument covers actual and draft plan approaches, to gain an accurate indication of existing and emerging practice. However, only local government respondents are able to answer questions relating to draft plans or other local or state policies applying to their area, so the complete data set (including responses collected by administrative assistants) relates only to the main statutory land use planning instrument for each local jurisdiction. Both data sets (full survey responses returned by local planners and questionnaires completed by research assistants with professional planning expertise) are maintained separately, but able to be analysed as a combined sample in relation to questions focusing on the primary planning instrument.

Key issues in terms of the validity of the research are the reliability of the measurement tool (i.e. the questionnaire) and the reliability of responses. The reliability of the questionnaire depends on accurate conceptualisation of the range of Australian planning techniques, so in addition to the researchers' previous research on the spectrum of planning approaches to environmental sustainability and housing (Gurran, 2003; Gurran et. al., 2006), the development of the survey involved content analysis of a cross-section of five planning instruments from each Australian jurisdiction. Professional input through a small professional reference group, including alumni from the University of Sydney planning program and the professional board of the University's Planning Research Centre, substantiated the interpretation of key planning approaches and the transferability of categories across jurisdictions. This group verified the validity and reliability of the survey.

Web-based survey administration enables interaction in ways that are similar to a face-to-face survey, through the use of pop up explanations of terms and questions. This is associated with less potential for respondent error and item non-response (where a participant chooses not to answer a specific question) (Burkey and Kuechler, 2003; Iraguen and Ortuzar, 2003). With reference to the reliability of responses, as local planners have professional responsibility for the planning instruments they are referring to, their knowledge is expected to be accurate. The potential for a dishonest response, or asserting the existence of a particular local approach when none has been implemented, is minor because the survey deals with statutory instruments that are publicly available.

Further information about the survey questions and rationale for their inclusion is contained in the following section, which presents the interim results of the survey. It focuses firstly on questions regarding sustainable urban form, secondly, on questions relating to biodiversity conservation, and thirdly, questions relating to climate change adaptation and mitigation.

Planning for urban form in Australia

The survey includes a number of questions concerning approaches to sustainable urban form, including provision for mixed use zones; higher density surrounding public transport or services; provisions for footpaths, bicycle paths and facilities; reduced parking requirements near public transport; energy, water efficiency and sustainable waste management controls. Questions about specific mechanisms to manage

Figure 30: Survey questions about sustainable urban form

Sub-question regarding plan & policy content	Explanation
Mixed use zones	Reduces separation of functions & need for motor journeys
High/medium density residential development zones in proximity to public transport, major nodes or corridors	Reduces car dependence
Incentives for mixed commercial/residential development in well located areas	Reduces separation of functions & need for motor journeys
Requirements for bicycle paths/dedicated lanes for new subdivisions or other applicable developments	Promotes cycling as an alternative to motor journeys
Requirements for bicycle facilities in employment buildings	Promotes cycling to work
Requirements for footpaths/walkways in new subdivisions or other applicable developments	Enables pedestrian journeys to reduce car dependence and promote public health
Reduced parking requirements for applicable developments in areas near public transport	Promotes public transport use
Requirements for passive energy use/energy savings in the design of buildings	Reduces carbon impact of development
Requirements for water saving approaches	Reduces domestic water use, lowers demand for potable water supply
Requirements for water sensitive urban design in new subdivisions/redevelopment areas	Reduces need for major new water infrastructure, promotes water conservation
Requirements for waste minimisation strategies in the construction and operation of new developments	Reduces need for new carbon producing land fill; promotes sustainable reuse of materials and resource recovery
Urban Growth Boundary	Technique for limiting urban expansion
Green building criteria/performance targets	Flexible technique for promoting sustainable building design

growth or to require sustainability features in new development, including urban growth boundaries, and green building criteria were also asked. Figure 30 outlines and explains each of the sub-questions relating to sustainable urban form. Respondents were asked to indicate whether the provision is contained within their principal statutory land use plan, a draft plan, guiding policy, draft guiding policy, or covered by state policy. Multiple responses are permissible by local government respondents, although as noted the data set collected by research assistants focuses only on the primary plan itself.

Figure 31: Approaches to sustainable urban form and containment

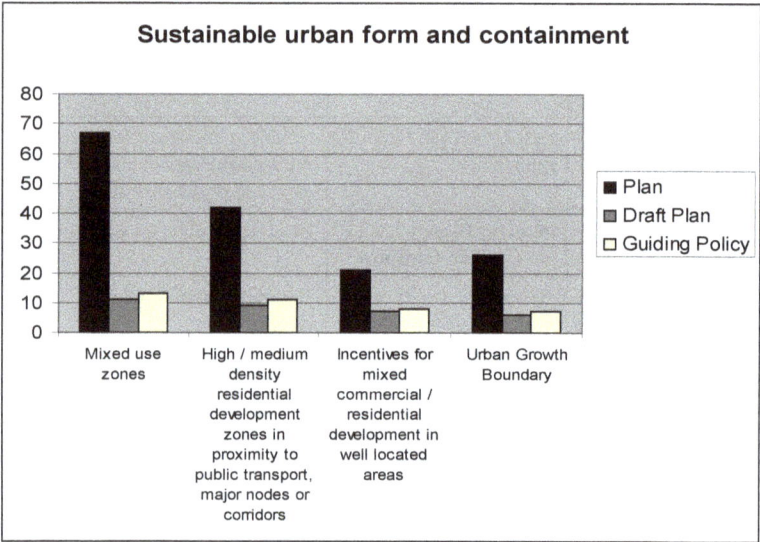

Source: Gurran and Phibbs (2008). N=129.

Sustainable urban form and containment

The most common approach for promoting sustainable urban form is to encourage mixed use areas through land use zones or equivalent categories, enabling a range of residential and commercial activities. Although this was anticipated to be a standard measure across Australian plans, in fact it was contained in just over half (67) of the 129 plans sampled (Figure 31). This may be explained by the higher number of regional cities and towns represented in the sample (78) as compared to metropolitan areas (51), reflecting the higher number of non-metropolitan government units in Australia overall. The smaller proportion of metropolitan areas in the sample might explain why only a third of the sample actively promote high or medium density residential development close to public transport. The final two mechanisms shown in the graph, incentives for mixed development and urban growth boundaries, are applied by 21 and 26 local government areas respectively, although there is no particular reason why these tools should be confined to metropolitan areas.

Figure 32: Planning levers for sustainable transportation

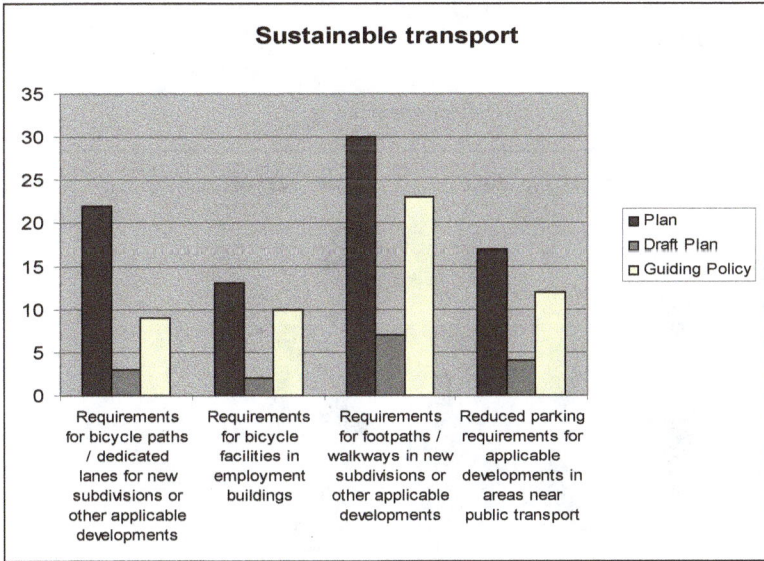

Source: Gurran and Phibbs (2008). N=129.

Sustainable transportation

Although there is a high level of policy emphasis in Australia on the need to promote sustainable transportation and reduce car dependency (e.g., Newman and Kenworthy, 1999; Transport NSW et al., 2001), the interim results of our study suggest that the use of planning mechanisms to achieve these goals is relatively limited. Only 30 plans surveyed actually require footpaths or walkways to be included in new subdivisions or other applicable developments, and an additional 23 of the local government area respondents indicate that provision for footpaths is addressed by guiding policy (Figure 32). It may be assumed that footpaths or walkways may be a matter for negotiation in the other local jurisdictions but the absence of statutory requirements or formal policy is a matter of concern.

A mere 17 of the plans included in the sample have adjusted their car parking requirements for developments located in proximity to public transport. Similarly, only a fifth of plans in the sample (22) include specific requirements for bicycle paths or dedicated lands in new subdivisions.

Figure 33: Energy, water and waste performance

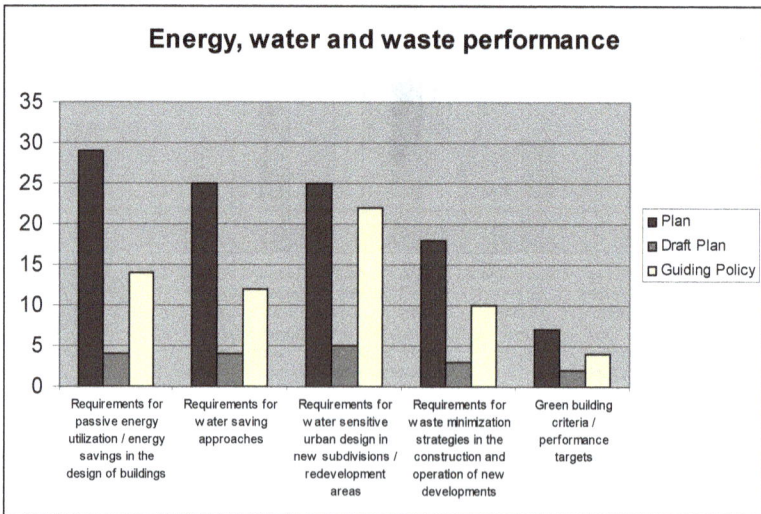

Source: Gurran and Phibbs (2008). N=129.

Energy, water and waste measures

Despite increasing emphasis on the need for energy efficient and climate appropriate building design in Australian planning, only a quarter of the plans sampled include requirements for passive energy utilisation or energy savings in the design of buildings (Figure 33). Results for water conservation were even lower, with only 25 plans including requirements for water saving approaches and water sensitive urban design measures in new development or redevelopment areas. Eighteen of the plans sampled include specific requirements to minimise waste in the construction and operation of new development.

Some local government respondents, particularly those in NSW, indicated that energy and water savings requirements are addressed by state policy under the State Environmental Planning Policy – Building Sustainability Index (BASIX) (see DOP, 2007). Seven plans include environmental or 'green' performance criteria, while 12 local government respondents indicated that this approach was achieved through state policy, and again the majority of these were from NSW.

Planning for biodiversity conservation in Australia

Approaches to biodiversity conservation in local plans are measured by the inclusion of specific measures to protect important biodiversity, like wildlife habitat, wetlands, native vegetation, catchments, coastal features and processes, and the interface between protected natural areas and surrounding lands. A set of sub-questions address the specific tools or environmental offsets to promote biodiversity protection outlined above, including provisions for tradable development rights, clustering on less sensitive areas of environmentally significant sites, population caps linked to environmental carrying capacity, and incentives for voluntary conservation agreements, which can all be effective inducements to biodiversity conservation – see

Figure 34 (Gurran, 2007; Noosa Shire Council, 2004). A series of sub-questions also focus on direct approaches to mitigate contributions to climate change, and provisions to promote adaptation to changed climatic conditions, including vulnerability to bushfire (Figure 35).

Figure 34: Survey questions about biodiversity conservation

Sub-question regarding plan and policy content	Explanation
Requirements for retention of/planting of endogenous species in sensitive areas	Enhances local biodiversity and avoids intrusion by exotic species
Protect wildlife habitat, wetlands, native vegetation, catchment values, landscape values, coastal features/processes	Specific tools – zones, overlays, development prohibitions, special assessment requirements, or referrals needed to ensure protection of these attributes
Manage interface between protected natural areas and surrounding lands	Interface controls or mechanisms to reduce potential conflicts between protected areas and neighbouring lands, such as the spread of exotic species, fire, visual degradation, and adjacent habitat loss

Figure 35: Survey questions about environmental tools/offsets

Sub-question regarding plan and policy content	Explanation
Environmental offsets/trade-offs	Incentive to enable development while achieving overall net environmental benefit
Tradable development rights	Enables compensation for removal of development rights in areas where development no longer appropriate
Clustering on less sensitive areas of environmentally significant sites	Enables reasonable development without compromising overall environmental integrity
Population cap	Allocates land for new urban development according to environmental capacity of local area
Incentives for conservation agreements	Encourages land holders to voluntarily conserve land

Figure 36: Survey questions about climate change

Sub-question regarding plan and policy content	Explanation
Climate change adaptation provisions (zones, zone objectives, overlays, development prohibitions, or special assessment requirements)	Specific mechanisms or objectives within goals to consider the need to adapt to future climate change impacts increasingly required as an important element of local planning, particularly in coastal areas
Climate change mitigation provisions	Ensures that planning authorities consider the carbon impact of new development
Reducing vulnerability to bushfire provisions	Land use plans need to consider potential for increased bushfire risk associated with climate change

Many of the questions relating to biodiversity conservation were tagged to a range of possible planning mechanisms, including zones or equivalent, mapped overlays (which introduce additional requirements), development prohibition, environmental impact assessment or other special assessment requirements, referral to other agencies for their views or endorsement, or other non-specified approaches. Respondents were also asked to indicate whether the issue is addressed through guiding local policy or via state policy requirements. Again, multiple responses were accepted.

Biodiversity protection

Zones or equivalent land use categories are the most common tool used by Australian local governments to protect biodiversity, including wildlife habitat, wetlands, native vegetation, catchment, landscape values, and coastal features. Although less than half of all plans sampled include such measures (Figure 37), inclusion also relates to the environmental features of the local government area, so many are unlikely to be used in metropolitan locations. Exceptions include metropolitan locations containing or adjoining national parks or reserves. Over a quarter of the plans sampled include specific zones or equivalent to protect the interface between these protected areas and adjacent land uses.

Figure 37: Biodiversity protection

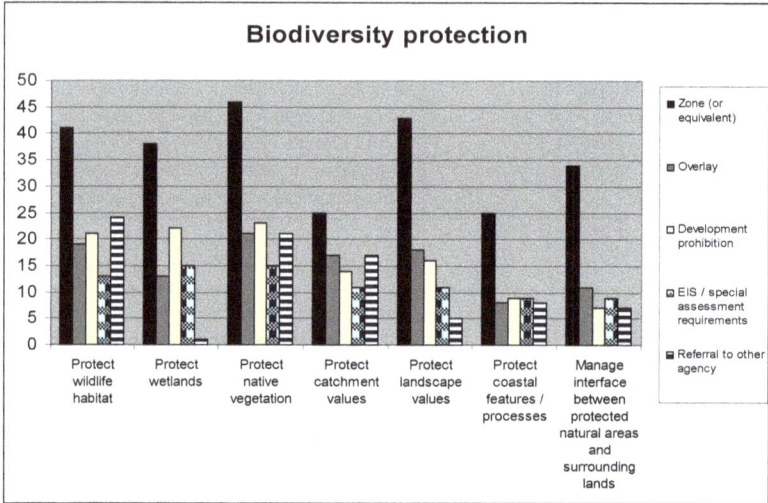

Biodiversity protection

Source: Gurran and Phibbs (2008). N=129.

Other approaches to biodiversity protection include referral to other agencies (particularly common for wildlife habitat, protecting vegetation, and catchment values). Many of the local government areas with planning provisions in place actually prohibit development that may affect wildlife habitat, wetlands, native vegetation or landscape values.

Environmental tools/offsets

The use of environmental tools or offset approaches is relatively limited across the plans included in the sample. As such approaches are regarded to be innovative, and may face legislative barriers in some jurisdictions, these results were not surprising. Indeed, the fact that a small but not insignificant number of plans across Australia do contain provisions for environmental offsets (10 plans), clustering (14 plans), incentives for conservation agreements (10 plans), and requirements for the retention of or planting of endogenous species (44 plans) demonstrates that such tools are feasible, depending on legal and resource constraints within specific local government areas.

Figure 38: Environmental tools/offsets

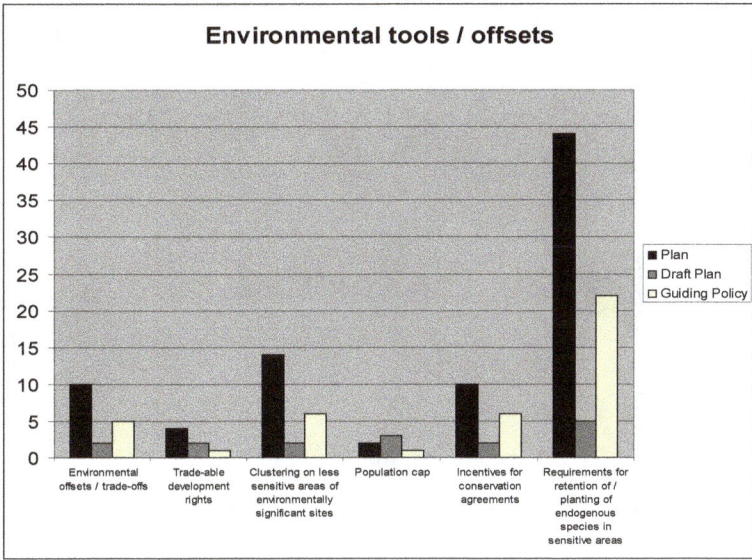

Source: Gurran and Phibbs (2008). N=129.

Climate change mitigation and adaptation

Broader provisions in Australian plans for climate change mitigation through sustainable urban form and building design were outlined above, noting surprisingly limited evidence of tangible planning requirements to achieve these goals. As shown in Figure 39 below, the extent to which climate change has been specifically included in Australian local plans appears extremely limited. Only three local plans refer to climate change mitigation or adaptation as a consideration when assessing development. Several respondents referred to state government requirements in South Australia (provisions for considering sea level rise), but none of the other states were identified by local government participants as promoting specific planning requirements relating to climate change.

Figure 39: Climate change adaptation and mitigation

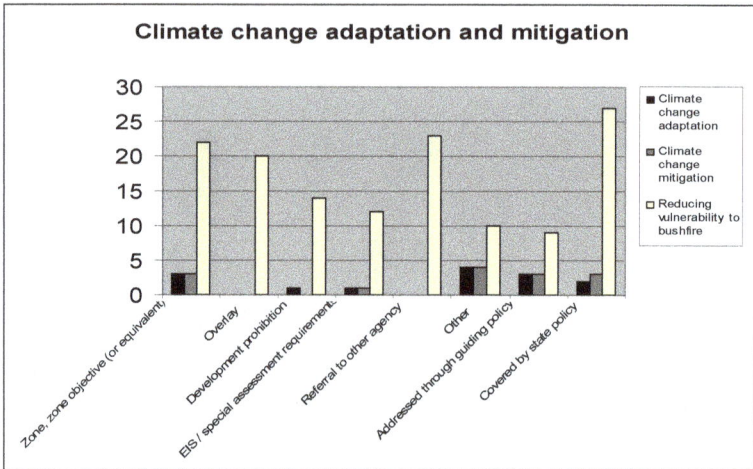

Climate change adaptation and mitigation

Source: Gurran and Phibbs (2008). N=129.

Provisions for bushfire protection is an important consideration in reducing community vulnerability to climate change, though not always recognised as such. Less than a quarter of plans include specific provisions for reducing vulnerability to bushfire, of which 22 use zones or equivalent, 20 use overlay mechanisms, and 23 require referral to another agency. Twenty seven local government respondents (across all of the jurisdictions) report that bushfire protection is addressed by state policy.

Conclusions

The interim results of this national survey of Australian land use plans demonstrates that knowledge of sustainable planning approaches exists in a considerable number of local government areas but that actual implementation of such approaches is limited. It may be difficult to transform pre-existing development control frameworks. Nevertheless, the fact that between a quarter to half of local authorities surveyed have implemented approaches for urban containment, energy and water efficiency, waste minimisation or biodiversity conservation within their plans demonstrates models for broader application across other local jurisdictions. Promoting such practice more widely across Australian local planning authorities will require education and information sharing strategies to promote awareness of existing models and approaches. The Australian Urban Land Use Planning Policy Monitor is intended to contribute to this goal. The act of completing the survey itself exposes practitioners (and planning students) to the range of potential approaches to sustainability planning. When the database is complete, more detailed research on the impacts of sustainable planning policies will be possible by drawing on other data sources available at local government area scale. For instance, the influence of sustainable transport policies will be able to be tracked over time against journey to work data from the census.

Strong state and territorial policy directions and requirements (particularly in relation to climate change mitigation and adaptation), dedicated resources to local government to assist in planning reform and innovation, and effective consultation processes are needed to build political and industry support for such models. It may also be necessary to remove legal barriers to innovative planning tools, for local authorities able to demonstrate effective models for environmental incentives and offsets that result in net benefits for local biodiversity. Such action must take place immediately, as environmental challenges – from biodiversity loss to global climatic change – are gathering pace. A rapid and widespread transformation in existing planning frameworks is needed if Australian local governments and communities are to successfully adapt to these impending challenges.

References

Australian Local Government Association (ALGA) (2005) *Survey of coastal councils*. Canberra: ALGA.

Baker, R., Davies, J., and Young, E. (2001) 'Managing country: an overview of the prime issues,' in R. Baker, J. Davies and E. Young (eds.), *Working on country: contemporary indigenous management of Australia's lands and coastal regions*. Melbourne: Oxford University Press.

Beatley, T. (1995) 'Planning and sustainability: the elements of a new (improved?) paradigm.' *Journal of Planning Literature*. 9(4): pp. 383–395.

Beatley, T. (2004) *Native to nowhere: sustaining home and community in a global age*. Washington DC: Island Press.

Beatley, T. and Manning, K. (1997) *The ecology of place planning for environment, economy and community*. Washington DC: Island Press.

Burkey, J. and Kuechler, W. (2003) 'Web-based surveys for corporate information gathering: a bias-reducing design framework.' *IEEE Transactions on Professional Communication*. 46(2): pp. 81–93.

Commonwealth of Australia (1992) *National strategy for environmentally sustainable development*. Canberra: available at http://www.environment.gov.au/esd/national/nsesd/strategy/index.html (consulted 11th December 2007).

Department of Communities and Local Government (2007) *Planning policy statement: planning and climate change. supplement to planning policy statement 1* available at http://www.communities.gov.uk/publications/planningandbuilding/ppsclimatechange.

Department of Planning (DOP) (2007) *BASIX fact sheet*. Available at www.sustainability.nsw.gov.au/information (consulted 12th June 2007).

Dyck, R. (1998) 'Integrating planning and sustainability theory for local benefit.' *Local Environment*. 3(1): pp. 27–43.

Ewing, R., Bartholomew, K., Winkelman, S., Walters, J. and Chen, D. (2007) *Growing cooler: evidence on urban development and climate change*. Urban Land Institute available at http://dnr.wi.gov/environment protect/gtfgw/documents/GrowingCoolerEs.pdf (consulted 3rd March 2008).

Fallding, M., Kelly, A. Bateson, P. and Donovon, I. (2001) *Biodiversity guide for NSW local government.* Hurstville: NSW National Parks and Wildlife Service (NPWS).

Gurran, N. (2003) 'Housing locally: positioning Australian local government housing for a new century.' *Urban Policy and Research.* 21(4): pp. 393–412.

Gurran, N. (2007) *Australian urban land use planning: introducing statutory planning practice in New South Wales.* Sydney: Sydney University Press.

Gurran, N. and Phibbs P. (2008) *Australian urban land use planning policy monitor interim data May 2008.* Unpublished data report strip available at http://ppm.usyd.edu.au.

Gurran, N., Squires, C., Blakely, E. (2006) *Meeting the sea change challenge: best practice models of local and regional planning for sea change communities.* Report for the National Sea Change Task Force. Sydney: University of Sydney, Planning Research Centre.

Hennessy, K. B., Fitzharris, B. C., Bates, N., Harvey, S. M., Howden, L., Hughes, J., Salinger, J. and Warrick, R. (2007) *Australia and New Zealand, climate change 2007: impacts, adaptation and vulnerability.* Contribution of Working Group II to the Fourth Assessment Report of the Intergovernmental Panel on Climate Change in M. L. Parry, O. L. Canzaiani, J. P. Palutikof, P. J. ven der Linden and C. E. Hanson (eds.). Cambridge: Cambridge University Press. pp. 507–540.

Holloway, D. and Bunker, R. (2006) 'Planning, housing and energy use: a review.' *Urban Policy and Research.* 24(1): pp. 115–126.

Holper, P., Nolan, L. S., Senese, M. and Hennessy, K. (2006) *Infrastructure and climate change: Risk assessment for Victoria.* Victoria: CSRIO.

Iraguen, P. and de Dios Ortúzar, J. (2003) 'Willingness-to-pay for reducing fatal accident risk in urban areas: an Internet based web page stated preference survey.' *Accident Analysis and Prevention.* 36(4): pp. 513–524.

Kay, E., Wong, T., Johnstone, P. and Walsh, G. (2004) *Delivering water sensitive urban design through the planning system.* Available at www.wsud.org/downloads (consulted 12th June 2007).

Low, N., Gleeson, B., Green, R. and Radovic, D. (2005) *The green city: sustainable homes, sustainable suburbs.* Sydney: UNSW Press.

McManus, P. (2005) *Vortex cities to sustainable cities: Australia's urban challenge.* Sydney: UNSW Press.

Newman, P. (2006) 'Sustainable transport for sustainable cities.' *Issues.* vol. 76: pp. 6–10.

Newman, P. and Kenworthy, J. (1999) *Sustainability and cities: overcoming automobile dependence.* Washington DC: Island Press.

Noosa Shire Council (2004) *Population carrying capacity in Noosa Shire.* Noosa: Noosa Shire Council.

NSW Greenhouse Office (2005) *NSW greenhouse plan.* Available at http://www.greenhouse.nsw.gov.au/__data/assets/pdf_file/0016/2662/28-11_FINAL_NSW_GH_Plan_web.pdf.

NSW National Parks and Wildlife Service (NPWS) (1999) *NSW biodiversity strategy.* Hurstville: NPWS.

Office of the Deputy Prime Minister (ODPM) (2004) *The Planning response to climate change: advice on better practice.* London: Office of the Deputy Prime Minister.

Rogner, H. H., Zhou, D., Bradley, R., Crabbe, P., Edenhofer, O., Hare, B., Kuijpers, L. and Yamaguchi, M. (2007) 'Introduction,' in *Climate Change 2007: mitigation.* Contribution of Working Group III to the Fourth Assessment Report of the Intergovernmental Panel on Climate Change. B. Metz, O.R. Davidson, P. R. Bosch, R. Dave and L. A. Meyer (eds.). Cambridge: Cambridge University Press.

Town and Country Planning Association (TCPA) (2006) *Survey of local authorities: planning for on-site renewable energy and sustainable construction.* London: TCPA.

Transport NSW, Roads and Traffic Authority and Department of Urban Affairs and Planning (2001) *Integrating land use and transport: improving transport choice – guidelines for planning and development.* Sydney: NSW Department of Urban Affairs and Planning.

Troy, P. (1990) *The perils of urban consolidation: a discussion of Australian housing and urban development policies.* Annandale: The Federation Press.

Williams, K., Burton, E. and Jenks, M. (2000) *Achieving sustainable urban form.* London: F & N Spoon.

World Commission on Environment and Development (WCED) (1987) *Our common future.* New York: Oxford University Press.

Chapter 7

PUBLIC HEALTH AND THE SUSTAINABILITY OF CITIES: SYDNEY AIRPORT'S NOISE POLLUTION AND COMMUNITY WELLBEING

Deborah Black and John Black

The development of international airports is a driving force behind globalisation. But growth in air traffic is also a threat to sustainable community health in the vicinity of airports. Airports are an increasingly important dimension to the economic sustainability of cities but the health and wellbeing of its citizens must also be considered in the process of development assessment and impact mitigation.

Human health impacts (that are both positive and negative) should be accounted for in the planning, development and management of urban environments (Capon and Blakely, 2007). Public health and environmental health impacts clearly have a spatial dimension. Capon and Blakely (2007, p. 54) describe a 10-point checklist for the planning and development of healthy and sustainable communities. The ten domains in the checklist are essentially physical characteristics of places: outdoor air quality; water supply and sanitation; housing and buildings; food; local shops and services; schools and other educational institutions; community spaces; transport and street connectivity; communication technology; economy and employment.

The complexity of these emerging public health problems presents a major new challenge for sustainable development. Integrated solutions will require health care professionals, epidemiologists, engineers, environmental scientists, urban planners, designers and managers, policy specialists, economists and social scientists to grapple with working together in new ways. We have already argued for the application of the trans-disciplinary approach that is advocated in medical science by Higginbotham et al. (2001) to research into quality of life and environmental health (Black and Hayashi, 2005; Issarayangyun et al., 2005a) – a framework that is helpful in the formulation of common conceptual approaches and for integrated solutions that match the spatial scale and pace of these emerging health problems in urban environments.

The issues of event, time and place are the basis of public health and environmental health studies, as noted over a century and a half ago by Dr John Snow, the founder of geographical epidemiology. In this chapter, we use space to articulate how geographers, urban planners and urban managers might, at the local, neighbourhood scale, comprehend the close interrelationship between human activity, industry, the physical environment and human disease, ill health and mortality. To do this we review the fundamental approaches adopted by public health specialists. Both the University of Sydney and the University of New South Wales have contributed substantially to the literature on public health (next section). In the following section, concepts from the new public health curriculum at Sydney University are illustrated by the case of aircraft noise at Sydney International Airport and noise impacts on individual stress and hypertension. Whilst we see the contemporary approach in forging greater collaboration between planners and public health specialists as a desirable step in the right direction, we conclude the paper with suggestions on more integrated solutions that emphasise the importance of GIS (Geographic Information Systems), the modern-day equivalent technique so powerful in Dr Snow's towering intellect and painstaking site investigations.

Public and environmental health – new approach

Innovation is necessary to achieve socially-sustainable solutions. As pointed out by Kearns et al. (2007, p. 49) partial solutions generated by traditionally distinct professional disciplines are unlikely to result in real innovation. Therefore, our suggestion, in responding to the challenges posed by Capon and Blakely, is that urban planners and urban managers might start with the public health literature, in particular, the diagrammatic representation of the way in which a variety of influences (including the social environment and the physical environment) interact to affect individual health and wellbeing (Baume and Irvine, 1995: p. 9) and examples of the non-health sectors (including housing and public planning) which may have a role in working with the health sector (Bauman, 1995). Furthermore, it should be noted that there has been a change in approach to environmental studies within public health that emphasises the close interrelationship between human activity, industry, the physical environment and human disease, ill health and mortality (Frith, 1995: p. 104). This background is explained using a public health paradigm developed by the University of New South Wales. The population health integration within the medical curriculum at the University of Sydney similarly aims to bridge the gap between the traditional, individual-level health care approach and population-based health care (Trevena et al., 2005).

We believe the eight key concepts of the population-health learning outcomes of this new curriculum are equally applicable to the way that research studies of the public and environmental health issues in cities could be designed so as to promote sustainable outcomes. The concepts are: 1) *distribution* – How common is the problem in the total population and in different subgroups?; 2) *cause* – what causes the problem?; 3) *prevention* – How can the problem be prevented?; 4) *management* – What is the most appropriate management of the problem at individual system and population levels, and how can systems be continually improved?; 5) *evidence base* – How strong is the evidence about the distribution and cause of the problem, its prevention and its management?; 6) *personal effects* – What are the personal effects of having the problem?; 7) *societal effects* – What are the effects of the problem (and its management) on, and in, society?; and 8) *societal response* – How does (and could) society respond to the problem? Later, these concepts are illustrated with reference to aircraft noise in communities around Sydney airport, but firstly we review contemporary research and practice.

Contemporary planning and public health approach

There is a body of literature that links urbanisation and urban layout with obesity (for example, Frank et al., 2003). There is also an increasing awareness of the need for planners and health specialists to work together more closely. Kearns et al. (2007) have defined some of the research challenges for urban researchers from a socio-ecological perspective as:

> The spatial and temporal dynamics of social and environmental determinants of human health in urban systems. Who gets sick and where do they live? What are the

relative contributions of social versus environmental factors? What types of interventions are available and appropriate?

Measures of health in different urban forms. What contribution does urban pattern and social–ecological processes in urban environments make to the functionality of urban habitats? Can we identify the characteristics of dysfunctional and functional urban landscapes and incorporate this knowledge into better urban planning, design, construction and management?

Harris et al. (2007: p. 150) consider that a range of practical actions from a public health perspective are required, such as:

- a shift towards 'healthy' public policy that increases the capacity of the health sector to engage inter-sectorally with urban planning;

- understanding the regulatory framework that governs urban planning and development;

- learning from past lessons (literature review) concerning advocating for health as part of the urbanisation process; and

- building on the strengths of, and meeting the challenges set by, health impact assessments.

There is already a body of knowledge from which to respond to the challenges articulated by these authors. The influence of built-form factors on health (and wellbeing) is already established from evidence cited in the literature, locally in Sydney for Granville (NSW Health, Sydney West Area Health Service, 2006: pp. 24–25; see also Appendix 2), and, more generally, in the international literature (Meade and Earickson, 2000: pp. 136–140; Jackson, 2003; Frumkin et al., 2004; Galea and Vlahov, 2005a, 2005b; Giles-Corti, 2006; Capon and Dixon, 2007; Harris et al., 2007). The Granville Health Impact Study (NSW Health, Sydney West Area Health Service, 2006) considers five themes: transport, traffic and parking, and pedestrians; business, industry and neighbourhood nodes; community facilities, medical services, child care and schools; landscape, parks, recreation, access to a local river; and housing and urban design.

Within this broad literature linking urban development and public health sits the more specific and widely researched topic of the social and environmental impacts of transport (see Chapter 2). For example, the eight concepts from the University of Sydney's medical curriculum that are applicable to the way studies of the public and environmental health issues in cities can be designed so as to promote sustainable outcomes can be illustrated from our broadly-focused research, such as: road traffic noise (Black et al., 1997); lead in petrol and the impact on children's IQs (Cowie et al., 1997); accident risk to pedestrians crossing the road (Black and Black, 2001); and the stress and hypertension caused by aircraft noise (Black et al., 2007; Black and Black, 2007).

All events that impact on the health and wellbeing of the urban population, whether they have been a result of the built form in general or motor vehicles or jet aircraft in particular exhibit a geographical pattern of incidence. It is the appropriate management of such factors that contribute to more sustainable cities. To further illustrate patterns of geographical incidence and management, we focus on one specific illustration of an individual heath problem in environmental health that is literally in Sydney University's backyard (or over its backyard): that is, aircraft noise at Sydney Airport.

Aircraft noise and environmental health

Aircraft noise is one of the best illustrations of the important health issues that are a major component of sustainable health in cities. Our research on aircraft noise was of sufficient social importance to be included in *The Sydney Morning Herald, Sydney Magazine* (Issue #60 of April, 2008: p. 58). The example is also a timely reminder that in cities the 'dose', in this case aircraft noise, may have variable spatial impacts over time. The research was undertaken when all three runways were operational so as to share the noise north-south and east-west of the airport. In November 2007, immediately after the results of the federal election were announced, the Sydney Airport Corporation Ltd notified that the East-West Runway would be closed for two years from 2008 to complete some necessary safety construction works at the ends of the runways. As a consequence, those suburbs north and south of the airport will be exposed to substantially more flights under parallel runway operations and hence more noise events.

Distribution

How common is the noise problem (annoyance, quality of life, stress and hypertension) in the total population (spatial patterns) and in different subgroups (socioeconomic status and equity)? These are important questions for both urban geographers and planners. Aircraft noise has been a vexing health and wellbeing issue for residents near major commercial and military airports in cities throughout the world especially with the introduction of commercial jets in the 1950s. Construction and operation of the third runway at Sydney airport in the mid-1990s highlighted this issue for the University of Sydney's backyard neighbours.

Figure 40: Aircraft noise at Sydney Airport, 1999

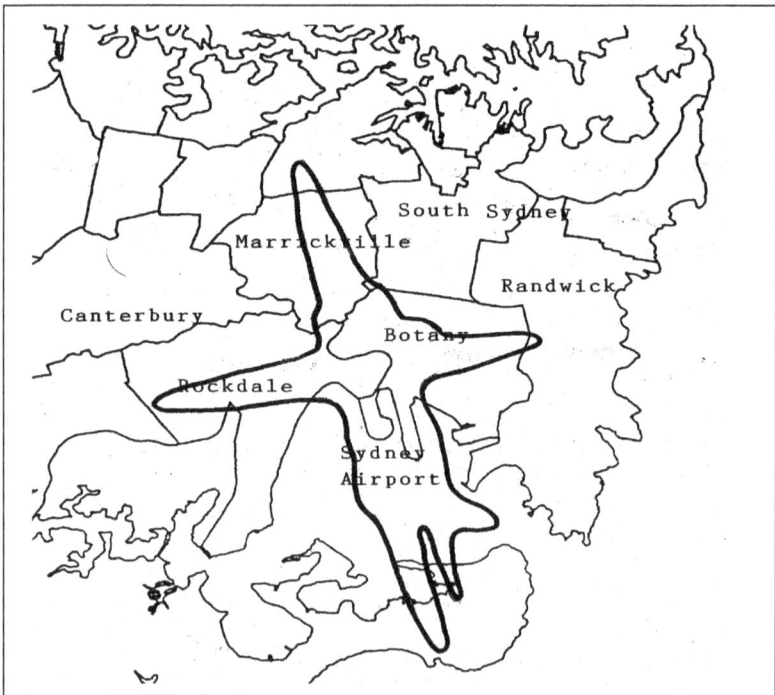

Source: based on http://www.airservicesaustralia.com/reports/anei/eo20_085.pdf

Figure 40 shows the 1999 ANEI (Australian Noise Exposure Index) 25 contour from which detailed demographic analyses of census data will reveal the number and categories of people highly affected by the annoyance from aircraft noise.

The Australian Noise Exposure Forecast (ANEF) is the metric, calculated from a standard computer program, and used in compatible land use planning in the vicinity of airports based on projections of air traffic growth and the types of jet aircraft flying in the future (AirServices Australia, 1999). The ANEF 25 contour is a critical piece of information because social surveys throughout the world demonstrate a high proportion of residents living within this boundary are 'highly annoyed' or 'moderately annoyed' from aircraft noise (Fidell et al., 1991). When the actual aircraft movements (aircraft type, flight tracks, etc.) recorded for one year at the airport are fed into the same computer software, the noise contours produced are called the ANEI.

The Number-Above (NA) metric is defined as the number of noise events during a given period that are louder than a selected threshold level and provides another approach to the distributional question. Our research (Issarayangyun et al., 2005b) obtained the average annual day of N70 contour maps around Sydney Airport which are periodically produced by AirServices Australia (see Figure 40. The level of 70 dB(A) was chosen because it is commonly the case that the outdoor sound level will be attenuated approximately 10 dB(A) by the structure of a house. An internal noise level of 60 dB(A) is the sound pressure level of a noise event that is likely to interfere with conversation or with listening to the radio or the TV (Southgate et al., 2000).

Cause

The source of aircraft noise is obvious, even to the casual observer, although the area of air traffic control and noise management is a highly specialised area of engineering as it entails the measurement, modelling and estimation of aircraft noise. Airport noise is caused by aircraft in their cycle of landing, taxiing and taking-off. There is additional noise from an airport as an industrial land use, especially where ground running of aircraft takes place during routine maintenance. Traffic control in terminal airspace conforms to international regulations (ICAO). However, there are additional local operational procedures aimed at minimising aircraft noise on surrounding land uses, such as the arrival flight paths for jet aircraft arriving at Sydney airport (the use of flight paths over Botany Bay where possible).

Prevention

How this noise problem for those living and working in the vicinity of Sydney Airport, in general, and in Sydney University's backyard, in particular, can be eliminated is purely a political, not a technical, question. The prevention involves building a second Sydney airport outside of the Sydney metropolitan basin. For example, Goulburn has been evaluated as a potential site some 20 years ago and Newcastle Airport at Williamstown – which is currently shared by the RAAF with civilian flights – has been mooted recently with suggestions of a high-speed rail to Sydney (*The Sydney Morning Herald*, 13 June, p. 15).

Closing down the existing airport at Mascot is unlikely. Despite the political statements about a second Sydney airport that have been made since the 1970s, and detailed assessments of alternative sites undertaken, there is still no resolution to this issue. A Commonwealth Green Paper on Australian aviation is scheduled for release later in 2008. The practical reality is that aircraft noise at Sydney Airport cannot be prevented by its relocation: noise can only be mitigated as discussed next under management. By 2020, 62 million annual passengers are projected to use Sydney airport and the number of aircraft movements will increase considerably.

Management

What is the most appropriate management of the noise problem at the individual system and population levels, and how can systems be continually improved? These are critical questions given that the most likely prospects are for civil aviation operations to continue for a long time at Sydney airport, where already there are several management strategies in place. The first planning instrument is the dose-response relationship which uses the Australian Noise Exposure Forecast (ANEF) as the relevant metric to define land use compatibility surrounding airports. This is a land use regulation designed to make sure new residential dwellings are not approved in proximity to the airport by local governments.

The Long Term Operating Plan which incorporates a noise-sharing principle with the use of 10 modes of runway operations (AirServices Australia, 1996) aims to avoid concentration of noise impacts for existing residents near the airport as would be the case under parallel runway operations affecting primarily residents to the north and south of the two parallel airport runways. The federal government has imposed an hourly cap on aircraft movements of 80 at Sydney Airport. The Sydney Airport Noise Amelioration Program also aims to reduce noise at the point of reception. From 1995 to the end of 1997, 93 public buildings (schools, religious buildings, such as churches, and health care facilities) and 4600 residences were provided with acoustical treatment at a capital cost of nearly $400 million, approximately the cost of the construction of the third runway at Sydney Airport. The eligibility criterion was location within the 30 ANEF contour.

It should be noted that adverse community reaction to aircraft noise within the 25 ANEF contour is substantial (Commonwealth of Australia, Senate Select Committee, 1995). Airport environmental management systems initiated by the owners of Australian privatised airports are designed for continuous improvement in performance, but the noise from arriving and departing aircraft is regulated by Commonwealth Government laws. Hence, any future innovative systems are likely to come from federal government initiatives.

Evidence base

The evidence about the world-wide distribution and cause of the aircraft noise problem in suburbs surrounding airports is compelling (Southworth, 2007: p. 3) and renders further discussion unnecessary. However, elimination of aircraft noise is impossible given the role of international aviation in the expansion of the global economy. Even given technological advances in aircraft engine design (for example, jet engines on the A380), there is no such thing as a 'quiet aircraft'.

Personal effects

What are the personal effects of experiencing the problem of aircraft noise? Annoyance is well documented in the literature (Hede and Bullen, 1982; Fidell et al., 1991), but stress and hypertension has only been identified in more recent years (Meister and Donatelle, 2000; HECS,

2001; Rosenlund et al., 2001; Issarayangyun et al., 2005b; Jarup et al., 2005). In our research fully discussed in Black et al. (2007), a self-reported questionnaire using the validated instrument SF-36 measured health quality of life, prevalence of hypertension, chronic noise stress, noise sensitivity, noise annoyance, confounding factors, and demographic characteristics. After controlling for confounders, subjects around Sydney airport (aged 15–87) who have been chronically exposed to high aircraft noise level have the odds of 2.61 (95% CI 1.42–4 .80) of having chronic noise stress, and these chronic noise stress persons have the odds of 2.74 (95% CI 1.55–4.84) of having hypertension compared with those without. The control group was surveyed in an area of similar demographic characteristics not affected by aircraft noise.

Societal response

How could society respond to the problem of alleviating stress and hypertension? One possibility proposed here is the practice of meditation, a form of 'mind body therapy' that has arisen from the ancient Eastern spiritual tradition. It is important to define 'meditation' as there has been a recent shift by the US National Centre for Complementary and Alternative Medicine (NCCAM) from a Western understanding of meditation as 'a conscious mental process that induces a set of integrated physiological changes termed the relaxation process' to a definition more consistent with the traditional Eastern concept of 'in meditation, a person learns to focus his attention and suspend the stream of thoughts that normally occupy the mind' (National Center of Complementary and Alternative Medicine, 2007; Manocha, 2002). Health professionals are enthusiastic about meditation; a survey of Australian GPs in 2000 found that almost 80% of respondents had recommended meditation to patients at some time in the course of their practice yet less than 35% had any formal training or education in the field (Pirotta et al., 2000).

The authors have designed a research study that uses mediation techniques to reduce stress from suffers of aircraft noise around both commercial and military airports. The hypothesis to be tested is that the impact of stress associated with aircraft noise can be alleviated by meditation. This has proven successful with asthma, work stress and menopause (Manocha et al., 2002). The aim is to demonstrate that meditation, whose central characteristic is the experience of mental silence, can alleviate stress in adults caused by long-term exposure to aircraft noise. A secondary aim is to look at the cost of such an intervention and compare the cost to prescription medication for stress. To our knowledge, no study has attempted to determine how stress from airport noise can be alleviated from methods other than pharmaceutical drugs.

Subject to funding, people aged 55 years or more in aircraft noise exposed suburbs will be recruited to four focus groups. The research is targeting those adults most likely to be at home during the day and exposed to aircraft noise. It would draw on members of this network, plus advertisements placed in local newspapers, to assist in the recruitment of the elderly is noise affected suburbs near Sydney Airport. The purpose of the focus groups is to identify attitudes to aircraft noise and methods used to ameliorate the effects of aircraft noise. Knowledge of, and attitudes towards, behavioural modification techniques will also be explored.

The intervention group will be taught a meditation technique called Sahaja Yoga. The Sahaja Yoga meditation technique is proposed because it utilises a 'classical' understanding of meditation, in which 'mental silence' is regarded as the defining feature, vis-a-vis the conventional understanding of meditation as method of relaxation. The technique uses a simple series of silent affirmations based on a traditional understanding of yogic psychophysiology. Subjects will be encouraged to meditate while sitting quietly in a chair or in a comfortable position that facilitates their meditation experience. They will be encouraged to develop a sustainable state of 'mental silence' (Sanskrit 'nirvichara samadhi' or *thoughtless awareness*). Each subgroup will meet separately for 2 hours each week over an 8 week period, and will be given supporting tapes and asked to devote 10–20 minutes per day to this practice.

The questionnaire will be designed to capture all potential confounders. Questions concerning employment status, exercise activities, smoking status, alcohol consumption, nutrition and demographic characteristics will be adapted from the Australian Bureau of Statistics, but some questions will be designed specifically for this research. For instance, a question measuring smoking status of other members of the household will be included to eliminate the impact of passive smoking. A question asking how long the respondent has lived in his/her house will be included to satisfy the research assumption that long-term aircraft noise exposure has negative impacts on human health. A noise-confounding question (which is: 'Have you recently insulated your house from noise?') will be added to the questionnaire to eliminate the effect from acoustic insulation (which has been a feature of the noise management plan at Sydney Airport).

Participants in the intervention and the control group will be followed up using the same mail-out procedure of the three questionnaires at 6 months and at 12 months. At 6 months, we will measure whether stress, hypertension and health and wellbeing measures are significantly different between the two groups. At 12 months, the research team will ascertain whether the hypothesised lower stress levels and general health and wellbeing have been maintained in the intervention group.

Suggestions for integrated solutions

Whilst aircraft noise is especially annoying in residents' backyards, there was definitely one place and backyard not to be: in the vicinity of Broad Street, London in 1854. Henry Whitehead located 700 deaths within a 250-yard radius and showed that use of water from the Broad Street pump was strongly correlated with death from cholera, as Dr John Snow had once hypothesised (Newson, 2006: p. 211). Thus, 'geographical epidemiology' began. One can imagine John Snow asking: how serious is the problem of cholera in the total population (deadly!)? What caused the problem (faeces in the water supply)? How can the problem be prevented (clean water)? What is the most appropriate management of the problem at individual system and population levels, and how can systems be continually improved (sanitary engineering)? How strong is the evidence about the distribution and cause of the problem (highly), its prevention (public hygiene), and its management (mapping)? What are the personal effects of having the problem (death)? What are the effects of the problem (and its management) on, and in, society? Finally, how does (and did) society respond to the problem (public health, engineering, and urban planning)?

Through exploring these questions, Snow pioneered 'geographical' epidemiology. The breadth of his work has made him one of the most revered scientists of his age. UCLA School of Public Health has devoted a website to his life and work. The backyard of Broadwick Street contains the 'John Snow' pub with a first floor display devoted to his work, a replica of the famous pump, and his picture on the inn's sign. What might modern 'geographical epidemiology' look like with the availability of today's technologies?

Many of these questions have been partially answered by the University of Sydney population health integration within the Medical Curriculum, as outlined above. In addition, we suggest that an initial research project would be to classify evidence on public health and urban form with particular reference to geographical location, as we have provided in the example of aircraft noise, and tease out built form effects from socioeconomic confounders, including the role of the law in supporting urban dysfunction (for a US example, see Buzbee, 2003).

In order to properly plan, manage and monitor any public health program, it is vital that up-to-date, relevant information is available to decision-makers at all levels of the public health system. As every public or environmental health event requires a different response and policy decision, information must be available that reflects a realistic assessment of the situation at the local level. This must be done with the best available data and taking into consideration demographics, availability of, and accessibility to, existing health and social services as well as other geographic and environmental features, including climate change impacts.

Geographic information systems (GIS) provide ideal platforms for the convergence of public and environmental health information and their analyses in relation to urban settlements, surrounding social and health services and the natural environment (Zhan et al., 2006). They are highly suitable for analysing epidemiological data, revealing trends and interrelationships that would be more difficult to discover in tabular format. Moreover, GIS allows policy makers to easily visualise problems in relation to existing health and social services and the natural environment and so more effectively target resources. The World Health Organisation (WHO) has a public health and GIS mapping program but this is at the global or national scale and not at the spatial resolution of the city, or parts of the city, that is necessary in our research design.

There is a clear need to create public health informatics that focus on problems of public and environmental health. Whilst this is an ambitious research and development agenda, it is also at the forefront of international competitive research where there are obvious gaps. Figure 41 provides a picture of dominant topic areas of research in health informatics in the United Kingdom, United States and Canada. These countries are at the cutting edge of research in this area according to the Queensland e-health strategy. The international classifications and codes are:

AI	Artificial Intelligence
BCS	Biomedical Cognitive Science
BIO	Bioinformatics
CBT	Computer Based Training
CCT	Coding, Classification, Terminology
CGL	Computerised Clinical Guidelines
CHI	Consumer Health Informatics
CIM	Clinical Information Management
DI	Dental Informatics
DSS	Decision Support Systems
EDU	Education and Training
EPR	Electronic Patient Records
IR	Information Retrieval
IRV	Imaging, Robotics, Virtual Reality
MLP	Medical Language Processing
NI	Nursing Informatics
OA	Outcomes Assessment
PHI	Public Health Informatics
SIG	Signal processing
SSL	Standards, Social and Legal Issues
TEL	Telemedicine

The gaps identified in Figure 41 of particular relevance to integrated solutions for the sustainability of cities and regions include public health informatics and outcomes assessment (see, for example, Scotch and Parmanto, 2006). There is also a clear practical need for public health informatics systems (Waitakere City Council, 2005). A stakeholder survey of 522 leaders and professionals in the 25 largest cities of the world found that health care is a major infrastructure challenge

(Lofthouse, 2007: pp. 44–49), and furthermore noted that IT in health care has a major role to play, supporting both treatment and administration (p. 48).

Figure 41: Classification of research fields on health informatics

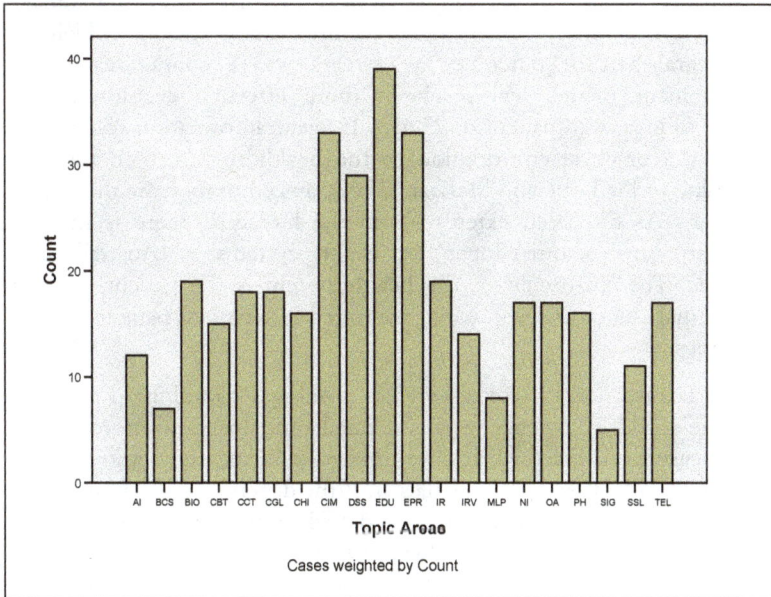

Cases weighted by Count

Source: web searches undertaken by authors. Data from Canada, the United Kingdom and the United States

The logical extension of this challenge is to incorporate visualisation for decision makers. As a starting point in the development of such systems, there are books on GIS and public health (Cromley and McLafferty, 2002), public health information visualisation technology (Lu, 2005), and a range of recent University initiatives linking geography, web-based spatial analysis (GIS) and epidemiology (for example, Grigg et al., 2006; Maclachlan et al., 2007). Cutchin (2007) suggests a number of geographic perspectives on health and environment that could create useful connections between geography and public health via social epidemiology.

Health service providers argue consistently that improved information systems will assist in providing more efficient ways of rationing health services. An important question less frequently asked about such information systems is: will improved health information systems make the services more effective? Improved information systems, which are an integral part of outcomes assessment and a continuous quality improvement model, will result in more effective decision-making leading to improved patient outcomes. If health information systems are to make a practical contribution to the health system, then there is, according to De Lone and McLean (1992), a need to measure the output concisely. As discussed extensively in the literature, there is now an emphasis on 'customer-focus' in health systems in Australia and overseas. The 'customer' in the health system is the patient, so it is argued that the output should be measured in terms of patients' health outcomes.

> If information system research is to make a contribution to the world of practice, a well-defined outcome measure (or measures) is essential. It does little good to measure various independent or input variables … if the dependent or output measure … cannot be measured with a similar degree of accuracy (De Lone and McLean, 1992: p. 61).

Conclusions

The issues of event, time and place are the basis of epidemiological studies. Integrated solutions, based on a trans-disciplinary approach and using the power of computers to link data and GIS to produce visualisation, need the specialised contributions of different professions working with a common conceptual framework. From a public health perspective, integrated solutions for the sustainability of cities and regions include public health informatics and outcomes assessment. Eight key concepts are applicable to the way that research studies of the public and environmental health issues in cities could be designed so as to promote sustainable outcomes.

The concepts are: 1) *distribution* – the problem in the total population and in different subgroups; 2) *cause* – the causes the problem; 3) *prevention* – interventions to prevent the problem; 4) *management* – determine the most appropriate management of the problem at individual system and population levels, and identify how to continually improve the systems; 5) *evidence base* – determine how strong the evidence is about the distribution and cause of the problem, its prevention and its management; 6) *personal effects* – specify the personal effects of having the problem; 7) *societal effects* – analyse the effects of the problem (and its management) on, and in, society?; and 8) *societal response* – How does (and could) society respond to the problem?

We have illustrated this methodology and each of the eight concepts with an example of aircraft noise at Sydney airport and an individual's health and quality of life in, what has been described as, the 'noise sewer' of the University of Sydney's backyard. The further development of public health informatics and the assessment of outcomes could be thought of as a fertile backyard meeting place of urban planners, geographers, health informatics specialists and epidemiologists. Dr John Snow pioneered 'geographical' epidemiology, and he breadth of his work has made him one of the most revered scientists of his age. Today, innovation across once traditionally separate disciplines is necessary to achieve more economic, social and environmentally sustainable cities and regions.

Notes

This chapter was written specifically for this book, although some of the research on aircraft noise was based on previously peer-reviewed published work with Dr Stephen Samuels (University of New South Wales) and Dr Tharit Issarayangyun (Institute of Transport and Logistics Studies, University of Sydney).

References

Airservices Australia (1996) *The long term operating plan for Sydney (Kingsford Smith) airport and associated airspace*. Canberra: Airservices Australia.

Airservices Australia (1999) *The Australian noise exposure forecast system and associated land use compatibility advice for areas in the vicinity of airports*. Canberra: Airservices Australia.

Bauman, A. (1995) 'Working across sectors,' in P. Baume and A. Bauman, A. (eds.), *Public health: an introduction*. Sydney: Eriador Press, pp. 54–57.

Baume, P. and Irvine, S. (1995) 'The concept of health,' in P. Baume and A. Bauman (eds.) *Public health: an introduction*. Sydney: Eriador Press, pp.8–17.

Black, D. A. and Black, J. A. (2001) 'Main street redesign and pedestrian accident risk'. *24ᵗʰ Australasian Transport Research Forum (ATRF), 17– 20 April, Hobart, Zero road toll – a dream or a realistic vision?* (CD-Rom).

Black, D. A. and Black, J. A. (2007) 'Aircraft noise and public health: a research design for innovative airport environmental management'. *11ᵗʰ World Conference on Transport Research, University of California Berkeley, CA, 24–28 June, 2007* (CD-Rom).

Black, D. A., Black, J. A., Issarayangyun, T. and Samuels, S. E. (2007) 'Public health responses to aircraft noise and its mitigation.' *Journal of Air Transport Management*. 13(5): pp. 264–276.

Black, J. and Hayashi, Y. (2005) 'A trans-disciplinary framework: challenges in modelling the sustainable city'. *Proceedings of the 9th International Conference on Computers in Urban Planning and Urban Management, University College London, 29 June to 1 July, 2005*.

Black, J. A., Samuels, S. E., Masters, E., Trinder J., Morrison, J. C. and Tudge, R. (1997) 'Road traffic noise prediction using object oriented and geographic information system technologies'. *Transportation Research Record, No 1601 Environmental Issues in Transportation*. Washington DC: National Academy Press. pp. 77–83.

Buzbee, W. W. (2003) 'Urban form, health, and the Law's limits.' *American Journal of Public Health*. 93(9): pp. 1395–1399.

Capon, A. G. and Blakely, E. J. (2007) 'Creating healthy, just and eco-sensitive cities,' *New South Wales Public Health Bulletin:* 18(3–4): pp. 51–54.

Capon, A. G. and Dixon, J. M. (2007) 'Cities, sustainability and health (special edition)'. *New South Wales Public Health Bulletin.* 18(3–4): pp. 37–72.

Commonwealth of Australia, Senate Select Committee (1995) *Falling on deaf ears: report of the Senate Select Committee on Aircraft Noise in Sydney.* Canberra: Department of the Senate, Senate Select Committee.

Cowie, C., Black, D. and Fraser, I. (1997) 'Blood lead levels in preschool children in Eastern Sydney.' *Australian and New Zealand Journal of Public Health.* 21(7): pp. 755–761.

Cromley, E. K. and McLafferty, S. L. (2002) *GIS & Public Health.* New York: Guilford Press.

Cutchin, M. P. (2007) 'The need for the "new health geography" in epidemiologic studies of environment and health.' *Health & Place.* 13(3): pp. 725–742.

De Lone, W. H. and McLean, E. R. (1992) 'Information systems success: the quest for the dependent variable.' *Information Systems Research.* 3(1): pp. 60–95.

Fidell, S., Barber, D. S., and Schultz, T. J. (1991) 'Updating a dosage-effect relationship for the prevalence of annoyance due to general transportation noise.' *Journal of the Acoustics Society of America.* 111(4): pp. 1743–1750.

Frank, L., Engelke, P. and Schmid, T. (2003) *Health and community design: the impact of the built environment on physical activity.* Washington DC: Island Press.

Frith, J. (1995) 'Environmental health,' in P. Baume and A. Bauman (eds.) *Public health: an introduction.* Sydney: Eriador Press, pp. 104–128.

Frumkin, H., Frank, L., and Jackson, R. (2004) *Urban sprawl and public health: designing, planning and building for healthy communities.* Washington DC: Island Press.

Galea, S, and Vlahov, D. (2005a) *Handbook of urban health: populations, methods and practice.* New York: Springer.

Galea, S. and Vlahov, D. (2005b) 'Urbanization,' in H. Frumkin (ed.) *Environmental health: from global to local.* San Francisco: Jossey-Bass, pp. 387–413.

Giles-Corti, B. (2006) *The impact of urban form on public health: Current or emerging issues paper.* Paper prepared for the 2006 Australian State of the Environment Committee, Australian Government, Department of the Environment and Water Resources, Canberra.

Grigg, M., Alfred, B., Keller, C., and Steele, J. A. (2006) 'Implementation of an internet-based geographic information system: the Florida experience.' *Journal of Public Health Management & Practice.* 12(2): pp. 139–145.

Harris, P. J., Harris-Roxas, B. F. and Kemp, L. (2007) 'Health impact assessment in urban settings.' *New South Wales Public Health Bulletin.* 18(10): pp. 149–150.

HECS (2001). *Noise from civilian aircraft in the vicinity of airports: implications for human health, I. Noise, stress and cardiovascular disease.* Ottawa: Minister of Public Works and Government Services Canada.

Hede, A. J. and Bullen, R. B. (1982) 'Aircraft noise in Australia: a survey of community reaction'. *National Acoustics Laboratory Report, No. 88.* Canberra: Australian Government Publishing Service.

Higginbotham, N., Albrecht, G. and Connor, L. (eds.) (2001) *Health social science: a trans-disciplinary and complexity perspective.* Melbourne: Oxford University Press.

Issarayangyun, T., Black, J., Black, D. and Samuels, S. (2005a) *Aircraft noise and environmental health: a trans-disciplinary approach.* 28th Australasian Transport Research Forum Sydney, 28–30 September 2005 (CD-Rom)

Issarayangyun, T., Black, J., Black, D. and Samuels, S. (2005b) 'Aircraft noise and methods for the study of community health and well-being.' *Journal of the Eastern Asia Society for Transportation Studies.* vol. 6: pp. 3293–3308.

Jackson, L. E. (2003) 'The relationship of urban design to human health and condition.' *Landscape Urban Planning.* vol. 64: pp. 191–200.

Jarup, L., Dudley, M. L., Babisch, W., Houthuijs, D., Swart, W., Pershagen, G., Bluhm, G., Katsouyanni, M., Cadum, E. and Vigna-Taglianti, F. (2005) 'Hypertension and exposure to noise near airports (HYENA): study design and noise exposure assessment.' *Environmental Health Perspectives.* 113(11): pp. 1473–1478

Kearns, A., Beaty, M. and Barnett, G. (2007) 'A social–ecological perspective on health in urban environments'. *New South Wales Public Health Bulletin.* 18(4): pp. 48–50.

Lofthouse, G. (ed.) (2007) *Megacity challenges: a stakeholder perspective: a research project conducted by GlobeScan and MRC McLean Hazel sponsored by Siemens.* Munich: Siemens A.G. Corporate Communications.

Lu, X. (2005) 'A framework of Web GIS based unified public health information visualization platform.' *Computational Science and Its Applications.* Volume 3482/2005. Berlin: Springer.

Maclachlan, J. C., Jerrett, M., Abernathy, T. Sears, M., and Bunch, M. J. (2007) 'Mapping health on the internet: a new tool for environmental justice and public health research.' *Health & Place.* 13(1): pp. 72–86.

Manocha, R., Marks, G. B., Kenchington, P., Peters, D. and Salome, C. M. (2002) 'Sahaja Yoga in the management of moderate to severe: a randomised controlled trial.' *Thorax.* 57(2): pp. 110–115.

Meade, M. S. and Earickson, R. J. (2000) *Medical Geography.* New York: The Guilford Press.

Meister, E., and Donatelle, R. (2000) 'The impacts of commercial aircraft on human health: a neighborhood study in metropolitan Minnesota.' *Journal of Environmental Health.* 63(4): pp. 9–15.

National Center of Complementary and Alternative Medicine (2007) http://nccam.nih.gov/health/meditation/overview.htm (consulted 5th December, 2007).

Newsom, S. W. B. (2006) 'Pioneers in infection control: John Snow, Henry Whitehead, the Broad Street pump, and the beginnings of geographical epidemiology.' *Journal of Hospital Infection.* 64(3): pp. 210–216.

NSW Health, Sydney West Area Health Service (2006) *Health impact assessment report: Greater Granville Regeneration Strategy: Stage 1 consultants report.* NSW Health, Sydney West Area Health Service.

Pirotta, M. V., Cohen, M. M., Kotsirilos, V. and Farish, S. J. (2000) 'Complementary therapies: have they become accepted in general practice?.' *Medical Journal of Australia.* 172(3): pp. 105–9.

Rosenlund, M., Berglind, N., Pershagen, G., Jarup, L., and Bluhm, G. (2001) 'Increased prevalence of hypertension in a population exposed to aircraft noise.' *Journal of Occupational and Environmental Medicine.* vol. 58: pp. 769–773.

Scotch, M. and Parmanto, B. (2006) 'Development of SOVAT: a numerical-spatial decision support system for community health assessment research.' *International Journal of Medical Informatics.* 75(10–11): pp. 771–784.

Southgate, D., Aked, R., Fisher, N. and Rhynehart, G. (2000). *Discussion paper: expanding ways to describe and assess aircraft noise.* Canberra: National Capital Printing.

Southworth, M. (2007) *Urban forms and metropolitan spaces.* Berkeley.it università degli studi di roma sapienza, facoltà di ingegneria, 2nd–3rd April, 2007.

Trevena, L. J., Sainsbury, P., Henderson-Smart, C., Clarke, R., Rubin, G. and Cumming, R. (2005) 'Population health integration within a medical curriculum: an eight-part toolkit.' *American Journal of Preventive Medicine.* 29(3): pp. 234–239.

Waitakere City Council (2005) *Towards sustainable urban form: connecting research and practice II: workshop summary 15 April 2005.* Waitakere City: Waitakere City Council.

Zhan, F. B., Brender, J. D., Han, Y., Suarez, L. and Langlois, P. H. (2006) 'GIS-EpiLink: a spatial search tool for linking environmental and health data.' *Journal of Medical Systems.* 30(5): pp. 405–412.

Chapter 8

SUSTAINABLE PLANNING FOR POOR COMMUNITIES: URBAN DESIGN STUDIOS AS A CATALYST FOR DEVELOPMENT IN COLOMBIA

Rafael E. Pizarro

This chapter addresses the potential role of sustainable urban design studios as catalysts for development in slum communities of the developing world. Understanding urbanisation processes in the developing world is important to our sustainability challenge because most of the world's population will live in these places. Moreover, world urbanisation patterns are both a key problem as well as a primary resource. Urban proximity makes sustainability with density possible, however urbanisation is both energy intensive and destructive to natural resources.

Two urban design projects for two fishing villages in the Caribbean coast of Colombia, developed by second year architectural students at the University Tadeo Lozano in Cartagena, Colombia, serve as examples of how student studio projects can help fill the vacuum left by a government's lack of resources, or unwillingness, to provide slum communities with specific plans to address their planning problems. These include infrastructure, environmental protection, basic services and the aesthetic quality of the urban environment.

The studio also showed how student studio projects may be the vehicle to build consensus on development goals among community members and to raise awareness among governmental officials about the infrastructure and services needs in those communities. The two student projects tested whether marginal communities abandoned by their local governments can envision a brighter future in terms of their social, economic and cultural conditions, to improve their physical infrastructure, and to preserve their surrounding natural environment. The paper concludes that university projects can help fill the governmental void by providing slum communities with local development plans.

Introduction

The usefulness of central planning to address infrastructure, economic, environmental and social issues in the developing world has often been debated in developing world literature (Payne, 2002; Richardson, 1977; Van der Linden, 1986). Many 'successful' plans for metropolitan regions often bypass the poorest neighbourhoods in those regions benefiting only the elite residential suburbs in those cities. The outcomes of these plans are counter to the U.N. fundamental tenets of sustainable development in the countries of the global South (U.N., 1992a, 1992b). This common neglect frequently accentuates deep economic, social, cultural, and physical divisions in many cities of the developing world (Ward and Gilbert, 1988).

In Latin America, official neglect of slum communities is not new. In fact, it can be considered part of the legacy from Spanish colonisation. In the founding of new cities, Spaniards laid out reticular urban structures placing colonial institutions and the socioeconomic elite at the centre of the new settlement surrounding the Plaza Mayor (or main town square). Beyond that immediate centre of power there lay the districts of merchants, regular residents, and some common facilities such as slaughter houses, tanneries, and warehouses. Further beyond, however, laid a vast 'periphery' of indigenous populations and other underclass. Under this urban scheme, the elite at the centre would benefit from its location near the inner sphere of colonial power while the neighbourhoods on the periphery would become permanently under-served (Low, 1993).

Today, although the urban structure of Latin American cities have changed, and this micro version of a centre-periphery model has been replaced, in many cases, by a poly-nucleated model, a 'periphery' still exists. It exists, literally, in the string of shanty towns so common in many Latin American cities or, figuratively, in the inner city slums. Many neighbourhoods in that literal or figurative periphery continue to be bypassed by central planning and are left to their own devices in dealing with their problems of infrastructure and services.

Another factor that exacerbates Latin American urban inequalities is the lack of formal planning education in some Latin American countries. In Colombia, for example, planning is generally done by architects who 'learned the ropes' of the profession out of personal interest. Or else, the profession is practiced by planners trained in North America or Europe where the economic and social conditions of their case studies vary widely from the social and economic realities of the country. This lack of planning professionals adequately trained to address the peculiarities of not only Colombia but many Latin American cities is generally reflected in the production of urban plans that do not address the needs of the poorest segments of those societies. In this way, the combination of historical neglect, the unpreparedness of local planning practitioners to deal adequately with a social group they are also supposed to serve and, in many cases, the literal abandonment of these groups by planning officials become more acute in regions with already low human development indicators. Colombia ranked 75 in 2008. The Human Development Index gives an indication of the level of development by a country in the United Nations, taking into consideration life expectancy, literacy, education, and GDP per capita (UNDP, 2008).

Figure 42: Map showing Colombian case study

This is the case of the Caribbean coast of Colombia which holds the lowest HDI in the country (Abello and Giaimo, 2000). Although it is true that residents of slum communities in such territories often devise means to look after themselves through self-help organisations (Perlman, 1976), their efforts are often piecemeal and do not include long-term plans to appropriately address deeper structural problems as would, or should, small-area plans prepared by planning professionals. The complexity of such problems demand nothing less than well-crafted projects designed by planners trained to address the complexity of marginal communities and in close cooperation with the residents of those communities. See location map, Figure 42.

Figure 43: Aerial view of La Boquilla

Note: the photographs in this chapter were taken by the Author

Background of the Tadeo Lozano University projects

Mindful of the neglect of slum communities by planning agencies in Colombia and aware of the possibilities of providing quasi-professional urban plans through university-based studios, I set out to approach two slum communities, La Boquilla and Manzanillo, in Cartagena, Colombia in my capacity as adjunct faculty in the School of Architecture, Urban Design Program, at the Universidad Tadeo Lozano. Images of the two villages are shown in Figure 43 and Figure 44.

Figure 44: View of Manzanillo del Mar

Although in Cartagena there are many other communities that deserve the same attention, the case of these two was urgent because they are at risk of disappearance under the bulldozers of upscale beach resort and residential development rapidly approaching their area (Figure 45).

The primary goal of this effort was to donate a plan to the leaders and residents of both communities in the belief that the project could be a catalyst to set in motion economic, environmental, social and cultural processes of revitalisation geared to nothing less than saving those communities from extinction.

Figure 45: Upscale resort encroaching upon La Boquilla's beaches

The objective was to produce a basic urban design plan for each community and give the scale-models and drawings to their leaders to be used as master plans so that the community could negotiate with the city's government a more promissory future.

Their principal problem, as villagers and leaders explained to my group of students, was that, with no development plans of their own, the fate of their communities was subjected to the larger plans of Cartagena's metropolitan area which did not contain provisions to address their problems, let alone to offer them a promissory future. They argued that the city's General Plan (locally called Territorial Ordering Plan) did not contain specific elements tailored to address their problems. Furthermore, they were seriously concerned that the General Plan contained elements and policy that would actually lay the legal ground for eradicating their communities to leave room for upcoming beach resorts and upscale high-rise apartment buildings. Local leaders claimed that when they met with local city planning authorities to air their concerns, they responded that if the community could provide the planning agency with alternative development options the city would consider revising the part of the General Plan affecting their area. The local city planners argued that they did not have enough resources to revise the General Plan and to produce area-plans for their communities. But given that neither of these communities have resources or the technical knowledge to produce any kind of alternative plans, they felt their destiny was sealed and fateful. Against such a gloomy backdrop, the University's offer to prepare an alternative plan for their communities was most welcomed.

Background: La Boquilla and Manzanillo

La Boquilla is a very poor fishing village of 15,000 people of African descent. The older residents track their origins back to the 18th century when runaway slaves from Spanish colonial Cartagena formed refugee camps (called 'palenques') in the swampy lands and mangrove lagoons far away from the Spanish settlement. The economic base of both communities used to be traditional fishing and small scale agriculture. This economy was operational for over two centuries but, due to development pressures coming from nearby Cartagena, today it is dwindling and its nature is changing. Their rich fishing and handicraft traditions are being replaced quickly by the catering to local and foreign visitors who visit the beautiful community's beaches.

Another reason for this switching to a different trade as a new means of sustenance is the gradual deterioration of the formerly rich wetland ecosystem surrounding the community. The ever-growing urban perimeter of Cartagena is encroaching upon the mangrove lagoon, degrading and contaminating the body of water and annihilating the fishery in the system. Today, the lagoon and mangrove forest that the community had exploited so successfully and sustainably for generations have entered a steady process of decay. In addition, the construction of a major interstate highway and the land filling of wetlands to lay firm grounds for the construction of international resorts and high-end apartment buildings blocked waterways between the lagoon and the Caribbean Sea, thus further degrading the ecosystem. As a result, the community's fishery has been drastically reduced.

181

As for public services, both La Boquilla and Manzanillo have limited electricity, no potable water, and no sewage infrastructure. Electric supply is shut off up to twelve hours a day, sometimes four days a week, which causes spoiling of food and the warming of cold drinks the community sells to tourists as another form of livelihood. In addition, given that the natural conditions in both communities are those typical of tropical coastal regions with average daily temperatures of 30° centigrade and relative humidity of 80–90%, residents complain that during power blackouts night-time is sometimes unbearable with no electricity to power fans and with mosquitoes swarming the village.

Paradoxically, the prime location of both communities has made their future uncertain. La Boquilla is only five minutes from Cartagena International Airport and has three kilometres of white sandy beaches facing the Caribbean Sea. There is the beautiful Cienaga de la Virgen lagoon and mangrove swamps lie opposite the Bay of Cartagena. A very important interstate highway (between Cartagena and Barranquilla) also runs in the vicinity of the community. These location advantages, however, have made La Boquilla prime land for upscale development. The ongoing construction of resorts and high-end apartment buildings threatens the future existence of the community. To make matters worse, those types of developments are well within the General Plan's projections for the area classified as 'lands for urban expansion'.

To counteract this situation is difficult. Given the poor economic conditions of La Boquilla, developers have it easy to buy residents out, offering well-below market values to local farmers. Furthermore, given that many of the La Boquilla residents actually squat on lands marked as flood-prone (for being too close to the mangrove lagoon), some of the residents are all too eager to sell their properties for whatever money they are offered before governments officials initiate processes of eviction. In the case of the residents with land titles, the opportunity to sell land that was formerly a squatter settlement is taken as a life-time opportunity to improve their lives by selling and moving out to another urban location. The combination of fast moving resort and residential development on the fringes of the community and the environmental degradation of the mangrove lagoon have induced a gradual process of social, cultural and economic deterioration forecasting a future for the community that is rather hopeless and bleak (see Figure 46).

Figure 46: Environmental degradation on flood-prone areas

Manzanillo (population 1200) is just five kilometres from La Boquilla but faces similar problems. The area is equally classified in Cartagena's General Plan as Land for Urban Expansion. Residents' livelihood out of traditional fishing and handicraft production is also shifting to catering the insipient tourism attracted to their beaches. The fishing industry has also deteriorated due to the degraded mangrove fishery and the inability to fish in deeper waters for lack of appropriate vessels. Basic infrastructure is also deficient in Manzanillo. The community has electricity but no sewage or potable water. Its seaside is vulnerable to sea storms that occasionally wash off the road on the seaside edge of the community (see Figure 47).

Just like in La Boquilla, the residents of Manzanillo feel helpless to secure the future of their village. Leaders and residents are afraid the approaching high-end developments will eventually force them out and thus lose their community. In meetings with the university students, the residents expressed the same fears that surfaced in the meetings with the residents of La Boquilla: they feel powerless to convince Cartagena's central government of their right to stay there. They are also eager to convince the government that Manzanillo could become a tourist asset if they were given the resources to restructure their cottage fishing industry, their handicraft production, their cultural traditions, and improve the physical appearance of their village. They feel their town and way of life are part of Colombia's cultural heritage with potential for becoming tourist attractions for national and foreign visitors.

Figure 47: Sea surges ravage edge of town for lack of a breakwater

The community meetings with both villages (see Figure 48) underscored their drive to bypass central authorities to find solutions to their problems on their own. The issues identified by the community leaders and residents in those meetings yielded a long list of unmet wants and desires long neglected by planning authorities and local politicians. What was most remarkable about those meetings, however, was the residents' display of creativity to articulate solutions to their problems, indeed not too different from what urban planning professionals would prescribe in a similar situation.

Figure 48: Meeting with residents and local leaders

Urban design plans

In both communities, the list of issues and their potential solutions ranged from the very policy-oriented, such as declaring their communities sites of Afro-Colombian Cultural Heritage to preserve traditional handicraft and fishing techniques, to the very physical such as the building of jetties to preserve the beach area or the dredging of a natural channel that connects the lagoon to the sea to allow the free flow of water between both systems.

In the final product, the plans for both communities included the standard elements of a comprehensive urban design plan including land use, housing, circulation, infrastructure, and services, but focused on specific elements that addressed their particular problems.

The environmental design for both La Boquilla and Manzanillo, for example, included the recuperation of the mangrove swamp and lagoon by dredging the clogged watercourse connecting lagoon and sea.

Blocking the waterway causes flooding in parts of the community during the rainy season. By opening the watercourse permanently and allowing stormwaters to move freely out to sea, they would maintain stable water levels inside the lagoon all year and stop the flooding.

Figure 49: Sand-clogged connection, Manzanillo del Mar

In the dry season, the free movement of sea water back into the lagoon would maintain a deeper level of water and allow fishermen to dig out pools for fish-farming inside the mangrove swamp. The farmed fish could then be sold to neighbouring communities. This solution proposed by residents of both communities demonstrates that local residents have sophisticated knowledge of the hydraulics of wetlands ecosystems and the benefits of better agricultural production to their economy.

Figure 50: Model of Manzanillo del Mar showing dredged canal

An environmental strategy was part of the economic strategy. The residents were aware that with the reopening of the water flow between both natural systems, the lagoon fishery would recuperate and the fishing industry revive. Along with this strategy, residents suggested the construction of a long needed fishing cooperative with a shipyard to build fishing boats more adequate to venture on deeper sea waters.

Presently, they can only fish in the proximity of the beach due to the vulnerability of their canoes to sail further out. By the same token, harvesting fish from the lagoon is currently done in a very rudimentary fashion resulting in poor quality and quantities of the fish harvested and in further environmental degradation of the mangrove lagoon ecosystem (see Figure 51).

Figure 51: Lack of appropriate fishing ponds limits fish harvest

To this end, the project featured a band of properly designed and constructed aquiculture ponds to address both problems. To take advantage of the tourist potential of both communities, the economic element of the plan included development of a cultural-tourist program where national and foreign visitors, lodged in cabins near the fishing coop, would pay for week-long workshops to learn traditional fishing, fish-net weaving, manufacture of local handicrafts, and folk dances.

Figure 52 shows properly designed and constructed aquiculture ponds to increase productivity and quality of fish harvested. At the far end of this image, there is the fishing coop and eco-tourism centre with boarding cabins to house participants in traditional fishing and crafts workshops.

The housing element of the plan included a relocation project for a large group of community residents currently living in shacks on the border of the lagoon. Those residents would gradually move to new stilt-housing in the same location so that social networks would not be disrupted and planning officials would not have an issue with seasonal flooding of the area. Figure 53 shows the proposed residential rehabilitation and construction of new housing following existing traditional settlement pattern in the region.

The circulation element of both plans included not just the pavement of some dirt roads in the community but the rather innovative system of stone-paving the strip of roadway in front of the houses, in lieu of conventional sidewalks. This way, given that car ownership in the community is low, the roadway itself might be used as public space for social gatherings and as playground for children. Although they acknowledged this solution contradicts conventional prescriptions about street design, they argued they wanted to keep the old social practice of gathering and playing in the streets, actually very common in many poor communities of the developing world. An added advantage to this solution, community designers claimed, is the considerable savings in the construction of other more conventional recreational spaces such as parks. Although the issue of parks was debated in those meetings, some residents' argument that 'the beach is our park' settled the issue.

Figure 53: Construction of new housing

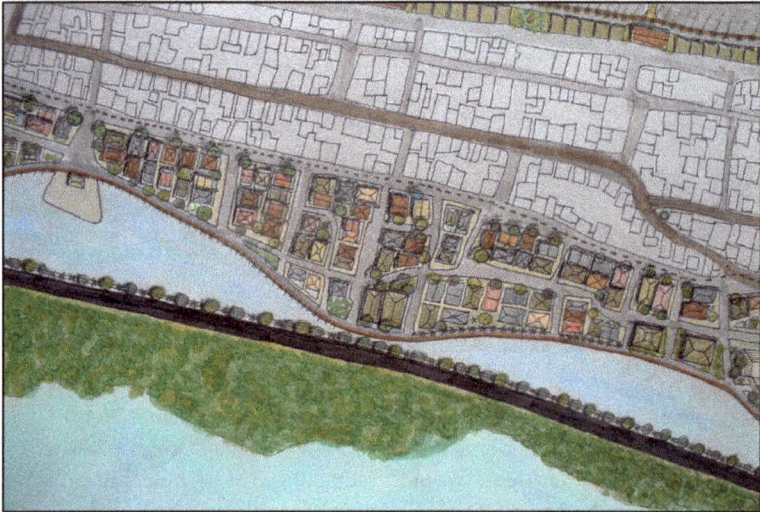

The cultural component of the plan took the form of a cultural complex with spaces to teach their youngsters and visitors traditional music and dancing. This suggestion came out of their concern for the dwindling interest in the part of their youth to practice those cultural expressions. They claimed that the lack of support and facilities for those activities was swaying teenagers and kids towards imported forms of rap music. They worried that if the trend continued, their traditional culture would eventually be forgotten.

Regional development was a strategy also considered by both communities and captured in the projects. They proposed to establish a network of seaside villages along the coast of Cartagena. The proposal was to start by connecting La Boquilla with Manzanillo through the natural network of water channels crisscrossing the mangrove swamp. The lagoon banks would also be landscaped and designated as a scenic route connecting to hiking trails in the nearby woods. The path would end in a coloured-paved boardwalk along the beach in the community of Manzanillo. They thought the aquatic ways, the hiking trails, and the beach boardwalk could be pitched to Cartagena's City Council as a tourist amenity for the entire region.

Student project outcomes

At the end of the semesters, students produced elaborate models and plans that were handed in to community leaders and residents. Delivering the projects to the villages turned out to be larger events than expected (see Figure 54). For the residents of both communities, it was the first time that their ideas had been listened to and their own solutions to their problems materialised in scaled-models and drawings. As expressed by one community leader, 'it is as if there is actually a government in the city and they were listening to us'. The students presented the projects to the community in public meetings held in one the resident's homes in each village. The high point of these presentations was the sight of a large crowd of community residents gathering around models and plans pointing with their fingers at their tiny scaled houses, chatting enthusiastically about the impact the proposed trails, streets, scenic routes, restored ecosystem, and other elements of the project would have on their particular properties.

Following these public presentations, word got out to the local media that the Tadeo Lozano University was crafting plans for La Boquilla and Manzanillo. A few weeks later, Cartagena's main newspaper, *El Universal* (2004), published a full page article featuring both projects. Following that publication, government officials and two non-government organisations (NGOs) doing work for the development of slum communities in Cartagena contacted the community leaders and the Faculty of Architecture to inquire about the projects. The public planners suggested the projects be lodged in the city's Planning Department to be considered in future plans about the area. And, one NGO requested the models to be permanently displayed in their facilities as examples of slum redevelopment.

The lesson for La Boquilla and Manzanillo from the year-long process and for the local planning agency and NGOs is that planning matters. The attention raised by the two projects among government planners showed community leaders and residents the importance of materialising into scaled-models and drawings community-based ideas to address their own problems.

To date, however, a revision of the General Plan for the city has not been called for by the City Council, so it is uncertain whether government officials will eventually give those student projects the attention they deserve to actually include in the City's plans for the area. Unfortunately, it seems the label 'student project' is a handicap that prevents government officials from taken the projects seriously. For La Boquilla and Manzanillo, then, the next challenge is to find resources to turn 'student' into 'professional' projects to have more leverage before politicians and planning authorities.

Conclusions

Cartagena Planning Department's response to these two modest student projects highlights the potential role university-led sustainable urban design projects can play in the improvement of slum communities in the developing world. The materialisation of actual models, drawings, and policy documents reflecting solutions to the problems of under-served social groups can make the difference between wishful thinking on the part of slum dwellers, unmet promises on the part of public officials, and real hope for improving the living conditions of those groups.

The overriding lesson from this experience was that government-abandoned communities armed with urban design and planning documents can potentially change their usual fateful destiny. If countries of the southern hemisphere are to heed the United Nations Development Program's recommendations towards sustainable development (UN NSDS, 2002), they must attend to the development potential of their poorest and most under-represented communities. However, given the lack of financial and human resources in the part of local governments to produce sustainable development plans for their slum communities, the resources available in public and private universities must be put to service to make up for such deficiency.

References

Abello, A. and Giaimo, S. (2000) *Compiladores, poblamiento y ciudades del caribe Colombiano.* Barranquilla, Colombia: Fonade y Universidad del Atlantico.

El Universal Newspaper (2004) *La boquilla y manzanillo tienen sueños para 2011.* Cartagena de Indias, Colombia, June 7th 2004.

Low, S. (1993) 'Cultural meaning of the plaza,' in R. Rotenbergand G. M. McDonogh (eds.), *The cultural meaning of urban space.* Amherst: Bergin and Garvey, pp. 75–94.

Payne, G. (ed.) (2002) *Land, rights and innovation: improving tenure security for the urban poor.* London: ITDG.

Perlman, J. (1976) *The myth of marginality: urban poverty and politics in Rio de Janeiro.* Berkeley: University of California Press.

Richardson, H. (1977) *City size and national spatial strategies in developing countries.* Washington DC: World Bank.

UNDP (2008) *Human development index.* Available at: http://hdr.undp .org/en (consulted 1st May 2008).

U.N. (1992a) MDG Millennium Development Goals. *Conference on environment and development.* Rio de Janeiro, Brazil. Available at www.undp.org/mdg (consulted 1st May 2008)

U.N. (1992b) Agenda 21 *Conference on environment and development.* Rio de Janeiro, Brazil. Available at www.un.org (consulted 1st May 2008).

U.N. (2002) NSDS. *United Nations national sustainable development strategies.* Conference on Environment and Development. Rio de Janeiro, Brazil. Available at www.un.org (consulted 1st May 2008).

Van der Linden, J. (1986) *The sites and services approach reviewed: solution or stopgap to the Third World housing shortage?* Aldershot: Gower.

Ward, P. and Gilbert, A. (1988) 'Land for the rich, land for the poor,' in J. Gugler (ed.), *Urbanization of the Third World.* Oxford: Oxford University Press.

Chapter 9

SUSTAINABLE TRANSPORT PLANNING: ASSESSING TRANSIT ORIENTED DEVELOPMENT IN NORTH-WEST SYDNEY

Santosh Bista

The main aim of this chapter is to design a generic planning and assessment framework in economic perspectives to gauge the sustainability of Transit Oriented Development (TOD) around bus corridors in North West sector of Sydney – a case study of Sunnyholt Road in the city of Blacktown. It further elaborates the potential for increased development in the vicinity of Sunnyholt Road that could be associated with the Parramatta-Rouse Hill-Blacktown Transit Way (T-Way) which is currently under construction. In order to gauge the sustainability of TOD, indicators in six categories should be analysed, which are: institutional performance indicator, quality of the built environment and accessibility indicator, economic performance indicator, environmental performance indicator, social diversity and public perception indicator, and travel behaviour indicator. This chapter focuses only on the economic performance indicators.

Sustainable goals and TOD definition

The concept of Transit Oriented Development emerged relatively recently. Originating in US planning theory, it has at times struggled for understanding amongst the development industry and public sector. Dittmar and Ohland (2004) provide a range of late 20th century American TOD case studies, including major projects in Arlington Virginia, Dallas Texas, Atlanta Georgia and San Jose and San Diego, California. The principles for successful TOD precincts can, however, also be observed in the transit-rich city centres of Western and Central Europe. The integrated land and transport planning that has been pursued post-World War II in Europe provides clear lessons for current attempts to establish something similar in the new world context (Hale and Charles, 2007).

Figure 55: Transit oriented development definitions

Literature	Definitions	Is TOD Goals Correspondent with Sustainable development		
		Eco.	En.	So.
Salvensen (1996)	Development within a specified geographical area around a transit station with a variety of land uses and a multiplicity of landowners.	✓		✓
Bernick and Cervero (1997)	A compact, mixed-use community, centered around a transit station that, by design, invites residents, workers, and shoppers to drive their cars less and ride mass transit more.	✓	✓	
Boarnet and Crane (1998)	The practice of developing or intensifying residential land use near rail stations.	✓		
Boarnet and Compin (1999)	TOD is consistent with the mixed-use, pedestrian-friendly character.	✓		
Maryland Department of Transportation (2000)	A place of relatively higher density that includes a mixture of residential, employment, shopping and civic uses and types located within an easy walk of a bus or rail transit center. The development design gives preference to the pedestrian and bicyclists, and may be accessed by automobiles	✓	✓	
Bae (2002)	A means of reducing automobile dependence, promoting more compact residential development and fostering mixed land uses.	✓	✓	
Belzer and Autle (2002b)	TOD focus on desired functional outcomes, not just physical characteristics, is an important next step. Three main outcomes or goals of TOD: location efficiency, choice, and value capture/financial return.	✓		✓
California Department of Transportation(2002)	Moderate to higher density development, located within an easy walk of a major transit stop, generally with a mix of residential, employment and shopping opportunities designed for pedestrians without excluding the auto.	✓	✓	
Still (2002)	A mixed-use community that encourages people to live near transit services and to decrease their dependence on driving.	✓	✓	
Cervero et al.(2004)	TOD is a tool for promoting smart growth, leveraging economic development, and catering to shifting housing market demands and lifestyle preferences.	✓	✓	✓
Lund et al.(2004)	TOD is intended to increase transit ridership, increase walking and biking, and decrease the share of automobile trips. The design and mixed-use features of TOD may reduce both work and non-work automobile trips.	✓	✓	

NOTE: Eco. =Economical Efficiency; En. = Environmental Protection; So. =Social Equality.

Source: Li, C. and Lai, T. (2006)

Transit oriented development has been defined as a set of urban design and land use characteristics conducive to generating journeys undertaken other than by car (Calthorpe, 1993). Various terms have surfaced over the years to convey the idea of TOD, such as 'transit villages', 'transit-supportive development' and 'transit-friendly design'. Some authors use the term TOD quite liberally, referring to any form of 'transport-oriented development,' including bus- and rail-oriented development as well as development along freeways (Lefaver, 1997). While there is no single, all-encompassing definition that represents the TOD concept in its many forms, most definitions of TOD nonetheless share common traits. Figure 55 highlights definitions of TOD used by researchers.

While such definitions vary in scope and specificity, most TOD definitions share several common elements including: *density* (raising, density within 400mm to 500m of transit stations; *diversity* (mixed land use, extensive choices of housing and commuting); and *design* (pedestrian or friendly oriented design). It is also known as 3Ds, referring to density, diversity and design, as shown in Figure 56. Strategies of 3Ds are intended to increase transit ridership, increase walking and biking, and decrease the share of automobile trips. The design and mixed-use features of TOD may reduce both work and non-work automobile trips. Furthermore, these potential benefits can help amortise multi-billion dollar investments in rail transit infrastructure. TOD strategies are based on a theory that land uses near a rail transit stop will produce a different travel pattern than land uses in an automobile focussed area. The best way to ensure that TOD can help solve urban challenges is to provide solid analytic evidence about its effectiveness (Lund et al., 2004). In other words, wide and varied benefits of TOD contain economical, environmental and social effectiveness. Thus, it can be seen that strategies of TOD are able to achieve goals of smart growth and sustainable development.

The main goals of TOD are also to carry out dreams that our cities and countries are smart and sustainable. Cervero et al. (2004) defined it as a means of promoting smart growth, injecting vitality into declining inner-city settings, and expanding lifestyle choices. Basically, there are three key components in sustainable goals of TOD. Firstly, environmental protection means that TOD will restrain land development from environmentally sensitive areas and guide it to corridors and stations of transit in order to protect the ecological environment. Secondly, economic efficiency means that high density and mixed development of land use around transit stations and corridors will raise transit ridership, promote economic development and improve location efficiency. Thirdly, social equality means that TOD will offer affordable housing with diverse types and more choices of transportation modes to keep social justice. Finally, the comprehensive and ultimate goals of TOD are sustainable development, as shown in Figure 56.

Figure 56: Achieving urban sustainability

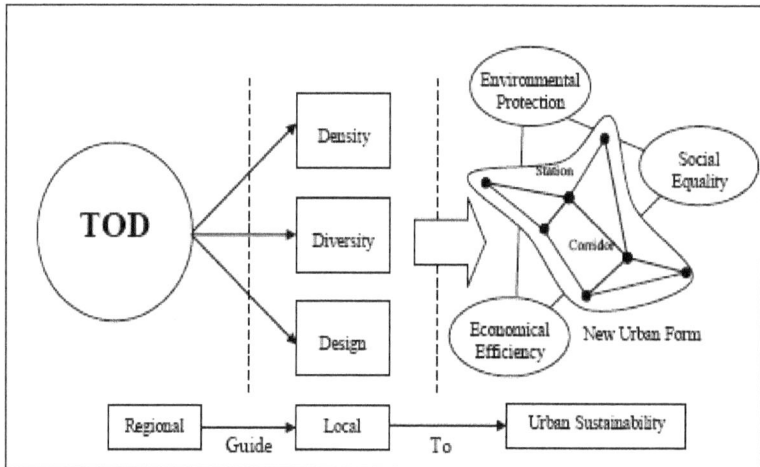

Source: Cervero et al. 2004

Bus corridor TOD

Calthorpe (1993) identified both an 'urban TOD' associated with rail stations and a 'neighbourhood TOD' associated with bus. Dittmar and Ohland (2004) suggest a hierarchy of transit modes related to a hierarchy of TOD types. While bus services are provided at every level, rail is more closely related to high-density/large-scale development and bus with low density/small-scale development. This is repeated in much of the literature. The term 'transit oriented development' (i.e., associating low density with bus) has also been associated with this. Cervero et al.

(2004) identified consistently lower density expectations for bus than light rail in San Diego, Portland, and Washington Country, Oregon.

The collocation of bus services and bus terminals at some major rail stations has been suggested as a potential spur for TOD (Porter, 1997). Bus Transit Oriented Development was also commonly associated with bus stations in cities without rails. Bus Transit Oriented Development (BTOD) is more commonly associated with bus ways or Bus Rapid Transit (BRT). The ability of large scale bus transit systems to encourage land development has been identified as a major benefit of these forms of transit technology (Levinson et al., 2003).

The Ottawa transit system is a major icon of BTOD. Ottawa's policy of combining integration of land use and transport planning with an emphasis on transit development over road construction is to be admired regardless of transit modes involved. Nevertheless, it was a bus way that achieved densification of development around bus way stations. Curitiba and Bogota are the other major icons of both BRT and associated BTOD (Bonsall, 1997). Evidence of development benefits of these systems has been identified (Rodriguez and Targa, 2004; Smith and Raemaekers, 1998).

Successful bus based transit systems such as Ottawa's, Curitiba's, Brisbane's, and Adelaide's all offer train-like trunk services on reserved corridors, along with buses that operate as feeder services in local communities, then join the transit corridor for express travel to a limited number of major stops. It all represents the 'state-of-art' in bus way design, infrastructure, and operations management. Guided bus way systems such as in Adelaide provide a high quality service, but the most noticeable aspect is the minimum space required for the guideways. This high capacity infrastructure has a cross-section of just 6.2m between outer edges of guideways (Adam, 2004).

It is appropriate here to compare conventional bus with its rail counterpart. Figure 57 compares the positive and negative aspects of both modes. While bus offers flexibility in routing and is cost effective, its routing tends to be complex and it has a poor public image. Rail, while considered inflexible, benefits from a positive public image, is seen as easy to understand and is permanent.

Figure 57: Comparison of conventional bus and rail attributes

	Bus	Rail
Pros	Flexible Cost-effective Accessibility	Simple Permanent Positive image
Cons	Complex Lacks permanence Poor image	Lacks flexibility Costly Poor accessibility

Planning and assessment framework

Any study of TOD must recognise the context of government policies and programs, and also the government's goals for bus transport development and land uses associated with it. Integrated land use and transport developments should contribute towards a more sustainable city and monitoring of the key performance indicators as mentioned above. In any practical application of this approach, the end product is an outcomes report to the government (See Figure 58). Among the six indicators, only economic indicators are analysed in this chapter.

Transit Oriented Development is increasingly becoming a solution across Australia and overseas for encouraging more sustainable cities and extracting maximum value from public transport investment. TOD facilitates higher-density, mixed-use development well designed to encourage walking, bicycling, and public transport use within a ten-minute walk of major public transport nodes. TOD integrates land use with transport – a key objective of the NSW State Government's Transport Planning and Metropolitan Strategy. Research in the past has shown that TODs have potential to create safer pedestrian environments, reduce private vehicle dependency, and create more vibrant communities.

In Australia, TOD-type examples have emerged almost 'by accident'. Revitalisation of historical inner-city areas as locations of choice for residences and offices has occurred, largely due to transit advantages and the attractiveness of pre-car development patterns. Increasingly, low-density outer suburbs, poorly served by transit, are recognised as locations of economic vulnerability (Dodson et al., 2006), and lack of lifestyle and cultural choice. From the supporting components in evidence in European cities, and in many other locations throughout Australia and the world, common 'success factors' emerge for TOD locations. These success factors should be studied and replicated wherever TOD is attempted or where urban renewal is pursued (Hale and Charles, 2007). They are: (a) *high frequency, high capacity public transit* linking the precinct to the wider metropolitan area and providing good access. The Transit should be integrated sympathetically with the precinct;

Figure 58: Transit oriented development outcome analysis

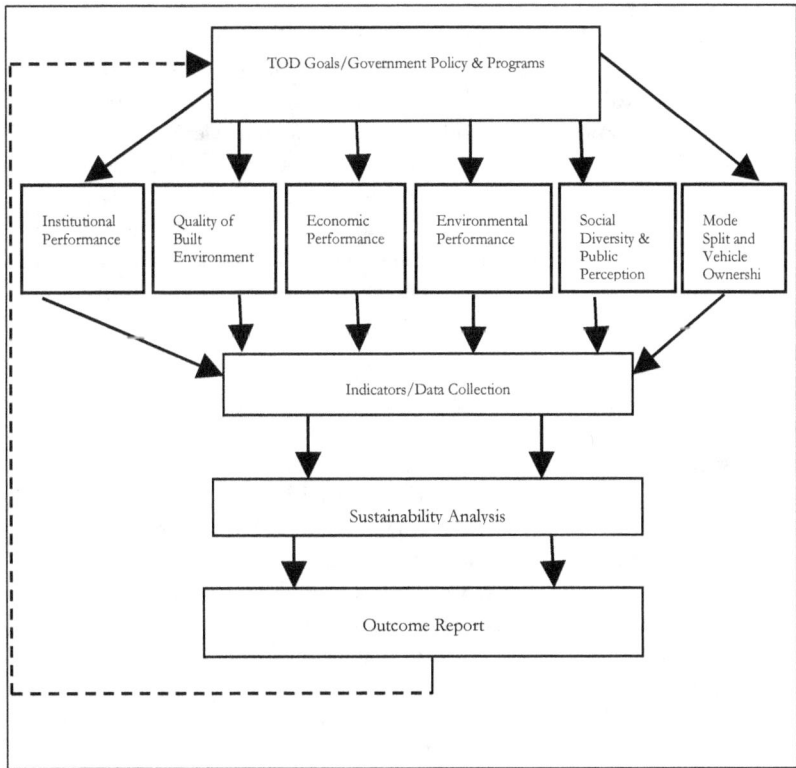

Source: Renne (2005)

(b) *mixed-use development* with street-front retail. Longer opening hours are an indicator of success. Offices and workplaces provide a support base of customers. Residential accommodation provides additional patrons who hold a stake in the liveability of the precinct. The development needs to be competitive and viable in the open property market; and (c) *public space* provision that, while generous, is never too large that the space becomes empty and loses its lively character. Cafés and restaurants should intermingle with public space. Up-market design is required for public space, incorporating climate compatibility, quality hard-scaping and considerate planting.

NSW Government programs

In 1998, the NSW Minister for Roads and Minister for Transport released a strategic transport plan for New South Wales, 'Action for Transport 2010'. It placed a special focus on Western Sydney where rapid growth in population and commercial activity demanded new and improved public transport investment. A network of dedicated bus transit way corridors was proposed in this document to create direct public transport connections across the West, Southwest and Northeast of Sydney. As the first and second stages of this program, the Liverpool-Parramatta Transit way is now operational, and the North-West Transit Way network is currently under construction.

The NSW Government is making a substantial investment in road-based public transport through the Transit Way network, Strategic Bus Corridors (for example, the recently announced Hurstville corridor), and bus service reform initiatives. In order to ensure the success of these initiatives, this investment needs to be matched by complementary land use and urban form initiatives. A TOD-related Urban Change Strategy and limited site investigations have already been carried out along the Liverpool–Parramatta T-way by the Roads and Traffic Authority (RTA) and other agencies. TOD can also be viewed as a pragmatic approach to implementing the State Government's Integrating Land Use and Transport Policy, Sydney Regional Environmental Plan No 18 – Public Transport Corridors, and initiatives contained in the Metropolitan Strategy. In terms of broader government objectives, the application of TOD aims to slow the rate of land consumption on the urban fringe, minimise vehicle kilometres travelled and assist in meeting air quality targets – all key government transport objectives. Successful TOD projects depend upon a strong partnership between local and state government and a commitment to working closely with private developers and local communities towards practical solutions to constraints and eventually implementation.

Figure 59: Transit oriented development indicators

Indicator	Measure
Range of businesses	Number of retail, commercial and industrial firms (possibly on GIS)
	Suitability of local retail for residents (Index of Retail Variation)
Business Success	Rate/number of vacant buildings/units (retail, commercial, industrial)
	Number of jobs in area (by categories, full-time/part-time)
	Number of people in home-based employment
Range of Housing	Number of residential units (houses/flats/apartments)
	Number of rental and owner-occupied residences
	Number of affordable housing units (to be defined) Range of 1, 2 and 3+ bedroom
Solid financial base	Property value (over time)
	Percentage of income spent on housing and transport
	Rates collected by local government ($)

Economic benefits of TOD

Figure 59 outlines an outcomes framework with the number of indicators which are desirable to analyse for any case study application of TOD along bus ways. It also classifies its benefits under different outcome headings. Its benefits under economic perspectives are analysed in more detail below.

A successful TOD is not merely a dormitory suburb, but is one where a wide range of businesses are thriving. A range of housing (both owner-occupied and rental) will be available, including affordable housing for lower income earners. For home owners, strong property values will ensure a solid financial base for future household prosperity as well as maintaining a healthy revenue stream for local government. Success against these aims could be measured using the following indicators.

Case study: Sunnyholt Road, Blacktown

Sunnyholt is located in the City of Blacktown, situated approximately 35 km west of Sydney CBD. It is defined by the M7 on the north, Richmond railway line to the west, the Western railway line to the south, and Johnston Avenue to the east. It covers the suburb of Kings Langley, Lalor Park and parts of Blacktown, Marayong and Seven Hills.

Figure 60: Map showing Blacktown study area

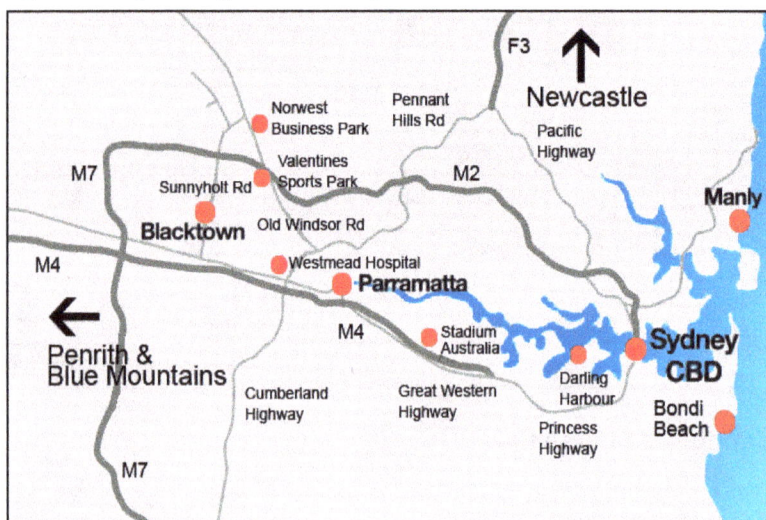

Source: Author

The two main motorways in the region are the M4 and the M7. Blacktown is connected with Sydney CBD both by the M4 via Prospect Highway and the M7 and the M2 via Sunnyholt Road. The Great Western Highway connects Blacktown CBD to Penrith on the west and

Parramatta to the east via Reservoir Road, and Richmond Road connects the Blacktown CBD with Richmond. Sunnyholt Road is a major arterial road connecting Blacktown with the M7 and with Old Windsor Road.

The Western rail line connects Blacktown with Parramatta and Sydney to the east and with Penrith and Blue Mountains to the west. The Richmond line originates from Blacktown and connects to Richmond. The proposed North West Rail link will in some years time connect Rouse Hill to Epping via Northwest Business Park and Castle Hill. The proposed Northwest Transit Way will connect Parramatta to Rouse Hill and Blacktown along Old Windsor Road and Sunnyholt Road.

There is a wide range of job opportunities in the subregion, however few of these areas are readily accessible by public transport and the journey to work is mostly by car. Industrial areas near the study area are at Seven Hills, Baulkham Hills and Castle Hill. Major retail and business areas are located at Norwest Business Park and Castle Hill. There are small town centres at Kings Langley, Quakers Hill, Stanhope and markets at Parklea.

The topography of the Blacktown study area to the east of Sunnyholt Road is gently rolling; the streets are pleasant and there is reasonable street tree cover. It was largely developed after 1945 and the predominant building form is small cottages. In the earlier subdivisions, the street pattern is geometric, whereas areas developed later are characterised by a street system that respond to contours and contain cul-de-sacs.

A successful TOD in economic perspective possesses a wide range of retail opportunities for residents enabling them to meet their day-to-day needs from local establishments. Strong property values for home owners will ensure a solid financial base for future household prosperity as well as maintaining a healthy revenue stream for local government. Success against these aims could be measured using the subindicators detailed below:

Population and demographics

Blacktown has experienced considerable growth in recent years and it is anticipated that this will continue for some time. It is necessary to understand enough about the age and changing nature of the Blacktown population to anticipate the range of possible demand for medium or higher density housing over a long period. The population of Blacktown grew by 23,689 persons (10.2%) between 1996 and 2001, representing an annual growth rate of approximately 2%. The total population of the Sunnyholt study area (four suburbs combined) was 58,166 persons at the time of 2001 Census, representing around 22.8% of the total Blacktown LGA population (See Figure 61). In 2001, the most dominant age group in both Blacktown Local Government Area (LGA) and Sunnyholt area is represented by 0–14 age groups. But one interesting trend in the case of the Sunnyholt study area is its significant contribution to the ageing population. It has 11.7 % of the total population who are over 65 in the 2001 Census as against 7.6 % in Blacktown during the same period.

Figure 61: Population distribution: Blacktown and Sunnyholt, 2001

Year	Blacktown LGA			Sunnyholt *		
	Population	Projected population	Inter-period growth rate (%)	Population	Projected population	Inter-period growth rate (%)
1981	181,139					
1986	192,054		6.0			
1991	211,361		10.1			
1996	231,509		9.5			
2001	255,195		10.2	58,168		10.2
2005		283,536	11.1		64,102	11.1
2010		303,277	7.0		71,218	7.0
2015		322,338	6.3		76,203	6.3
2019		337,169	4.6		79,709	4.6

*Source: Computed using ABS Census Data, 2001. * The study area comprises the suburbs such as Blacktown, Lalor Park, Kings Langley and Kings Park combined.*

Of those reporting their weekly household income in 2001, there is no significant difference between Blacktown LGA and the Sunnyholt study area in the income bracket of A$0–A$299. Blacktown has less percentage of households in this category (i.e., 10.7%) as compared to 12.2% in the Sunnyholt area, whereas it is the opposite in the case of the higher income bracket of A$1500–A$1900. Blacktown LGA has 14.1% of the total population as against 13.4% in the Sunnyholt study area.

Figure 62: Job stocks by industry, 2001

Employment Sector	Blacktown LGA		Sunnyholt	
	Number	%	Number	%
Agriculture, forestry, fishing	486	0.7	98	0.4
Mining	43	0.1	18	0.1
Manufacturing	14,281	20.1	4,207	16.5
Electricity, gas, water supply	1,394	2.0	207	0.8
Construction	4,800	6.7	2,084	8.2
Wholesale trade	6,815	9.6	2,118	8.3
Retail trade	12,806	18.0	3,757	14.7
Accommodation, cafés etc.	1,960	2.8	891	3.5
Transport & storage	3,837	5.4	1,355	5.3
Communication services	992	1.4	717	2.8
Finance & insurance	1,247	1.8	1,455	5.7
Property & business services	4,915	6.9	2,564	10.1
Government & defence	2,131	3.0	865	3.4
Education	5,865	8.2	1,377	5.4
Health & community services	5,295	7.4	2,421	9.5
Cultural & recreation	1,196	1.7	404	1.6
Personal & other services	2,375	3.3	971	3.8
Total	71,190	100	25,505	100

Source: NSW Transport Data Centre, based on ABS Census, 2001

Housing types

In 2001, the highest proportions of households in both places were found residing in separate houses: 83.1% in Blacktown LGA and 80.2% in the Sunnyholt study area. Although the total number of separate dwellings in Blacktown LGA increased from 1996 to 2001 (approximately 5399 dwellings), the percentage as a total of all dwellings in Blacktown LGA has declined from 85.6% to 83.1% in 2001.

Job opportunities

Blacktown is strategically located at the heart of a western region of more than 1.5 million people. Its outstanding features include transport infrastructure which provide road and rail network to Northern and Southern markets as well as to the Sydney CBD. The completion of the Sydney Orbital M7 and also the proposed TOD of the Sunnyholt study area will further enhance the accessibility of the city to market.

The manufacturing sector provides the largest segment of employment generation in Blacktown LGA with 14,281 jobs making up more than 20%. It has also the same ranking in the Sunnyholt study area, providing 4,207 jobs representing 16.5%. The second major employer in the Sunnyholt study area is property and business services (10.1%), whereas Retail represents this rank in Blacktown LGA. Finance & business sector employment in the Sunnyholt study area is also significant. There is little difference between the percentages of employed people in both places though the unemployment rate is slightly higher in Blacktown LGA compared to the Sunnyholt study area (See Figure 63).

The majority of people (more than 72%) use the car as the main mode of transport to work either in Blacktown or the Sunnyholt area (See Figure 64). Except the median household size, which is 3.1 in Blacktown LGA as against 2.9 in Sunnyholt, all other key averages in both places are similar such as median monthly housing loan repayment (i.e., $1000–$1199) and median weekly household income (i.e., $800–$999).

Figure 63: Employment: Blacktown and Sunnyholt, 2001

Description		Blacktown LGA		Sunnyholt	
		Numbers	%	Numbers	%
Employed:	Full-time	75,875	69.7	18,137	69.6
	Part-time	28,889	26.5	7,011	26.9
	Not stated	4,113	3.8	909	3.5
Total		108,877	100	26,057	100
Total labour force		117, 930		28,001	
Unemployment rate (%)		7.7		6.1	

Source: ABS Census of Population and Housing, 2001

Figure 64: Methods of travel to work, 2001

Methods	Blacktown LGA		Sunnyholt Corridors	
	Number	%	Number	%
Train	8,792	10.3	1,923	9.4
Bus	1,196	1.4	334	1.6
Ferry	4	0.00	3	0.01
Tram	11	0.01	3	0.02
Taxi	196	0.2	62	0.3
Car, as driver	62,205	72.8	14,993	73.5
Car, as passenger	7,734	9.0	1,735	8.5
Truck	2,292	2.7	500	2.5
Motorbike/Motor scooter	486	0.6	109	0.5
Bicycle	321	0.4	89	0.4
Others	356	0.4	93	0.5
Walked only	1,879	2.2	551	2.7
Total	85,472	100	20,395	100

Source: Transport Data Centre, using ABS Census data, 2001

Economic output

It is interesting to note that in terms of economic output, unlike the manufacturing sector, property and business services in Blacktown generated the highest revenue (i.e., $3.1 billion in GRP) in gross real terms across all industries in Blacktown LGA. This may be due to the booming construction business in the City. Manufacturing represented the second largest contributors (i.e., $1.8 billion), followed by Finance & Insurance with $0.9 billion in 2002–03 (ABS, 2003).

Property market

The property market is at a very low point in the market cycle with sales dropping since 2003 according to the ReMAX real estate broker in Blacktown (2007). The sales in May 2006 are approximately 60% less than what they were in 2005. The real estate agents interviewed do not see the market improving until 2008–2009 and believe this could be an appropriate period to buy land or property as prices are very low and should start to increase next year (See Figure 65).

Figure 65: Sunnyholt property market, 2006

Description	Sunnyholt Study Area
Property Market	
2 bedroom units sell at	$250,000–260,000 ($290k–$320k last year)
Town Houses	$ 290,000
Detached Houses	$ 330,000
Rental Market	
2 bedroom units rent at	$230–$250pw
Town Houses	$230–$270pw
Detached Houses	$230–$250pw

Source: ReMAX Real Estate Office, Blacktown, 2007

A number of opportunities for higher density housing and for more intense commercial development exist along the stretch of the T-Way that extends between Blacktown and the M7. These development

Figure 66: Industry structure in Sunnyholt

Standard International Industrial Classification & Industry Types	(A) Population needed for one firm	(B) Potential businesses	(C) Number of businesses	(D) Gap (B − C)
Hardware store	15,818	11	6	+5
Lawn and garden supplies	20,082	6	2	+4
Department stores	51,221	2	1	+1
General merchandise stores	7,662	23	12	+11
Grocery stores	3,575	49	21	+28
Motor vehicle dealers	11,197	16	4	+12
Men's & boys' clothing	45,747	4	13	-9
Women's ready-to-wear	12,643	14	17	-3
Shoe stores	20,426	9	9	0
Furniture stores	12,530	14	11	+3
Drapery & upholstery	20,178	3	3	0
Household appliance stores	18,673	9	4	+5
Radio & TV stores	34,707	5	1	+4
Music Stores	42,382	3	2	+1
Drug stores	11,923	15	18	-3
Sporting goods & bicycles	44,973	4	10	-6
Book stores	41,478	2	3	-1
Stationary stores	40,424	2	3	-1
Hobby, toy & game shops	17,085	3	1	+2
Gift, novelty and souvenirs	20,725	8	11	-3
Sewing, needlework etc.	23,220	8	1	+7
Florists	18,286	10	15	-5

Source: www.yellowpages.com.au

opportunities could, over time, enhance its use and improve the quality and safety of the road.

Gap analysis

The gap analysis in Figure 66 is performed using the standard international industry classification of the firms' entry threshold norms. Column A represents the number of populations needed for one firm entry by types to compute gap analysis. The number of potential businesses by types in Sunnyholt is shown in Column B. The number of existing registered businesses by types in the area is represented in Column C. The gap analysis is performed in Column D by subtracting Column C from Column B. The positive entry in the gap analysis indicates a prospect of more new businesses of this type could be established in Sunnyholt whereas negative entry reveals its saturation. From the gap analysis, grocery store, motor vehicle dealership and general merchandise stores businesses are still a huge prospect in the Sunnyholt study area.

Conclusions

This chapter has connected sustainability and transit-oriented development planning. It also designed a generic planning and assessment framework in economic perspectives to gauge the sustainability of TOD around bus corridors in the north-west sector of Sydney – a case of Sunnyholt in the city of Blacktown. The planning and assessment framework of TOD in general and policy and programs of the NSW government in particular was also analysed in this chapter. Many economic variables associated with TOD have been analysed minutely to gauge sustainable economic benefits and development along bus corridors in the Sunnyholt study area.

In order to know the potential new businesses in the area, a gap analysis method has been undertaken. The positive entry in the gap analysis (as shown in Column D) suggests that there is a possibility of new business entry in the area whereas a negative sign shows its saturation by industry types. From the gap analysis, grocery store, motor vehicle dealership and general merchandise stores businesses were found to be a high prospect in the Sunnyholt study area. For this to happen, the whole corridor of Sunnyholt needs to be included, recognising that it is the whole road and its edges that need to be improved. There is a need to look at a broader range of issues prior to designing of transit facilities of this nature. Although politically more complex, a much wider range of the stakeholders who stand to gain need to be involved and committed to the implementation of a common set of outcomes. Finally, a study like this one should have been carried out prior to the concept design of the T-Way comprising all the indicators as mentioned earlier in the chapter.

Notes

This chapter follows from a larger research project commissioned by the NSW Roads and Traffic Authority from Sydney University's Planning Research Centre (2006).

References

Adam, J. (2004) *Orienting Sydney to bus transit: a policy and practice comparison and analysis*. A dissertation for the degree of MURP. Sydney: University of Sydney (unpublished).

Australian Bureau of Statistics (ABS) (2001) *Census of population and housing*. Canberra: Australian Bureau of Statistics.

Bae, C. C. (2002) 'Orenco Station, Portland, Oregon: a successful transit-oriented development experiment.' *Transportation Quarterly*. 56(3): pp. 9–18.

Belzer, D. and Aulter, G. (2002) 'Countering sprawl with transit-oriented development.' *Science and Technology*. 19(1): pp. 51–58.

Bernick, M. and Cervero, R. (1997) *Transit villages for the 21st century*. New York: McGraw-Hill.

Boarnet, M. and Crane, R. (1998) 'Public finance and transit-oriented planning: new evidence from southern California.' *Journal of Planning Education and Research*. vol. 17: pp. 206–219.

Bonsall, J. (1997) 'Planning for a transit-oriented city: lessons from Ottawa-Carleton.' *Transport Engineering in Australia*, pp. 12–18.

Calthorpe, P. (1993) *The next American metropolis: ecology, community, and the American dream*. Princeton: Architectural Press.

Cervero, R., Murphy, C. Ferrell, N., Goguts, T., Yu-Hsin, G.B., Arrington, J., Boroski, J., Smith-heimer, R., Golem, P., Peninger, E., Nakajima, R., Chui, R., Dunphy, M., Myrres, S., and Witenstein, N. (2004) *Transit oriented development in the United States: experiences, challenges, and prospects*, TCRP Report 102, Transportation Research Board.

Department of Infrastructure, Planning and Natural Resources (DIPNR) (2001) Department of Infrastructure, Planning and Natural Resources, Transport Data Centre, Government of New South Wales.

Dittmar, H. and Ohland, G. (2004) 'Defining transit-oriented development: the new regional building block,' in H. Dittmar and G. Ohland (eds.), *The new transit town: best practices in transit oriented development*. Washington DC and London: Island Press.

Dodson, J. and Sipe, N. (2006) *Suburban shocks: assessing locational vulnerability to rising housing fuel and mortgage interest costs*. Australian Transport Research Forum Conference, Gold Coast.

Hale, C. and Charles, P. (2007) *A step-by-step approach to TOD project delivery*. Paper presented at the 11th World Conference on Transport Research, University of California Berkeley, 24–28 June 2007.

Lefaver, S. (1997) *Private land with public partnerships for transit based development*. San Jose, California, The Mineta Transportation institute, San Jose State University, Report 01–05.

Levinson, R. (2003) *Bus rapid transit*, TCRP Report 90, Transportation Research Board.

Li, C. and Lai, T. (2006) 'Sustainable development and transit-orientated development cities in Taiwan'. Unpublished: available from the website of the National Ceng-chi University Taipei at www.nccu.edu.tw

Lund, H. M., Carvero, R., and Wilson, R. W. (2004) *Travel characteristics of transit-oriented development in California*. Caltrans Transportation Grant, State-wide Planning Studies, FTA Section 5313 (b).

NSW Government (1998) *Action for Transport 2010*.

Planning Research Centre (2006) *Transit oriented developments along bus corridors* A Research Report Prepared by the Planning Research Centre, University of Sydney and the Jackson Teece for NSW Roads and Traffic Authority.

Porter, D. R. (1997) *Transit-focused development*. TCRP Synthesis 20, Transportation Research Board.

ReMAX (2007) ReMAX Real Estate Office, Blacktown.

Renne, J. (2005) *Transit-oriented development in Western Australia: attitudes, obstacles, and opportunities*. Paper prepared for the Western Australia Department for Planning and Infrastructure: Planning and Transport Research Centre, Murdoch University.

Renne, J. and Wells, J. (2005) *Transit-oriented development: developing a strategy to measure success*. Research Results Digest *295*, Washington DC: National Cooperative Highway Research Program, Transportation Research Board of the National Academies.

Rodriguez, D. A. and Targa, F. (2004) 'Value of accessibility to Bogotá's bus rapid transit system.' *Transport Reviews*. 24(5): pp. 587–610.

Salvensen, D. (1996) 'Promoting transit oriented development.' *Urban Land*. July 1996, pp. 16–20.

Smith, H. and Raemaekers, J. (1998) 'Land use pattern and transport in Curitiba.' *Land Use Policy*. 15(3): pp. 233–251.

Chapter 10
PLANNING A SUSTAINABLE DOWNTOWN IN THE GLOBAL ERA: A CASE STUDY OF SAN FRANCISCO

Richard Hu

Sustainability has been a buzzword of urban planning for the past two decades. This is particularly true in the discourse of planning effort specifically focused on the downtown area. In the downtown discourse, the concept of sustainability is more comprehensive than it is generally understood as of ecological and environmental implications only. The essence of planning a sustainable downtown is how to combine the downtown's economic competitiveness with its social and environmental scenarios and make them mutually supportive. Downtown development practices in the post-war decades proved that narrowly-focused economic goals and downtown redevelopment could not be sustained without a balanced integration of considerations of social equity, physical environment and infrastructure provision. This sustainable planning approach for the downtown area has been becoming increasingly important in the context of accelerated globalisation and the rise of global cities in that a city centre's interaction moves from a regional scale to an international one.

The advances in information technology and transport technology accelerated the process of globalisation at an unprecedented speed in the last two decades of the 20th century. One direct impact of this globalisation process is the advent of a bunch of global cities whose influences are of global importance. The global importance is mostly understood in an economic sense, even though there are some global cities whose global influences are more through political or cultural means. These global cities are the command centres of globally dispersed activities and agglomeration centres of advanced producer service providers (Sassen, 2001). They are interconnected through the location choice of leading firms of services such as accounting, advertising, financing, insurance and management consultancy (Taylor,

2004). Global cities interact with each other and compete for location choices of the leading business, investment and people which produce or serve the advanced services. Downtown area, the powerhouse of a global city, now has to face dual competitions with global counterparts and regional centres.

Downtown is changing, no matter whether it is considered as a concept or as a place. Conceptually, downtown is often referred to as CBD (central business district). The sense of business, however, needs re-examining since a process of diversification of functions and activities is underway in the downtown area (Hu, 2006). The downtown is no more a place exclusively for business, particularly office activities as it was until the 1980s. The mode of production and the workforce of the knowledge based economy require an urban environment which can facilitate and attract a diversity of human activities of working, living and visiting.

A downtown's competitiveness is directly related to its sustainable capacity to create such features of diversification. Here, the competitiveness of downtown refers to its capacity to attract business, activities, and people, while the sustainability of the capacity is that the economic vitality is achieved without undesirable environmental and social consequences. So the sustainable capacity encompasses economic vitality as well as liveability and social diversity. In the past two to three decades, major global cities have been reshaping their downtown planning strategies to build their sustainable capacity to improve urban competitiveness.

In order to illustrate how sustainability is incorporated in the strategic planning to transform a downtown area, this chapter examines the City of San Francisco. San Francisco fundamentally transformed its planning strategy of the downtown area to improve its sustainability capacity in the 1980s and 1990s as a response to changed global and regional settings. The traditional downtown development model which was heavily focused on pro-growth office buildings was unable to sustain its long-term development and was thus criticised. Downtown planning stakeholders of the business, the government and the community gradually came to a consensus, notwithstanding deep conflicts in the early stage, that the re-tolling to a more sustainable approach for San Francisco's downtown was necessary in order to continue San Francisco's status as a global city and a regional hub. The overwhelming

217

scale of downtown redevelopment impacted negatively on urban infrastructure, environmental quality and liveability, and thus reduced its competitiveness. From the 1980s, San Francisco began to lose its corporate economy to the Bay Area regional centres. Meanwhile, San Francisco's economic base was shifting towards being more dependent on knowledge and experience sectors (ICF International, Economic and Planning Systems, 2007). In order to maintain and enhance its competitiveness and cope with the economic base transition, San Francisco released a series of plans to reposition its sustainable future.

Content analysis of plans is used for this research to reveal the contours of the planning process via the discourse used to articulate planning. I examine each of the major plans including the Downtown Plan 1985, the Proposition M 1986, and the South of Market Plan 1995. These three plans are the key planning documents that transformed the downtown development in the past two decades. The three thematic variables of economic planning, physical planning and social planning along with three imbedded characteristics of development, restriction and conservation are examined in the plan texts to explore common frameworks and patterns. In addition, a set of statistical tabulation based on the economy and demography are used to trace the contours of data that acted as backdrops for the planning process. Finally, I use informed assessments and judgements from these documents to reach conclusions about the intentions of the actors as the plans emerged.

The chapter is organised into an overview/introduction, followed by a historic narrative of the background of the plans, and a brief on the application of the method of content analysis. The chapter then analyses the three plans in detail to explore their thematic variables and characteristics. It finally concludes the common thematic patterns of the plans to showcase how the sustainable capacity of a downtown area was built to improve its competitiveness in the new context of global and regional competition.

Background

The post-war decades were another urban boom age for major American cities. For the City of San Francisco, the strategy was to build another Manhattan instead of the sprawling model of its southern rival city of Los Angeles. This Manhattan strategy was based on two basic propositions. For one, it anticipated the rise of the post-industrial economy. In this economic transition, San Francisco maintained its long-established status as a national and regional centre of financing, administrative and service sectors. The planning framework was for San Francisco to be a cosmopolitan city similar to New York with a dynamic downtown with high rise office buildings as the anchor to maximise land value, attract headquarters business, investment and people (McGovern, 1998). For the other, San Francisco should be an American gateway to the rising Asian Pacific area. San Francisco's geographical vicinity and historical links with this area would help build relationships with the emerging growth centres of Japan, Hong Kong, Taiwan, and Southeast Asia. A global city image with modern high-rise buildings would be an asset in facilitating trade, as well as attracting business and tourism.

The Manhattan model for San Francisco emerged in post-World War II as a consensus. This consensus was shared by the business, the government and the general public (DeLeon, 1992). They upheld the legitimacy of large-scale urban redevelopment and took a laissez-faire planning approach, believing in market forces as the determinants of urban affairs. Centred on this consensus, a pro-growth coalition was formed in San Francisco in the late 1950s and early 1960s. This coalition was initiated by the business, echoed by the government, propagated by the media and won the general support of the community (Hartman, 2002). This pro-growth coalition exercised pre-emptive power over the city's land use and development policy. Very swiftly, lands were cleared for redevelopment, and high-rise office buildings mushroomed. Within two decades of construction boom, a Manhattan grew on the West Coast – by the mid 1970s, San Francisco's present skyline had almost taken its shape. From the late 1950s, the growth heat continued until the mid-1980s for almost three decades with San Francisco's office space supply more than doubled.

The pro-growth planning culture dominated San Francisco without any challenge until the early 1970s. McGovern (1998) calls this planning culture a private hegemonism in that it was led and dominated by the private sector in the three post-War decades. However, since the early 1970s, some differences in opinions began to be voiced. Not surprisingly given San Francisco's liberal tradition, they were first voiced by some progressive activists (DeLeon, 1992). The activists expressed concerns over the loss of San Francisco's traditional aesthetic and environmental character with the advent of overwhelming modern building boxes and argued for growth control. These sporadic early voices were submerged in the construction boom. In the late 1970s, the negative consequences of urban redevelopment became more obvious. Apart from aesthetic considerations, the concerns expressed expanded to include environmental pollution, pressure on transport infrastructure and housing supply, and impact on social equity. Some progressive activists established community-based organisations to push forward the cause to harness the growth juggernaut. They proposed public ballots to change the course and although they all failed, they spread the message.

The attitude of the pro-growth groups towards downtown growth began to substantially change from the early 1980s. Businesses and the government were ready to review their pro-growth stances because the old model was straining public resources and leading to deep social cleavages between the haves and have nots. The office vacancy rate in the financial district climbed steadily from 1% in 1980 to 17% in 1986. The investment incentive of office construction lessened. Other negative impacts of urban growth on environmental and sustainability issues aroused stronger community reactions. Growth control for sustainability was widely discussed and was gradually accepted by more people.

The time was right to adjust the laissez faire approach towards urban affairs and take some interventionist actions in the mid 1980s. In 1983, the Planning Department of San Francisco released the Downtown Plan as a strategy to guide future downtown planning as well as a response to the increasing community pressure for growth control. The Downtown Plan was officially ratified by the Board of Supervisors, the legislative branch of the City's government, in 1985. It is clearly stated in the Introduction that 'the Downtown Plan grows out of an awareness of the public concern in recent years over the degree of change occurring downtown – and of the often conflicting civic objectives between fostering a vital economy and retaining the urban patterns and structures which collectively form the physical essence of San Francisco' (San Francisco Planning Department, 1985). It was the first comprehensive downtown plan of its kind in the US and put San Francisco at the forefront of American city planning and urban design efforts. It was on the front page of the *New York Times* twice and won the National Merit Award from the American Institute of Architects (AIA).

However, the growth control supporters were not satisfied with the development orientation set down in the Downtown Plan. They proposed another public initiative through popular voting in 1986. This time, they succeeded. The ballot initiative, which is generally known as the Proposition M as it was registered, was approved by the voters. It imposes the strictest limits on commercial office development ever witnessed in a major US city. The influence of Proposition M is fundamental: it represented not merely a change *in* the system but a change *of* the system (DeLeon, 1992).

One outcome of downtown growth in San Francisco is the incorporation of the South of Market Area (SoMA) as part of it. The SoMA had been traditionally one area of industry and warehouse, and a bastion of working-class residents, ethnic minorities, gays and lesbians. From the 1980s, the SoMA was gradually becoming a trendy centre of arts, museums, design studios, restaurants, bars, and nightclubs. It is becoming San Francisco's CSD (Central Social District) as a complement to the CBD (Terplan, 2007). In the 1990s, with the rise of hi-tech economy, the diverse lifestyle and cheap rent spaces made the SoMA the Mecca of hi-tech elites composed of computer programmers, visual artists, film makers, and media content producers. Dubbed as 'Multimedia Gulch', the SoMA was the driving force of San Francisco's economic growth.

The SoMA was the focus of urban development in the 1990s. The Downtown Plan clearly targeted the SoMA as a new office expansion zone and envisioned the Transbay Terminal area in the SoMA as the heart of the new downtown. In the old downtown core, no substantial office space was built during the second half of the 1980s in downtown San Francisco due to the Downtown Plan, particularly the restrictive Proposition M. The Proposition M was the result of the system of ballot initiatives in California in which the citizens could make proposals to intervene in government policy through public ballots. However, the growth pressure and market forces constituted a menace to the social diversity and the economic mix of traditional light industry and new hi-tech start-ups in the SoMA. The businesses in the SoMA are mostly location and rent sensitive and are not competitive with those higher rent paying commercial activities which require office space. It was in this context that the South of Market Plan was produced in 1995 to guide the development and conservation of the SoMA. As expressed in the Introduction, the Plan 'identified both existing community characteristics, problems and amenities as well as the types of development pressures and market forces that may affect the SoMA over the next 20 years' (San Francisco Planning Department, 1995).

These three plans – the Downtown Plan 1985, the Proposition M and the South of Market Plan 1995 – are the three benchmark planning documents which shaped the downtown development in the past two decades and are still working now.

Analytical approach

To examine the central themes of the sustainability debate, the San Francisco plans have been looked at through three lenses:

Figure 67: Classifications of thematic variables

Thematic variables	Thematic points	Exemplary contents
Economic planning	Business activities, Commercial space use, Employment	Maintain high quality, especially retail shopping facilities in the retail core. (Downtown Plan)
Physical planning	Infrastructure of transport, Housing, Urban form, Open space, Place amenity	Landmarks and historic buildings should be preserved. (Proposition M)
Social planning	Social life, Social equity, Cultural and community facilities	Promote making existing rental housing permanently affordable for low- and moderate-income residents. (South of Market Plan)

In order to measure the thematic variables in each planning document, a number of thematic characteristics are identified and defined. These thematic characteristics are key concepts which appear repeatedly in the text. Tabulation of the frequencies and percentages of these characteristics will demonstrate the trends and patterns of the themes, which is regarded as an invariable and crucial step in a content analysis (Leedy and Ormrod, 2005). In the case of San Francisco's planning documents, three thematic characteristics appear with very high frequency in the text. They are defined as thematic concepts of development, restriction and conservation, as classified in Figure 68. The texts are scrutinised to highlight and measure the frequency of the appearance of these concepts and their synonyms. The numerical frequencies of these thematic characteristics are the measures to indicate the thematic patterns of planning. The content analysis is a qualitative research method using very quantitative tools.

Figure 68: Classification of thematic characteristics

Thematic characteristics	Synonymous concepts	Exemplary contents
Development	Develop, encourage, provide, promote, improve, address, introduce, arrange, create, etc.	Create new parks and recreational facilities for the enjoyment by area residents, workers, and visitors. (South of Market Plan)
Restriction	Restrict, exclude, discourage, reduce, minimise, limit, etc.	Discourage development which has substantial undesirable consequences which cannot be mitigated. (Downtown Plan)
Conservation	Conserve, preserve, remain, maintain, protect, continue, keep, etc.	Ensure that existing housing and neighbourhood character is conserved and protected in order to preserve the cultural and economic diversity of our neighbourhoods (Proposition M)

Downtown Plan 1985

The Downtown Plan envisages downtown San Francisco as a centre of ideas, services and trade, and a place for stimulating experiences. Towards this goal, downtown San Francisco should 'encompass a compact mix of activities, historical values, and distinctive architecture and urban forms that engender a special excitement reflective of a world city' (San Francisco Planning Department, 1985).

Figure 69: Themes of the Downtown Plan, 1985

Thematic variables	Categories	Policy nos.	Frequencies of thematic characteristics			Key objectives
			Develop -ment	Restric -tion	Conser- vation	
Economic planning	Commercial space	11	8	6	3	Enhance commercial spaces
Physical planning	Housing	4	2	1	1	Expand and preserve housing
	Open space	12	12	0	0	Provide quality open space
	Historical preservation	3	1	0	3	Preserve historical architecture
	Urban form	14	11	0	3	Design attractive city
	Transport	34	31	5	3	Encourage public transit; discourage cars
	Seismic	4	5	0	1	Reduce hazards
Social planning	Social equity	1	1	0	0	Retail services for lower incomers

Before approving the plan, the Board of Supervisors insisted on a growth cap as a condition of approval. So the final Plan includes an annual limit of 950,000 square feet on construction of downtown office buildings of 50,000 square feet or larger. This is the most prominent thematic characteristic of restriction in the plan as a sustainability approach. The main body of the Plan includes seven sections: Space for Commerce, Space for Housing, Open Space, Preserving the Past, Urban Form, Moving About, and Seismic Safety, which in total cover 23 objectives and 82 policies. Figure 69 is the tabulation of the thematic characteristics of these 23 objectives and 82 policies.

Economic sustainability planning

The section of Space for Commerce exclusively covers the theme of economic planning. This section includes six objectives regarding the commercial spaces of office, retail, hotel and support commercial space. The overall objective is to enhance the total city living and working environment through economic growth and change management. In terms of major economic activities, downtown San Francisco should be a prime location for financial, administrative, corporate and professional activities, as well as a centre of specialised retail trade, tourist and visitor centre. Future land use and density for these commercial activities should be maintained and enhanced in and around downtown.

Of the 11 policies to implement the economic planning objectives, there are eight frequencies of thematic characteristic of development, six of restriction and three of conservation. It is a clear strategy to continue downtown development to sustain the economic vitality. In the mean time, some restriction measures are taken to control the development to an appropriate extent in order to 'minimise undesirable consequences' (Policy 1.1). This shows recognition that although prior growth did generate economic vitality, it also brought about environmental and social costs. Future office development is restricted within the downtown core of north and south of Market and is allowed to expand to the Transbay Bus Terminal in the SoMA. The quality retail core and local retail services are conserved from office encroachment. A compact downtown should be developed and maintained with a diversity of commercial activities of office, retail, hotel and support facilities, all of which are central to new urbanist sustainable planning approaches.

Physical sustainability planning

The theme of physical planning covers all the other sections in the plan of housing, open space, historical preservation, urban form, transport and seismic.

For housing, the policies are balanced between providing more housing and protecting existing housing. Lack of housing provision was becoming problematic for downtown's vitality at night and on weekends. This problem was worsened by the downtown office development pressure which had demolished or converted housing into commercial uses. As a result, San Francisco was short of affordable housing and some low and medium incomers were forced out of town.

The plan emphasises the importance of open space for a vital, comfortable and economically vigorous downtown. It has 12 policies which are exclusively about developing sufficient and sophisticated open space for downtown workers, residents and visitors. Details of design requirements are specified to make open space usable, accessible, and aesthetic.

Historical preservation is also emphasised in the plan. San Francisco is proud of its legacy of traditional architecture. Unfortunately, this urban character was impacted by the modern downtown redevelopment with large scale, square shape and heavy colour. The plan requires architectural continuity with history and classifies 251 buildings of architectural value for protection.

Apart from open space, urban form is another key component of urban design element in the plan. The plan claims to build San Francisco into the most visually attractive city in the world. Very detailed specifications are provided regarding height and bulk, sunlight and wind, building appearance, and streetscape. Considerations are made from the pedestrian perspective for visual aesthetics and sensual comfort. Traditional street patterns and street-building relations are preserved.

The category of transport covers 34 policies, the most of all categories, which can be partially translated into the importance of transport in the Downtown Plan. This is justifiable since transport plays a crucial role in determining the competitiveness of downtown. The transport objectives fall into three aspects: encourage transit use; discourage auto use;

enhance pedestrian and cyclist circulation. Most policies are about developing downtown transport in different modes as manifested in as many as 31 frequencies of the thematic characteristic of development. The five frequencies of thematic characteristic of restriction aim at restricting auto use and downtown parking.

Seismic safety is a special issue to San Francisco due to its geographical location on the earthquake belt. This is of particular importance for high-rise downtown area.

Social sustainability planning

There is no policy which specifically addresses social issues. Only Policy 3.2, which stipulates to 'encourage the retail businesses which serve the shopping needs of less affluent downtown workers and local residents', can be regarded as an effort to address social equity.

Sustainability summary

The Downtown Plan is predominantly a planning document of physical sustainability planning. Even though the category of commercial spaces is classified into the theme of economic planning in the analysis, it is essentially about land use and development orientation. The social planning theme is almost non-existent.

The Downtown Plan focuses on development, urban design and conservation. Development refers to the growth of commercial spaces, provision of housing and public transport, and provision of public space. Urban design refers to the emphasis on the design aspect of open space and urban form to create a pleasing environment for workers, residents and visitors as well as a global city image. Conservation refers to the protection of the historic urban character of architecture and street pattern, and the protection of housing and historic building from office development encroachment.

Economic competitiveness and liveability are the two primary goals of the Downtown Plan. Economically, downtown San Francisco should be the centre of activities of finance, insurance, administration, corporate and professional services, as well as retail and hotel. This is maintained and enhanced through a balanced and controlled land use of office, retail, hotel and support commercial services. The liveability is achieved through urban design of open space, urban form, and historical protection. The competitiveness of the city requires the kind of environment which is beautiful, compact, walkable and accessible.

Housing and transport are two basic supporting infrastructures for a sustainable downtown development. Enhancing housing supply and preserving existing housing from being encroached on by office development adds to the sustainable vitality of downtown. Efficient public transit facilities will sustain the downtown's competitiveness.

Proposition M, 1986

The Proposition M has four parts: growth limits, citizen participation, job training for local residents, and priority policies. With regard to growth limits, the Proposition M strengthens the restriction characteristics of the Downtown Plan by imposing a permanent annual 950,000 square feet cap on all new buildings of more than 25,000 square feet and reserving annual 75,000 square feet for small buildings. In social planning, the Proposition M empowers citizen participation by giving citizens the last word in deciding the fate of any large scale development projects. Other favourable measures for local residents include creating a coordinated training program for local residents to take newly opened jobs and responding to the primary needs and concerns of ethnic minorities, workers and low-incomers. The Proposition M further proposes eight priority policies to be included in the Master Plan of San Francisco. Figure 70 is the tabulation of the thematic characteristics of these eight policies.

Economic sustainability planning

Three policies touch upon the theme of economic planning. They are about economic diversity and neighbourhood-serving retail. Conservation is the strongest thematic characteristic – they mean to protect the existing diverse economic base and local serving retail from being encroached upon by office development.

Physical sustainability planning

The majority of the eight priority policies stipulate on the general physical planning issues of urban form, housing, open space, transport, and seismic protection. In terms of thematic characteristic frequency, it is clear that almost all physical planning policies are on conservation, that is, to conserve the existing physical features from being impacted.

Figure 70: Themes of Proposition M, 1986

Themes	Categories	Policy nos.	Frequencies of thematic characteristics			Key objectives
			Develop- ment	Restric- tion	Conser- vation	
Economic planning	Economic diversity	2	0	0	2	Protect economic diversity
	Retail	1	1	0	1	Retail for neighbourhood use
Physical planning	Urban form	2	0	0	2	Preserve city character and historic architecture
	Open space	1	0	0	1	Protect from development
	Seismic	1	0	0	1	Protect from earthquake
	Transport	1	0	1	0	Public transit priority
Social planning	Cultural diversity	1	0	0	1	Preserve cultural diversity
	Local employment + ownership of business	2	2	0	0	Enhance local employment and ownership
	Affordable housing	1	1	0	1	Preserve and enhance affordable housing

Social sustainability planning

There is a strong component of social planning theme in the Proposition M policies. In total, four policies stress the social issues of cultural diversity, affordable housing, and preference towards local employment and ownership of business. In terms of the thematic characteristics, there is a balance between development and conservation. The cultural diversity and existing affordable housing are protected. Local employment and business ownership as well as the supply of affordable housing are enhanced.

Sustainability summary

Of all the proposals and policies of the Proposition M, there is a strong prevalence of the theme of social sustainability planning over economic planning and physical planning. This is not surprising since the Proposition M came out as a community response to the Downtown Plan which is essentially a physical planning document as discussed above. The major social planning concerns of the Proposition M include citizen participation, social equity of employment and business ownership, affordable housing and development mitigation.

The issues of economic planning and physical planning replicate those in the Downtown Plan, but the focus is on the conservation rather than the development aspect. In this sense, the Proposition M is a planning document about conservation rather than development. In almost every piece of proposal or policy, the word 'conserve' or its synonyms occur. The Proposition M is the most restrictive planning document in the history of San Francisco for its permanent annual development cap.

South of Market Plan, 1995

The South of Market Plan includes goals, objectives and policies of development and conservation of the SoMA towards the 21st century. It is based on the recognition that the SOM as a healthy, vibrant and stable community of low-incomer residents and location- and rent-sensitive small businesses. It has a diverse employment base of industrial and service activities, an increasing number of which belong to the creative technology and artistic work. The plan is a true new urbanist sustainability approach that recognises the need to protect existing housing for local workers and residents.

Based on a thorough analysis of the physical, social, cultural and economic conditions and the forces within the SOM, the Plan outlines these four goals: (1) protect and facilitate the expansion of industrial, artisan, home and business services, and neighbourhood-serving retail and community service activities; (2) protect existing economic, social and cultural diversity; (3) preserve existing housing and encourage the development of new, affordable housing; and (4) preserve existing amenities and improve neighbourhood liveability for South of Market residents, workers and visitors.

These four major goals are embodied in more details in the objectives and policies of the four sections of the plan: Business Activity, Residential Activity, Transportation, and Area Liveability. Figure 71 analyses the policies through the spectrums of the three themes of economic planning, physical planning and social planning.

Figure 71: Themes of the South of Market Plan, 1995

Themes	Categories	Policy nos.	Frequencies of thematic characteristics			Key objectives
			Develop ment	Restric- tion	Conser -vation	
Economic planning	Business activities	6	5	2	2	Protect existing business activities
Physical planning	Housing	8	6	1	1	Preserve and develop housing
	Transport	8	8	1	0	Develop transit and restrict auto
	Liveability	13	12	0	8	Preserve and improve amenities
Social planning	Social equity	1	1	0	0	Preserve/develop affordable housing

Economic sustainability planning

The SoMA has been traditionally housing artisan, service and light industrial businesses which are small in employment number and space use. They are very rent- and location-sensitive and are vulnerable to higher rent-paying office activities. So their biggest challenge comes from the pressure of office conversion of the existing residential and industrial buildings which are normally low and small in size.

The first policy of the plan is to restrict office development within the SoMA which has already been integrated as part of the downtown so as to protect light industries and business service spaces from being encroached upon. Other conservation policies include protection of the live/work loft studio space of performing and visual artists and craftspersons. The existing mixture of business activities which should not be allowed in new land use is protected. The economic diversity as well as cultural diversity are preserved and enhanced through the planning of night entertainment activities and small businesses which are diverse and are mixed together.

Physical sustainability planning

Housing is crucial to the cultural, social and economic diversity of the SoMA. Like the space for traditional SOM industries and services, the biggest challenge of affordable housing also comes from the pressure of office conversion. On the one hand, existing housing should be conserved through discouraging their demolition for non-residential use. On the other hand, new housing provision should be expanded.

Transport development should help enhance the social and economic diversity of the SoMA. Transit should be the primary mode of travel, and auto traffic should not impact on the liveability of the SoMA. The liveability is a key element of physical planning of the SoMA through both conservation and development thematic characteristics. By conservation, the existing amenities should be preserved, such as urban form, architectural character, and landmark buildings. By development, essential community services and facilities should be improved.

Social sustainability planning

Social planning is implicit in most policies by preserving and enhancing social diversity. The need for affordable housing is emphasised for local low- and moderate-income workers and residents.

Sustainability summary

The South of Market Plan is a balanced sustainable approach among the three themes of economic planning, physical planning and social planning. Numerically, the policies exclusively expressing the theme of social planning is few, but the notion is embodied in most of the policies. The chief goal of the plan is to achieve social and economic diversity of the SoMA through physical planning measures.

To enhance and preserve the cultural and economic diversity and the physical character is the prevailing theme of the plan. The thematic characteristics of development and conservation converge to point to this purpose: conservation and development of vitality and diversity of the SoMA community. The thematic characteristic of restriction also points to this purpose: protection of the community character from office development pressures and market forces which would otherwise convert the area and thus cause undesirable social and environmental consequences.

Economically, the diverse economic base of small-scale light industrial, service and artisan business activities should be preserved and their expansion should be allowed through construction of new industrial and commercial spaces. Spaces for convenient retail and community service activities for residents, workers and visitors should also be provided.

The supporting infrastructures of housing and transport are crucial in sustaining the healthy, vibrant and stable community. The liveability of the SoMA is to be improved through providing more amenities and community serving facilities. The area liveability should not be negatively impacted by commercial development and auto traffic.

Social diversity and equity should be maintained through providing and preserving affordable housing, maintaining the mixture of employment, and the existing business space uses. The needs of low- and moderate-income residents and workers is especially protected.

Conclusions

The Downtown Plan, the Proposition M and the South of Market Plan collectively represent a fundamental sustainability orientation to planning of downtown San Francisco in the 1980s and 1990s. They have been shaping central San Francisco's urban landscape in the post-1980s period. Their ultimate aim is to strengthen San Francisco's sustainable urban competitiveness in order to continue its status as a global city and a regional hub of the Bay Area.

The three plans signify first of all a transformation of planning philosophy in San Francisco. Prior to the 1980s, San Franciscans believed in the market forces and adopted a laissez faire approach to planning. Behind this ideology was a strong pro-growth coalition, mainly composed of the business sectors and the government who prioritised urban redevelopment on the top agenda to drive a post-industrial economy. This stance was propagated by the media and acknowledged by the general community in the early stage. However, in this pro-growth hegemony, community participation and social equity were virtually absent. The very unsustainable nature of this planning philosophy had an increasingly negative impact on San Francisco's strategic status as a leading urban hub. The release of these plans is a strong message of redirection of the laissez faire tradition towards interventionism. Free market force was regulated and downtown development was mitigated. The community was empowered in deciding on the city's affairs. Figure 72 is a comparison of this planning philosophy transformation in San Francisco across the 1980s and 1990s which are collectively aimed at a sustainable downtown San Francisco.

The three plans led to a fundamental transformation of planning strategy, policies and practices in San Francisco to a more sustainable base. After three decades of office construction boom, the negative effects were becoming a barrier to long-term competitiveness. It was recognised that downtown development was not inherently positive. A competitive downtown relies on sustainable capacity building between economic development, environmental liveability and social equity. This imperative required a review of three decades of unfettered downtown development and repositioning of planning strategy and practices.

Figure 72: Planning transformations for a sustainable San Francisco

Philosophies	Beliefs
Laissez faire	Hegemonic privatism: business-dominated elite
	Laissez faire approach: market-driven and minimum government intervention
	Manhattan model for aesthetic appreciation and embracement of post-industrial economy
	Faith in market forces as a fair distributor of costs and benefits of development
	Minimal concern about the negative consequence of vigorous development
	Virtual absence of regulator and redistributive policies
	Expert skills
Interventionist	Progressive activism: grassroots and community-based
	Scepticism of market forces: government interventions guarantee a more equitable outcome
	Popular empowerment and citizen participation in downtown planning
	Downtown development is not inherently positive
	Growth limits and linkage policies to offset social and environmental costs of downtown development
	Popular initiative as a powerful tool to shape land use decision making

Thematically, the three plans try to reach a sustainable balance between economic planning, physical planning and social planning. This is an important differentiation from San Francisco's planning tradition which was exclusively focused on economics. Economically, the goal is to continue and strengthen San Francisco's status as a centre of financing, headquarters and service. Strong physical planning policies are adopted to enhance infrastructure of transport and housing supply, improve accessible and pleasing public space, and emphasise the aesthetic value of urban form to build a compact and walkable downtown San Francisco for workers, residents and visitors. Socially, favourable policies towards local residents, especially the low- and moderate-incomers, aim to protect them from being squeezed out of the city by market forces and commercial development. Similar favourable policies are also proposed for affordable housing, employment and local businesses.

The three plans guide urban development in such a way as not to cause undesirable environmental and social consequences. Office construction is restricted in terms of both volume and location. More development policies are devoted to urban design and downtown walkability. Meanwhile, conservation of existing economic and social diversity, and historical buildings and architectural aesthetics is enforced. They are plans for sustainable development, as well as conservation and restriction as shown in the analysis of their thematic characteristics.

These transformations mark important changes of urban planning philosophies and practices in San Francisco. They are meant to improve the urban competitiveness of the downtown area through its sustainable capacity building. This sustainable capacity building, in the case of San Francisco, is planned through a balanced approach between economic planning, physical planning and social planning.

References

DeLeon, R. E. (1992) *Left coast city: Progressive politics in San Francisco, 1975–1991*. Kansas: University Press of Kansas.

Hartman, C. (2002) *City for sale: the transformation of San Francisco* (Revised and updated ed.). Berkeley and Los Angeles: University of California Press.

Hu, Y. (2006) 'Reinventing the CBD: centralization, decentralization, and diversification,' in E. J. Blakely (ed.), *Dialogue in Urban Planning*. Sydney: Planning Research Centre, University of Sydney.

ICF International, Economic and Planning Systems, Seifel Consulting Inc. & Leslie Parks Consulting (2007) *Sustaining our Prosperity: the San Francisco economic strategy*. San Francisco: Mayor's Office of Economic and Workforce Development.

Leedy, P. D. and Ormrod, J. E. (2005) *Practical research: planning and design* (8th International edn.). Upper Saddle River, NJ: Pearson Prentice Hall.

McGovern, S. J. (1998) *The politics of Downtown development: dynamic political cultures in San Francisco and Washington, D.C.* Lexington: The University Press of Kentucky.

San Francisco Planning Department (1985) *Area plan: downtown, 2007*. Available at www.sfgov.org.

San Francisco Planning Department (1995) *Area plan: South of Market, 2008*. Available at www.sfgov.org.

Sassen, S. (2001) *The global city: New York, London, Tokyo* (2nd edn.). Princeton, New Jersey: Princeton University Press.

Taylor, P. J. (2004) *World city network: a global urban analysis*. New York: Routledge.

Terplan, E. B., Lisa (2007) *Framing the future of downtown San Francisco*. SPUR Newsletter, March.

Chapter 11

RECOVERY OF THE SOUL: SUSTAINABLE REBUILDING IN POST-KATRINA NEW ORLEANS

Edward J. Blakely

Although the notion of sustainable development is usually associated with the design and building of new settlements, this chapter illustrates how this notion can also be used to undergird the recovery strategies to rebuild a city struck by a natural disaster. The chapter shows how a sustainable development approach in post-Katrina New Orleans has helped frame post-disaster recovery efforts by applying the following five sustainability concepts: community participation in deciding best strategies for recovery to continue the healing; public safety and security for all neighbourhoods; 100-plus-year time-horizon infrastructure planning; a diverse economy; and sustainable settlement pattern.

Spates of new books and journal articles have attempted to capture the highs and lows of the Hurricane Katrina catastrophe. Some of this work has examined the physical characteristics of New Orleans and asked if the city was built in the wrong place (Vale and Campenella, 2005). Is it now time to rectify this accident of geography? In essence is New Orleans sustainable or can it be made sustainable?. Other work has examined New Orleans as a cultural icon where the forces of good and evil have shaped a unique culture which is under threat from the potential of modern rebuilding paradigms that might disturb the crucible from which the rich music and art spring (Sublette, 2007).

Some work reflects the real pathos of New Orleans with a seemingly intractable set of social problems co-existing in a fragile environment, especially John Barry's epic volume *Rising Tide* (1997). All of these emerge from different partially correct prisms from which one can assess this great old city in its time of crisis. But in essence, they miss the real New Orleans which is often described as the Soul of America (Soul City). It is a city with a magnetic past and a character and charm that is unique. Everyone in the world has some form of exposure to New

Orleans through the countless jazz, rhythm and blues, Cajun and other music that emanates from this cultural capital of the United States.

On August 29, 2005, New Orleans suffered from over exposure. As Hurricane Katrina hit, a new image of New Orleans was broadcast around the world. This was not the image most of the world held of Soul City. What the world saw projected, and to some extent exaggerated, was a City of disorder, racial inequality and poverty along with inadequate national responses to the disaster caused in large measure by the failure of federally built and maintained levees. So, the magic of New Orleans was challenged by the reality of the situation that was presented to the world. Two years have passed since the New Orleans tragedy. In those two years the issues of planning and re-planning have become central to the discourse on New Orleans. This article addresses the dimensions of the planning process and products that are underway, and the many complicated issues associated with trying to put New Orleans back together again. The future of New Orleans rests with its special past without denying its desperate reality if it has any hope of a real recovery.

What is a sustainable plan – New Orleans style?

Almost immediately after Katrina, a planning contest emerged between various New Orleans factions that felt strongly about what New Orleans was and what it should and could be. On one side were the traditional landed plantationists who still owned considerable assets in the form of real estate and business. In the middle were the local neighbourhood activists who viewed the city entirely from what happened in their neighbourhoods. Finally, there were African Americans of all classes who felt disenfranchised and acted as a group to develop and maintain political power.

Planning or re-planning New Orleans challenged the notion that the past is the only foundation for the future. Community interest groups who felt they owned the past; artists, African Americans, and preservationists were challenged by architects and planners who were shaping a new city form to meet the challenges of a new century. This chapter looks at sustainable planning through the prisms of contestants who use it as a vehicle to gain recognition, shape debates and move their agendas forward. It examines how they understand the meaning and opportunities for plans to garner an improved position for themselves. What will become evident is that planning and planning tools will shape the future of New Orleans in ways the residents never anticipated (Birch and Wachter, 2006).

Plan as a sustainable problem identification

There is a rich planning tradition of finding problems as the basis for planning (Baer, 1997). This tradition emerges from the systems theory literature. It is based in the concept that if the city, or whatever is being planned for, can be properly diagnosed then good data can be applied to find the correct course(s) of action. In New Orleans, the way one described the problem became a central component in shaping the discourse.

New Orleans had deep problems prior to Katrina. The city pre- and post-Katrina had one of the nation's highest poverty rates with 23.2% against 12.7% nationally. Moreover, the city segregated large portions of the black low income population in public housing or very substandard private government subsidised (HUD section 8) rental accommodations. The New Orleans median household income of US$27,000 compared to a national median of US$41,000 is among the lowest for major metropolitan areas in the nation. Homeownership rates also fall well below the national median at 45.6% versus the nation at 67.9%. Poverty, low wages and lack of housing are universally associated with crime and social issues in New Orleans. In the decade of the 1990s, New Orleans ranked at or near the top of the murder rate per 1000 with a murder rate 7.54 times the national average and comparable to some of the nation's largest cities (Earth Day Network, 2005).

All of these problems are compounded by the fact that the New Orleans City schools were taken over by the state of Louisiana because of constant low performance combined with administrative incompetence. One striking feature of New Orleans is that it has an illiteracy rate of 39% among the New Orleans Parish adult low income population (Earth Day Network, 2005). Many of these under skilled and illiterates are products of New Orleans Public Schools. New Orleans public housing authority is in federal receivership by the US Department of Housing and Urban Development (HUD).

The combination of poor schools, crime and low incomes in the city core has pushed both whites and blacks into the suburbs and private education over the last three decades leaving as many as 40,000 vacant lots or abandoned residential properties. The city has one of the nation's worst violent crime rates averaging over 200 murders per year for the last decade (Federal Bureau of Investigation, 2002). This blight depresses home values in all but the most exclusive neighbourhoods as well as acting as a magnet and safe haven for drug consumption and dealing. Moreover, New Orleans had the worst school test scores by grade in Louisiana, a state with one of the nation's lowest school performance rates (Earth Day Network, 2005).

Overlaying and contributing to the malaise of poverty, residential deterioration and socioeconomic disruption is a fragmented governmental system. At the time of Katrina, there were five different levee boards, which have since reduced to two. The small Orleans Parish of under 500,000 people had 7 tax assessors which will be reduced to one in 2009. There are a myriad of boards of commissions governing the delivery of public services from libraries to water and sewer and even public parks. Even the famous Superdome that graces the city skyline as a premier sporting facility is owned and operated by the state and not the city.

Sustainable planning theorists would immediately suggest that no plan can be formed that merely addressed the flood damage. Yet, some of the earliest approaches to recovering the city such as the *Bring Back New Orleans Plan* barely recognised these issues and the strong emotional weight that these problems carried for any attempt to deal with the future of the city (Nossiter, 2007).

There is little doubt that the problems of New Orleans have to be acknowledged as a first step in formulating a response to the recovery efforts. To do this, the Office of Recovery Management formed in January 2007, some 18 months after the crisis and headed by the author, offered a 5 point diagnostic framework as the basis for assessing the sustainable challenges from which the city needed to recover (Office of Recovery Management, 2007).

- *Continue the healing* – recognises that the deep underlying trauma of Katrina started well before the disaster and lay in the deep division across race and class. Healing the chasms across the community is an ongoing exercise that the Recovery Office has to play a central role in designing and carrying out. This process, including meetings of all city employees and community groups, is going on as part of the recovery efforts.

- *Public safety and security for all neighbourhoods* – The depth of fear of crime in the lowest income communities is impeding the return of residents to these areas. Crime is, however, a citywide contagion affecting all areas, so incorporating both crime prevention and crime stopping has become a critical element of the recovery. There are a host of programs including citywide crime cameras along with more community and neighbourhood policing strategies to engage young people in positive social and recreational pursuits. In addition, good schools near home are an important security issue for every parent. Schools are now the community core facilities, with libraries, to act as anchors and form more public open space, dense housing patterns and walkable communities. Finally, good hospitals and clinics are required to deal with both mental and physical health issues. Therefore, a core element of the strategy is to provide every community with access to better health facilities than in pre-Katrina New Orleans.

- *Infrastructure for the 21st and 22nd century* – Like many American cities, New Orleans has under-invested in the city's primary infrastructure such as sewers and water as well as other basics. This infrastructure is the bedrock for any new industries and balances the needs of all communities across income groups, as well as meeting the needs of emerging enterprises for better, cheaper and greener technologies.

- *Diversify the economy* – New Orleans' economy is based on tourism, energy and retail services. The largest job producers are in low wage service sectors. To combat crime and generate a healthy social economy, new jobs related to the city's future have to be sought in areas such as bio-medicine, advanced transportation and media.

- *Sustainable settlement pattern* – is the foundation of any good city. Cities with good neighbourhoods attract people and jobs. While some quarrel with aspects of Richard Florida's (2002) concepts, the basic message is correct. So, New Orleans has a special burden in crafting a re-settlement program that avoids the hazards of the past and builds new communities that are less segregated by income as well as being environmentally and socially sustainable.

These five sustainability concepts act as the problem reference points for taking all of the issues and data and articulating them in a clear way that is both compelling and accurate. In this way, the re-building program will emerge from a process of constructive engagement which the city has been undertaking for nearly two years.

Sustainable direction for planning

To some planning advocates, the process is the plan. How people are engaged in this process ranges from therapy to control (Arnstein, 1969). Engaging citizens with professionals and stakeholders is the core of planning. This engagement in itself has many positive aspects such as creating a collective consciousness as to what the future is and how to get to it. The New Orleans City Council began the planning process in some frustration as a release or therapy for citizen discontent. The Council engaged Lambert and Associates from Florida, a firm well grounded in citizen engagement process post disasters, to assist community groups in the re-planning process. The process planning orientation embedded in the Lambert approach orientation has many inherent problems such as who has a voice in the process. Do bigots have a right to control the outcomes of the process and thus the plan? Is this a consensus approach or do the most votes win? How and what information can be used as the process unfolds? All of these issues surfaced in New Orleans.

At the outset, citizen groups on their own started planning all over the city for their own neighbourhoods or districts. This was problematic in many ways. Firstly, how could these citizens speak for people who were still scattered over 37 states? Secondly, what was the planning goal? With governmental or other frameworks, citizen planning can and was Balkanising the city since each group set its own targets for the planning outcome they preferred with no reference to any other larger citywide goals or visions. The Lambert plans established a very good process of engagement but left open the need to find a customer or client other than each neighbourhood for the plans.

Sustainability discourse

Bent Flyvberg noted that: 'If you want more civic reciprocity in political affairs, you work for civic virtues becoming worthy of praise and others becoming undesirable' (1998, p. 121). Enter the Rockefeller Foundation with some urging from community leaders offering the city resources and a new set of planners to weave the Lambert and other work into a strategic tapestry to craft new civic virtue called 'The Unified New Orleans Plan' (UNOP) (Nossiter, 2007). The UNOP process took a very broad consultation and outreach approach that engaged New Orleanians across the nation. UNOP organised and prioritised citizen input into a wider and deeper document addressing physical, economic and social requirements for recovery. UNOP became the new sustainability discourse/civic virtue setting mechanism for people in all walks of life an opportunity to share their needs, frustrations and visions of what the city might be.

The UNOP process was crafted outside the formal city bureaucracy. In some ways, this was a good idea since bureaucrats tend to narrow agendas. On the other hand, it meant no one in the city government had ownership of it or accepted it as a mandate for recovery. As a result, UNOP became a stalking horse for funding priorities and not a plan for recovery from the Katrina natural disaster. UNOP shaped the discourse about what was needed to be actionable but not the steps to action.

Sustainable action planning

Good plans form good projects. However, we know from many studies that there can be a disconnection between what is planned and what actually happens. In many cases, this is not the fault of the planners or the plan but the decision makers (Innes and Booher, 2004). In the case of New Orleans, plans became an end in themselves. Plan after plan was rolled out by various groups that seldom showed what steps would be taken to implement them (Nossiter, 2007). In most cases, the plans were actually demands on resources rather than actionable problem solving. After nearly two years, there was no direct approach to implementation of any of the previously discussed plans – 'Bring Back New Orleans', Lambert, UNOP and others. In order to move beyond this conundrum, the newly formed Office of Recovery Management was tasked by Mayor C. Ray Nagin to pull visible actions in places from all of the documents that emerged over the nearly two years of planning at every level including Chamber of Commerce, Philanthropy, Education and a host of other plans by neighbourhood groups like Acorn. Good information and good ideas were contained in all of these plans but the task of organising was daunting.

Figure 73: New Orleans recovery areas

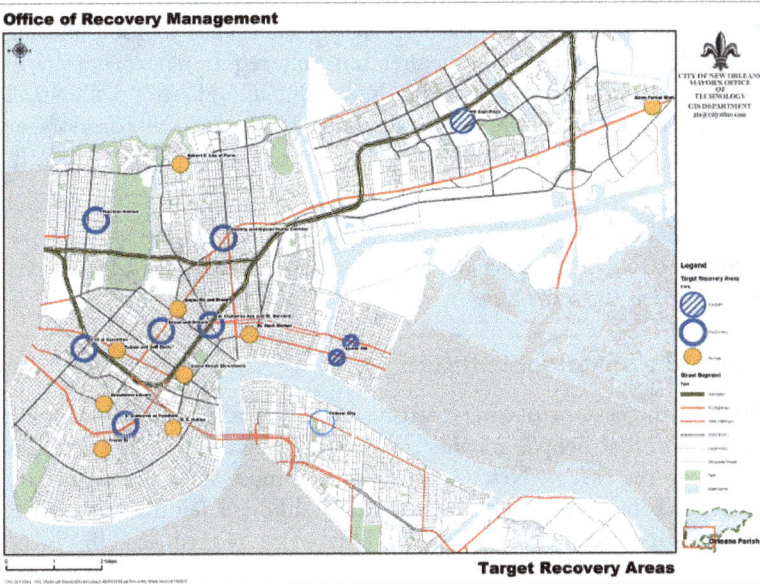

Source: Office of Recovery Management (2007)

The approach adopted by the Office of Recovery Management (ORM) was to take the plans from all the different groups and overlay them as problems and/or opportunities on the city geography. In essence, the staff took all of the plans to see where projects and places came together. While this was hard for some plans that did not identify specific implementation geography such as crime reduction of literacy and skill level improvements, each of these issues had a place or geographic node where the problem was more manifest or the

245

opportunities for intervention were more coherent. From this data bank, the ORM staff produced a map of places that could be intervention platforms of three logical Target Area types (see Figure 73).

- *Rebuild* – places heavily damaged by flooding with massive destruction that will require rebuilding from the ground up.

- *Redevelop* – areas that were blighted pre-Katrina and needed substantial revitalisation of both commercial and retail stocks.

- *Renew* – communities that were lightly damaged with good housing stock and other infrastructures but only require improvements in civic facilities such as schools, parks, and libraries with small incentives for business revitalisations in commercial corridors or strips.

This approach was vetted with planners and community activists and civic leaders to ensure that it met the spirit as well as the goals of the recovery effort. The Target Areas approach has been well received and is being used as the *action plan*.

Toward a sustainable future

Plans in the case of disaster need to embody a new sustainable future orientation that people gravitate to because they can identify with this future. In the case of New Orleans, this is a must. New Orleanians are very much in love with their past glory, although few of the current residents have seen or shared much of that glory. Nonetheless, this is the story. A substitute story has to feel good and look good too. In some ways, New Orleans has to recapture the imagination of the American people who have seen the old New Orleans as a parody of its past.

To create a new face and new space, in addition to the sustainable redevelopment strategies outlined above, the city is promoting a sustainable economic recovery by attracting new industries and new transportation technologies that are more modern and contribute to a sustainable economy that is non-polluting. The new New Orleans is one based on Media Technology – the *Hollywood South* with film studios growing in the old warehouse district; *Broadway South* based on the use of the central city large old art deco theatres and the strong working performing artists backdrop; *biomedicine* looking to the new opportunities in chronic diseases such as diabetes, heart disease and maladies related to local and increasingly international lifestyles; *transport technologies* oriented to the increasing freight – air, sea, rail and ship – moving between Latin America, Africa and China (with the wider Panama Channel) with New Orleans strategically located for this trade with a river, air and seaport connected to six rail roads. So, the new New Orleans is a Sustainable Phoenix rising out of the water to create a new future and a new sustainable dream.

References

Arnstein, S. R. (1969) 'A ladder of citizen participation.' *Journal of the American Institute of Planners*. 35(4): pp. 216–224.

Baer, W. (1997) 'General plan evaluation: an approach to making better plans.' *Journal of the American Planning Association*. 63(3): pp. 329–344.

Barry, J. (1997) *Rising Tide*. New York: Simon and Schuster.

Birch, E. and Wachter, S. (2006) *Rebuilding urban places after disaster: lessons from Katrina*. Philadelphia: University of Pennsylvania Press.

Earth Day Network (2005) Website of Earth Day Network 2005: www.earthday.net (consulted 28th May 2008).

Federal Bureau of Investigation (2002) *Uniform Crime Reports*.

Florida, R. (2002) *The rise of the creative class*. New York: Basic Books.

Flyvberg, B (1998) *Rationality and power: democracy in practice*. Chicago: University of Chicago Press.

Innes, J. E. and Booher, D. E. (2004) 'Reframing public participation: strategies for the 21st century.' *Planning Theory*. 5(4): pp 419–436.

Nossiter, A. (2007) 'New Orleans plans to invest in 17 target areas.' *New York Times*, March 30th 2007, p. B1.

Office of Recovery Management (2007) *Strategic Plan of the Office of Recovery Management, City of New Orleans, 2007*.

Sublette, N. (2007) *The world that made New Orleans: from silver to Congo Square*. New York: Lawrence Hill Books.

Vale, L. and Campanella, T. (eds.) (2005) *The resilient city: how modern cities recover from disaster*. Cambridge, Mass.: MIT Press.

INDEX